To Swanie
much Aloha
A.L. Kilgo
Dec 1983

HONOLULU
HEART of HAWAII

BY SCOTT C.S. STONE

HONOLULU
HEART of HAWAII

by Scott C.S. Stone

Publisher
Douglas S. Drown

Editor
Sharon R. Mason

Picture Editor
Mazeppa King Costa

Art Director
Rusty Johnson

Production Manager
Mickey Thompson

Project Directors
Tim Emmons
Ann England

Copyright 1983 by Continental Heritage Press, Inc., P.O. Box 1620, Tulsa, Oklahoma 74101. All rights reserved. Library of Congress Catalog Card Number: 83-070413. ISBN Number: 0-932986-34-X.

Honolulu: Heart of Hawaii is one of the American Portrait Series published by Continental Heritage Press. Others include:

THE VICTORY
LIBERTY LOAN

Lovely Honolulu ladies gather for Victory Loan opening day, April 1919.

A crew of outrigger canoeists paddle with precision off Ala Moana
Park, between downtown Honolulu and Waikiki.

SPONSORS AND BENEFACTORS

The following firms, organizations. institutions and individuals have invested toward the quality of this historic book and thereby expressed their commitment to the future of this great city and to the support of the book's principal sponsor, the Chamber of Commerce of Hawaii.

Abraham & Dunn, Ltd.
Academy Hawaiian Agency
Airport Quick Print
Alaska Pacific Ventures
*Alexander & Baldwin, Inc.
*Aloha Airlines, Inc.
Alum-Glass, Inc.
*American Hawaii Cruises, Inc.
American Scientific Products
AMFAC Drug Supply Co.—Honolulu
Wallace S. Amioka
Andrew's Restaurant
Ann Grubb Realtors,
    A Division of Mike Dietz Golf Shops Inc.
*Arthur Andersen & Co.
Associated Steel Workers, Ltd.
*Bancorp Hawaii
*Beretania Florist Inc.
*Bishop Insurance of Hawaii
*Bishop Trust Company, Ltd.
*E.E. Black, Ltd.
*C. Brewer and Company, Limited
*Cades, Schutte, Fleming & Wright
R.L. Caldwell
*Cannon's International Business College of Honolulu
*Capital Investment of Hawaii Inc.

Castle Medical Center
*Central Pacific Bank
*Chamber of Commerce of Hawaii
Chevron U.S.A. Inc.
*City Bank
Bruce M. Clark, Attorney
Coca-Cola Bottling Co. of Honolulu, Inc.
*Columbia Inn, Ltd.
Combined Insurance Company of America
*Consolidated Amusement Company Ltd.
*Coopers & Lybrand
*Crazy Shirts Hawaii
*Crossroads Press, Inc.
Daka Travel of Hawaii, Inc.
*Daniel, Mann, Johnson & Mendenhall
*Deloitte Haskins & Sells
DHL Cargo
DHL Corporation
DHL Worldwide Courrier Express
*Dillingham Corporation
Dreyers Ice Cream of Hawaii Limited
*Duty Free Shoppers Limited
*Eagle Distributors, Inc.
Edsung, Inc., DBA Edsung Food Service Co.
Edward Enterprises, Inc.
*Carl Erdman Travel Inc.
Exclusive Incorporated
*First Interstate Bank of Hawaii
First Federal Savings & Loan Association of Hawaii
The Flower Touch
Frito-Lay of Hawaii, Inc.
Garlow Petroleum, Inc.
*Gaspro

General Electric Company
Norman Goldstein, M.D.
*Goodsill Anderson Quinn & Stifel
H.S. Gray Co., Ltd.
*Greyhound Rent-A-Car
Mr. and Mrs. Lyle Guslander
*Hawaii Business Publishing Co.
*Hawaii Medical Service Association
*Hawaii National Bank
Hawaii Dental Service
Hawaii Kai Rotary Club
Hawaii Nut & Bolt, Inc.
Hawaii Tax Institute
*Hawaiian Airlines, Inc.
*Hawaiian Electric Company, Inc.
*Hawaiian Host Chocolates
Hawaiian Life Insurance Co., Ltd.
*Hawaiian Memorial Park Cemetery Association
Hawaiian Pacific Freight Forwarding, Subsidiary of
    Carolina Freight Carrier
*Hawaiian Telephone Company
*Hawaiian Trust Company, Ltd.
Hawaiiana Investment Co., Inc., a C. Brewer Company
*Heftel Broadcasting Corporation
J & M Higa & Sons Inc.
James M. Higa
Merle N. Higa
*Sam O. Hirota, Inc.
Dennis I. Hirota
Jed Hirota
*Honolulu Federal Savings & Loan Association
*HOPACO, Boise Cascade Office Products Division
IMUA Builder Services, Ltd.

*InterIsland Resorts, Ltd.
*International Savings & Loan Association, Ltd.
Masanobu Ishihara
*Island Movers, Inc.
Jardine Insurance Serv. Hi, Inc.
Kaiser Cement Corporation
Alden Kajoika
Douglas Kamiya
Kaneshiro Development Corp.
Kapalama Equipment Co.
*Kapiolani/Children's Medical Center
Lillian S. Kashiwabara
Florence S. Kaya
Robert M. Kaya
*Robert M. Kaya Builders, Inc.
*KGMB-TV, Division of Lee Enterprises, Inc.
*KGU 76 Communications of Hawaii, Inc.
*KHON-TV
*A.L. Kilgo, Inc.
*King's Bakery, Inc.
*KKUA Honolulu Radio
Frederick H. Kohloss & Associates, Inc.
*Kuakini Medical Center
Drs. Kuwabara & Yamane, Optometrists, Inc.
Joseph P. Leong
*Liberty Bank
Jim Lusk Pal Club
Manpower Temporary Services
Marlin Distributors, Inc.
*Matson Navigation Company, Inc.
*Maunalani Hospital
MEPC Hawaiian Investments Inc.
Micro-Metrics, Inc.

*Milici/Valenti Advertising, Inc.
Ming's, Inc.
John Mullen & Co., Inc.
*National Mortgage & Finance Co. Ltd./Island Insurance
   Co. Ltd.
Kataichi Ninomiya
Northwestern Mutual Life Ins. Agency
NOVVA Computer Systems, Inc.
*Oceanic Cablevision
Office of Council Services
*Pacific Construction Co. Ltd.
Pacific Development Company, Limited.
*Pacific Insurance Company, Ltd.
*Pacific Marine & Supply Co. Ltd.
*Pacific Resources, Inc.
Dr. H.Q. Pang
Paradise Park, Inc.
*Peat Marwick
*Pioneer Federal Savings Bank
*The Queen's Medical Center
R & F Enterprises, Ltd.
Ramsay Galleries
Rawley Frozen Foods, Inc.
Real Estators Ltd.
Realty Mortgage Corporation
Richards, Ltd.
Royal Adventure Travel
Royal Hawaiian Shopping Center, Inc.
*St. Francis Hospital
Major General William A. Schneider
Schuman Carriage Co. Ltd.
Security Title Corporation
*Servco Pacific Inc.

Herbert Z. Shiroma, Ph.D.
Denis T. Shiu
Steiner Corporation
John E. Stepp, Spl Agent/NML
Steven Paul Stepp
*Tai Hing Company Inc.
Mr. and Mrs. Theodore T. Takai Jr.
Glenn T. Takeuchi
Jane A. Tamashiro
*Theo. H. Davies & Co. Ltd.
3M
Tileco Inc.
Title Guaranty of Hawaii, Inc.
Steven Tomei
Tori Richard Ltd.
Dennis T. Toyomura, F.A.I.A.
Trattoria Restaurant
Travel House, Inc.
Wendy M. Tsuji
United Agri Products (Hawaii)
John S. Williamson, CLU
Winmar Company, Inc.
*C.S. Wo & Sons, Inc.
James W.Y. Wong
Wong, Sueda & Assoc., Inc.
Xerox Corporation—Honolulu Branch
Alan K. Yoshida, D.D.S., Inc.
Young Scale Co.
*Arthur Young & Company

*Denotes Corporate Sponsors. The histories of these organizations and
individuals appear in a special section beginning on page 185.

*Last of the old volunteer firefighters, members of Company Two, are
about to join King Kalakaua's Jubilee celebration, November 1886.*

Twenty-foot waves at Waimea on Oahu's North Shore, generated by storm fronts elsewhere, attracted hundreds of spectators and handfuls of the strongest, most skillful surfers during the winter of 1983.

8

9

Honolulu Harbor—Original 1849 watercolor rendering by Robert Elwes (below) is in Bishop Museum. The same vista captured on film in 1983 (right).

PROLOGUE

Late in the history of the earth—25 million years ago—a series of cracks opened northwest to southeast in the floor of the North Pacific Ocean. In paroxysms of explosions, and sometimes in quiet but fiery rivers, liquid magma poured out of the fissures and became lava flows that formed mountains under the surface of the sea.

No human eyes saw this drama, nor witnessed the titanic battles that followed. The lava mountains pushed above the surface and were attacked by the elemental forces of nature—the wind and the sea.

In a glacial period, the rise and fall of ice caps on distant continents helped raise and lower the level of the sea. Yet despite the erosion caused by wind and water, the islands persisted. In time, the islands would remain like beads on a string across 1,500 miles of open ocean.

Then there was a time of quiet.

At some unrecorded moment the mountains blew up again, and volcanic activity resumed. Vast lava flows rampaged down the mountainsides, flowing and tumbling in dazzling pyrotechnics. More land was being born.

The battering of the waves and the hard force of a wind that blew steadily out of the northeast began to cut deep valleys into the new land. Once-rounded mountains were carved into coves and inlets, volcanoes collapsed leaving only their tops, new eruptions changed the face of the old. Algae and coral began to build reefs around the islands.

That is the scientific explanation for the creation of the Hawaiian Islands. There are other accounts.

In a place where legends and history diffuse and meld, the legends become as important as the history.

Who would deny that a demigod named Maui—a mischievous, cunning fellow—fished the islands up from the bottom of the sea? No one who has seen the sun fracturing on the rim of the great volcano Haleakala, on the island named for Maui himself.

And who would deny the presence of the tempestuous, passionate and beautiful Pele, the fire goddess? No one who has watched a sudden burst of magma roar out of a mountainside and begin to spread across the land, the very stuff of creation.

One drama that can be confirmed began a millennium ago when strange sails appeared on the horizon to leeward of the islands that had been alone for so many centuries.

CONTENTS

Hawaiian plantation house.

CHAPTER ONE

WAR-CLUB
AND
CANNON

The feather cape and helmet of John Webber's "A Man of the Sandwich Islands, with His Helmet" (1779) identify him as a chief. The superb example of Hawaiian sculpture (inset) is thought by some to be the eighteenth-century wooden image of Kamehameha I's war god, Kukailimoku.

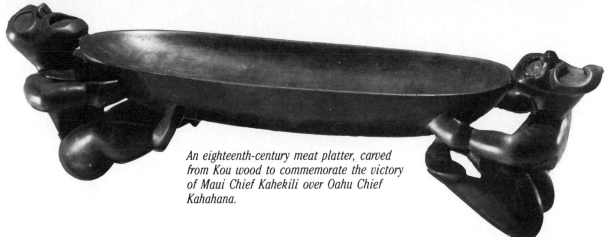

An eighteenth-century meat platter, carved from Kou wood to commemorate the victory of Maui Chief Kahekili over Oahu Chief Kahahana.

History did not record the name of that first adventurous Polynesian, and he has slipped forever into the mists of antiquity. But on some bright, ringing morning more than eleven centuries ago he stood on the deck of a double-hulled canoe underneath an odd, claw-shaped sail and looked in wonder on a new land.

It rose out of the sea like the realization of a dream—high and green islands that even at first glance appeared to be incredibly fertile. If that adventurer had approached from the west he might first have gazed on the Island of Kauai, noting its wet and massive interior and its reef-protected beaches. If he had come up from the south, he first would have sighted the massive volcanoes Mauna Kea and Mauna Loa, both nearly 14,000 feet high, on the largest island in the long chain. He would have been astonished, perhaps, at the sight of the mountains capped in something totally beyond his experience—snow.

In his wake came other Polynesians in canoes of 80 feet or more, arriving in this northern land after epic sea voyages and feats of navigation unequalled in the world at the time they were made. They came at first, in all probability, from the Marquesas Islands—fierce, pragmatic people who simply transplanted their culture into this new

and receptive land. Unchallenged, they evolved into a peaceable race and in time themselves succumbed to a new wave of invaders, the warlike and powerful chiefs from the islands of the Society group.

In a real sense, everything that flourished in the new islands was brought there. From the barrenness of the lava sprouted seeds that had washed ashore or were carried in the bellies of birds. To the indigenous plants, the Polynesians added variety and interest to their lives and their diets with dogs, chickens, pigs, bananas, sugarcane, coconuts, sweet potatoes, bamboo, ginger, the candlenut tree, yams and breadfruit. They also brought their gods and their glories and perpetuated a civilization that was both unified and rigid.

The life of the average Polynesian, the *makaainana,* was ordered by influences that he was powerless to change. The overriding one was the *alii,* the royalty, whose very countenances, when gazed upon, could be the cause of a swift and probably fatal retaliation. Another group which cast a fearful shadow was the *kahunas,* or priests. The *kahunas* were exempt from most laws and dealt in both the supernatural and the practical. As priests, they not only talked with gods and interpreted signs, but had mysterious powers which they were inclined to use when crossed. Each powerful chief had a *kahuna* as his advisor, which gave the *kahunas* political power as well.

CHARTING A COURSE THE OLD WAY

The ancient Polynesians crossed long seas without the aid of sextants, chronometers or other modern navigational devices. Their methods were effective, but hardly simpler.

Keen observers of the heavens, they were able to determine time by the stars' movements. Equally keen in observing the water, they were able to discern currents moving in the ocean, currents which could signal the presence of land.

The Polynesians watched land birds disappear over the horizon and, knowing they would not live in the water, deduced that land was near. From the color of the reflection of water on the undersides of clouds, they could estimate the water's depth—and discover a lagoon, which meant an atoll.

By watching the "set" of waves the Polynesians could determine directions; in various navigational areas of the Pacific the ocean swells moved from a specific place in a specific direction, hence the navigators could confirm to some degree their star courses. With a remarkable sense of time the navigators also knew in what part of the sky a certain star would be at a given time—hence finding direction again.

Each area of the Pacific had its navigational traditions and aids, such as "stick charts" from which a knowledgeable navigator could learn the direction of currents. While Melanesians and Micronesians were accomplished navigators in their own areas, the Polynesians became the most proficient and ranged the farthest from home.

In May 1976, a 60-foot replica of an old Polynesian canoe set out from Hawaii to Tahiti, navigating by the ancient methods. The Hokule'a *was a double-hulled craft manned by modern Hawaiians, and the voyage was three years in preparation.*

The preparations paid off, for 34 days after leaving Hawaii the Hokule'a *sailed into safe waters in Tahiti and was greeted by some 25,000 Tahitians, wildly cheering the craft's safe arrival.*

With a fresh crew the Hokule'a *sailed back to Hawaii, still using the old navigational methods, and found another enthusiastic welcome. The techniques are as viable today as they were more than a thousand years ago, and the* Hokule'a *had lived up to its name—"the star of gladness."*

Gods were numerous and powerful. The common people bowed in supplication before the omnipotent deities of Kane, Lono, Kanaloa and Ku; they also had personal, household gods called *aumakuas,* who were much more approachable and helpful in times of trouble. Society itself was regulated by a system of *kapus,* tabus, which defined the class and role of each *makaainana.* To break a *kapu* was to invite punishment, usually fatal.

A dark side of Polynesian society was the preference by chiefs for the excitement of war rather than the somnolent lifestyles enjoyed by many. Wars were intense and brutal affairs in which whole families could be wiped out. Battles were so frequent and so bloody that places of refuge were established where defeated warriors could go—often with their enemies in hot pursuit. If the warriors could reach a place of refuge they would be safe and, after rituals dictated by *kahunas,* could leave the sanctuary and again take their places in society without fear of harm from their former enemies.

But it was not altogether a grim life. Thriving in the most remote inhabited landfall on earth, the Polynesians knew moments that perhaps could never come again. In a healthy, uncrowded and astonishingly beautiful archipelago, they raised families and planted crops, rising to brilliant mornings and watching, at night, an enormous moon turn the land the color of frost. They grew into a statuesque and regal people who lived for the *makahiki,* the traditional games and dances. They revered their old people, their *kapunas.* Their blood flowed in rhythm with the tides and currents of the world's mightiest ocean, in which they found their food and their recreation.

Children of the land, they were also brothers to the creatures of the sea, and many households had as their *aumakua* the far-ranging *mano,* the shark. As the years passed the Polynesians developed splendid art forms and, like other "primitive" people, turned the making of the smallest artifact into a labor of joy. They dyed *tapa,* bark-cloth, into geometric designs and made an art form of the styling of a fishhook. From the irridescent feathers of birds they made enormous cloaks. Images they carved to represent gods appear somewhat crude to the Western eye today, but they were expressions of bold and fearsome dieties which quite satisfied the Polynesian psyche. Their thatched-hut homes, their utensils, the shaping of their distinctive canoes—all reflected an artistic integrity. Dances developed and evolved, were banned and resurrected, and their legacy today is the graceful and provocative *hula.*

The family unit was important. It was within the family that the common Polynesian found his joy and his satisfaction. Eventually the

The nineteenth-century stone fishing god (opposite, top) was typical of images made from stone, wood or basketry covered with feathers. In the 1819 Jacques Arago lithograph (opposite, bottom) punishment, probably for breaking a kapu, was swift and brutal. Henry W. Henshaw's circa 1895 photograph (above) depicts "A Calabash Carrier in Ancient Hawaiian Dress in the Fern Forest" whose progress was certainly slower than the canoeists in claw-shaped sail off Nihau in 1778 John Webber sketch, original in Bishop Museum (right).

The masked paddlers in the original pencil, pen and wash in Bishop Museum (left) were probably delivering gifts to Captain James Cook (right), whose tracks through the Sandwich Islands may be traced in a reproduction of the earliest (1778-79) historic map of Hawaii (below).

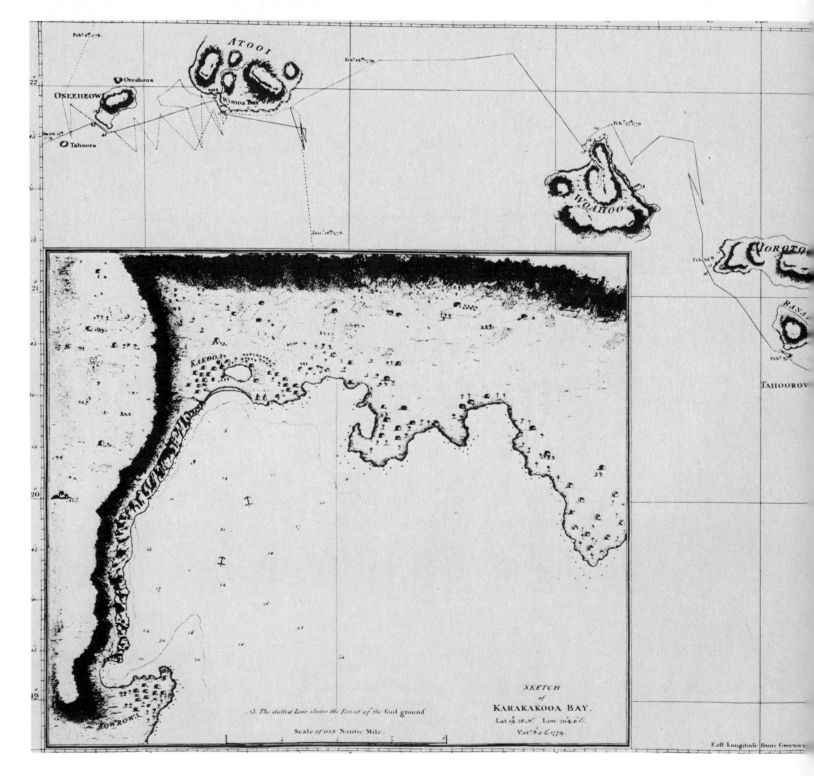

extended family, the *ohana,* became almost as important. Families labored together to satisfy the requirements of a chief, to gain wealth for important marriages, simply to pay their taxes and try to get ahead. In their common striving was a closeness which also became a legacy.

From the eighth century onward for a millennium, the Polynesians persisted in the new islands, remote and self-sufficient, but still Polynesians. They were not yet Hawaiians; that could come only with a true unity of the scattered islands.

And it came—thrust forward by yet another sail from a civilization distant in both miles and development, and by the birth of an infant who would rise to power through his own cunning and strength.

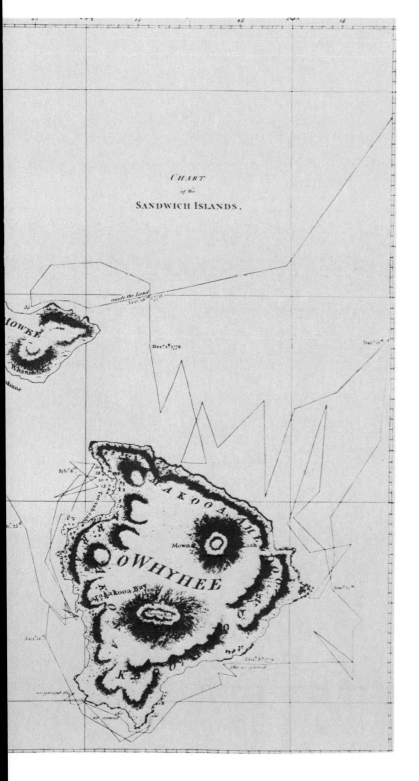

THE RETURN OF LONO

I f the Polynesian discovery of the Hawaiian Islands remains vivid only through modern researchers looking back in time, Western discovery is made striking by the men who took part in it. The journals of Captain James Cook are detailed and complete, leading up to that fateful moment in Kealakekua Bay, when Cook's life ended and his place in history began.

Artists and chroniclers aboard the ships *Resolution* and *Discovery* tell us much about the natives inhabiting these lonely islands in the North Pacific when Cook found them. At first sighting—on January 18, 1778—the islands reminded Cook of other lands he had discovered to the south. He was "agreeably surprised" to find the natives who approached in canoes speaking a recognizable dialect of the language he had heard in the Society Islands to the southeast.

The first sighting came at dawn when Cook's ships sailed within sight of the islands of Oahu, Kauai and Niihau at the western end of the major island cluster. The first contact was with the timid but curious natives of Kauai, from villages in the area of Waimea. Cook and his men were impressed by their openness and friendship.

Cook was at both the apex of the triangle that encompasses the Polynesian islands and the apex of his career. Born in obscurity but thirsting for distant shores, he had worked his way through British fleets until he was recognized as his nation's foremost mariner and navigator. He coupled these talents with an intelligence and a tolerance rare for sea captains of his day.

He would need all his forbearance in the weeks to come. The natives he met seemed mercurial and quixotic, although he recognized that the *haoles,* the white foreigners, probably mystified the natives equally as much. When his men traded iron nails for pigs and food, Cook approved; when the native women, *wahines,* came aboard with an innocent sexuality, he looked on with both understanding and dismay, the latter because he knew that members of his crew carried venereal diseases that would strike the natives down. Experience had taught him it was impossible to keep such liaisons from taking place, but he was humanitarian enough to deplore it.

The bemused Cook wrote of the natives' generosity at the same time he worried over their tendency to steal anything they could, often making a game of it. And before the visit had ended, Lieutenant John Williamson had killed a native for theft of a boathook. It was an old, sad story of the introduction of Pacific peoples to the power of the West —a confrontation the islanders would lose again and again.

Cook was also impressed with the islands themselves, taking note of the wooded uplands, the forests of bananas and the expanse of sugarcane. Of all his explorations—he had circumnavigated the globe three times, charted New Zealand, ranged in voyages of exploration from Antarctica to the Bering Sea—he thought these new islands must be as important as anything he had come across. In deference to his chief patron and supporter, he named them after the Earl of Sandwich.

Then he sailed away.

Cook spent the early part of 1778 with his ships far north, all the way through the Bering Strait and into the Arctic Sea, looking for a passage that did not exist. After months of snow and ice and the increasing danger of being trapped, Cook decided to return to the Sandwich Islands for the winter and come north again in the summer of 1779. He was never to see the north again.

Sailing back into familiar latitudes, Cook saw an unexpected sight—an island unknown to him. It turned out to be Maui—large, oddly shaped and bearing a huge volcano towering to some 10,000 feet. Surprisingly, the natives seemed to know about Cook, and sadly, some of them seemed infected with venereal diseases. Cook sighted the Island of Molokai and a few days later abandoned his plan to sail in the lee of Maui because another island had risen on the horizon —the last of the windward group of islands and the largest in the entire line. The natives called it Hawaii.

Cook sailed along its coast, admiring the snow on the summits of two enormous volcanoes, but frustrated by a coastline which afforded no safe anchorage. Working his ships along the windward coast and to the south, Cook finally was able to drop anchor in a sheltered bay at Kealakekua.

The welcome was tumultuous. Thousands of natives came down to the bay, singing and shouting; Cook had never seen anything like it in all his travels. The climax was an elaborate ritual in which Cook was the central figure at a *heiau,* a stone temple with wooden scaffolding lined with the skulls of sacrificial victims. The *kahunas* were making more of the visit than could be expected, and Cook kept hearing the word "Lono." Afterwards, everywhere he went he was accompanied by a *kahuna,* and the common people threw themselves on the ground as he passed. Cook's crew basked in the reflected glory and for several weeks there was genuine good feeling on all sides. When Cook weighed anchor to sail for Maui, he left with the sense that all had gone well.

Three days of beating up the western coast of Hawaii in the face of worsening seas and strong winds began to wear on the crew. The *Resolution* sprang her foremast and Cook, playing it safe, returned to Kealakekua to make repairs. This time, instead of a lavish welcome Cook found the villages under a *kapu,* the bay deserted. The crews went about the tasks of making repairs, which necessitated frequent trips ashore. The *haoles* now returned from shore talking about the "insolence" of the natives and how they had begun carrying throwing stones. Marines armed with muskets began to accompany the shore parties. Soon afterwards, shots were fired from the *Discovery* at a native who had stolen some tools. Cook himself was among the pursuers who went ashore, but this time there were no accompanying priests, no gifts, no prostrate natives. Instead, he was followed by an ugly mob, calling insults. The thief was never found.

The next morning a large cutter was stolen from the *Discovery.* Cook led an armed party ashore with the intent of taking as a hostage the ranking chief, Kalaniopuu, who after talking with Cook willingly started with him toward the beach. At this point Kalaniopuu's wife begged him not to go, and in confusion the old chief simply sat down. By now a crowd of several thousand natives had formed and appeared to be menacing the Marines who had accompanied Cook. A native stepped forward and threatened Cook with a long iron spike. Cooked fired his musket but the small charge was not strong enough to penetrate the native's body mat. The crowd began to throw stones.

Cook fired a second shot and killed a man. The Marines fired a volley and as they reloaded, the natives pushed forward. Cook turned toward the boats and was hit from behind, reportedly by a *kahuna* named Koa, who earlier had taken part in the elaborate ritual as a high priest of Lono.

Cook fell forward in the water and was pounced on by natives who killed him with clubs and knives. Four Marines died in moments, others managed to get into boats and stand off. Subsequent attempts to recover Cook's body ended in failure and in a matter of days, during an uneasy stalemate, portions of it were returned to the ships, wrapped in *tapa.*

The chiefs put a *kapu* on the area. A naval burial service was read and the ships' cannons fired in salute. Cook's remains were lowered into the water. When the *kapu* was lifted, canoes surrounded the two

John Webber depicts Kalaniopuu bringing gifts to Captain Cook (inset, left) and a sacrificial offering to Cook at a heiau *(inset, right). Pen and wash originals are in Bishop Museum. Engraving after work by Webber shows "The Death of Captain Cook" (below).*

foreign ships and a group of *alii* came aboard to express their regrets.

On February 22, 1779, eight days after Cook's death, the two ships bent on canvas and stood for the open ocean, sailing away from the scene of a tragedy that, in retrospect, was not remarkable in the chronicles of Oceania. In this instance, however, the dead man was the world's foremost explorer and navigator, about whom a *Resolution* crewman would write, "... on him all eyes were turned; he was our leading star, which at its setting left us involved in darkness and despair."

Cook's achievements were many and significant, but to the people of the "Sandwich Islands" his visit had awesome proportions—he had torn apart the curtain of secrecy which had hidden their islands for centuries. Willingly or not, they were now located, charted and reported. Their world would never be the same.

THE NAPOLEON OF THE PACIFIC

The realization that times were changing came swiftly to one who had witnessed the genesis of that change. Kamehameha, the nephew of old Kalaniopuu, the ranking chief whom Cook took as hostage at Kealakekua Bay, had also been reported in the crowd around Cook when the sea captain was killed. Certainly he was aboard the *Resolution,* where he traded a cloak for an iron knife. One report said he had asked for, and was given, Captain Cook's hair after the navigator's death.

As a nephew to Kalaniopuu, the young Kamehameha was not

Hook pendant excavated from Bellows Beach, Oahu, is believed to be about 1,000 years old.

expected to inherit his uncle's domains on Hawaii; the political control went to Kiwalao, Kalaniopuu's son. As things turned out, the old man's gift to Kamehameha was more than fitting—to his nephew he entrusted the war god Kukailimoku, a fiercely carved image with a mouth distorted in rage, showing sharp teeth. The image was cloaked in feathers and carried an aura of violence.

Kamehameha's own visage was not reassuring. The English sailors thought he had a "savage" look; he was indisputably strong, tall and fearless. Behind the warrior's mask was the mind of a tactician.

With the death of Kalaniopuu Hawaii was plunged into a series of battles between chieftains vying for control over the entire island. The battles began ritualistically with prayers and sacrifices and even some personal combat between champions. Before it was over, however, the battles became bloody hand-to-hand encounters with knives, clubs and bare hands. Kamehameha took part in these battles along with the rest, leading his own men into combat and engaging in personal contests with opposing champions. All the while, he was remembering the guns carried by Cook's men and their devastating effect when fired.

Kamehameha did not have long to wait to see the guns again.

In 1785, a ship carrying furs from the American Northwest called at the Sandwich Islands to refresh before going on to Canton to trade. Others followed, stopping at Kealakekua to bargain for water, meat and vegetables. The natives wanted guns in return, and the early traders suffered no guilt in trading not only guns, but ammunition. Often the guns were defective. Equally often, sailors were killed and their boats stolen with the idea of swapping the boats for guns and ammunition.

The climate of violence did not deter more ships from coming. Among them were the *Eleanora,* commanded by Simon Metcalfe, and the *Fair American,* under the command of Metcalfe's son, Thomas. After a series of incidents on Maui, the elder Metcalfe became enraged and off Olowalu, Maui, hit upon an idea for revenge. Encouraging trading canoes to come alongside the *Eleanora,* he suddenly turned his cannons and deck guns on the massed canoes and opened fire. As the ship came about to head for the Island of Hawaii, it left more than 100 natives dead or wounded and dozens missing.

By coincidence, the *Fair American* was in Hawaiian waters and having its own problems with the natives. One day a group boarded the ship, heaved Thomas Metcalfe and the crewmen overboard and beat them to death in the water. The lone survivor was an Englishman, Isaac Davis, rescued by a sympathetic native chief.

Kamehameha took possession of the ship and the arms she carried. Then, hearing that the *Eleanora* was at Kealakekua, Kamehameha laid a *kapu* on the area so that the ship's crew would not learn that the *Fair American* had been captured. The *Eleanora's* boatswain, another Englishman named John Young, came ashore to assess the situation and was taken prisoner by Kamehameha. After a few days of waiting, the *Eleanora* sailed without him. (Simon Metcalfe was later reported killed by natives in the Tuamotu archipelago.)

Kamehameha now had guns and a ship, and he had two foreign seamen who might prove useful. Although both Young and Davis tried to escape, they were brought back unharmed and in time were forced to accept their situation. They were now the vassals of a strong, cruel, ambitious and cunning warrior whose dreams began to transcend that of becoming ranking chief of the Island of Hawaii. Knowing of the intrigues on the other islands, knowing of the power of the war god Kukailimoku, knowing his own prowess, Kamehameha had begun to think in terms of conquest on the widest scale he could imagine. He wanted to become ruler of all the islands.

Vancouver's ships on voyage are illustrated by Thomas Heddington, circa 1794 (left), while Vancouver's "strong, tall, fearless" friend, Kamehameha I, wards off spears in a late eighteenth-century drawing (below).

The pali where Kamehameha I won the battle for Oahu was steel engraved by A.T. Agate in 1840 (below). "Man of the Sandwich Islands, Half Face Tattooed" (right) by John Webber, circa 1780 (original pen and wash in Bishop Museum), could have been one of Kamehameha's fierce warriors.

26

THE KINGDOM

With a number of enemies still extant on the Island of Hawaii, the bold Kamehameha nevertheless felt strong enough to launch his conquests. He began with an attack on Maui Island, whose strong ruler, Kahekili, was away on Oahu to the northwest. Kahekili's son, Kalanikupule, was left to bring the disastrous news to his father on Oahu—Kamehameha had invaded and was rampaging about Maui winning one fight after another. Kahekili immediately began planning his retaliation, but Kamehameha was forced to return abruptly to Hawaii where his arch-rival Keoua, was ravaging Kamehameha's land in his absence.

Kamehameha solved his most urgent problem by inviting Keoua to the dedication on the west coast of Hawaii of a new *heiau,* a temple to his war god Kukailimoku. For reasons still unclear, Keoua accepted, and when he stepped ashore one of Kamehameha's warriors struck him down with a spear. All but two of the 26 warriors who accompanied Keoua also were killed. Keoua's body was carried to the *heiau* at Puukohola and placed in sacrifice on the altar there. Whether Keoua's death was ordered by Kamehameha or simply an impulsive act by a Kamehameha lieutenant, it consolidated Kamehameha's hold on the island. He now reigned over all Hawaii Island and once more turned his attentions to the lands to leeward.

On Oahu, meanwhile, Maui's equally bold king, Kahekili, joined with his half-brother Kaeokulani of Kauai Island. Together they sailed for Hawaii with a fleet of war canoes and a group of wild, tattooed warriors who rampaged through the land, looting, burning and destroying grave sites—a horrible offense to Hawaiians. Kahekili also had brought a foreign gunner along, and off the spectacular Waipio Valley of Hawaii, Kahekili's gunners fought a great sea battle with Kamehameha's forces which had their own foreign gunners, John Young and Isaac Davis. The battle was indecisive but bloody enough to be called by the Hawaiians *Kepuwahaulaula,* the battle of the red-mouthed gun.

Kamehameha's campaigns got another assist in 1794 when Kahekili died in Waikiki on Oahu, leaving his son and his half-brother to divide the lands he controlled. It was a fateful move, for the two erstwhile rulers were at each other's throats quickly and bloodily. Kamehameha, knowing the moment to be at hand, sailed from Hawaii with a giant fleet of canoes and small ships. He invaded and conquered Molokai and Maui, then took his fleet to southern Oahu and over the reefs between Waikiki and Waialae. Marching his forces across the island, he pushed his enemies, under Kahekili's son, Kalanikupule, back into the long reaches of Oahu's Nuuanu Valley and finally to the *pali,* the thousand-foot cliff in the Koolau Mountains that divide Oahu's leeward and windard sides. It was an untenable position, with sheer cliffs on either side and the precipitous cliff behind. Kalanikupule's forces broke. Some fled to the mountains to search for elusive paths out of the trap, but many warriors jumped or were forced over the cliffs, to plunge to their deaths on the rocks below. Kalanikupule himself wandered through the mountains for several months, finally to be captured and killed.

From Nuuanu, Kamehameha went to another lovely valley, Moanalua, to rest beside a giant rock near a stream and contemplate his victories. He was now lord over Hawaii, Molokai, Lanai, Maui and Oahu. Only the northernmost Island of Kauai stood between him and the realization of his hopes. He vowed to take it, for with its annexation to his islands he would have seized all that he saw in his mind and heart.

It was to take a surprisingly long time.

Kamehameha I late in life was painted by N. Tikanov on Golovnin's expedition early in the nineteenth century.

In the spring of 1796, Kamehameha tried to move his forces across the rough, 100-mile channel separating Oahu and Kauai, only to see many of his canoes go under in the wild waves and strong winds. Bitterly, he turned back to Oahu to await a better time. On Oahu, he learned that a revolt on Hawaii needed his attention. He returned there and in a savage battle near Hilo, defeated a rebel army and sacrificed its leader.

Kamehameha was diverted by important events on his home island; he spent the next six years trading with foreigners and expanding his government. Through all the affairs of state he did not forget Kauai for a moment, and once again he appeared on Oahu with a fleet of special canoes, built to withstand the perilous crossing. Shortly before they were to be launched, an epidemic swept through Kamehameha's army, killing his warriors by the score and causing the king himself to fall ill. The invasion was postponed once again.

A third invasion attempt was in the offing in 1810 when the king of Kauai, Kaumualii, concluding the fates had spared him twice but would not a third time, sailed to Oahu where he worked out a treaty with Kamehameha. The treaty acknowledged Kamehameha's sovereignty put provided that Kaumualii would continue to govern Kauai as usual. It was an arrangement that recognized Kamehameha as the supreme ruler over his island kingdom.

Now at his pinnacle, Kamehameha made an abrupt about-face and declared his displeasure at the idea of war. He wanted peace, he told his subjects, and issued a famous decree in which he stated, "Let the old men, the old women, and the children sleep in safety by the

The faithful John Young, one of Hawaii's first resident haoles.

roadside." War being unprofitable, the wily king now turned his attention to the grand design for his islands. He wanted true unity, expansion, trade, a social order held in place by the *kapus,* and—perhaps with a heightened sense of his own mortality—he wanted his kingdom to continue after his death.

There followed nine years of the Kamehameha monarchy—years of relatively stable conditions and economic growth, a period far removed from the days when the young Kamehameha was avid for guns from the *haoles* to wage bloody war.

Kamehameha fell ill for the last time on the Kona coast of the Island of Hawaii, then and now a place of great beauty. Both *kahunas* and foreigners arrived to try their skill at saving his life, but on May 8, 1819, at approximately 70 years of age, he began slipping

FLYING THE RUSSIAN FLAG

*F*or a time, the flag of Imperial Russia flew over parts of the Hawaiian Islands, the result of a wild fantasy that ended in humiliation.

In 1815, Georg Anton Schaffer (or Scheffer), a German-born doctor working for a Russian company in Alaska, was sent by the company's Alaska manager, Alexander Baranov, to recover the cargo of a Russian ship wrecked on the Island of Kauai. Schaffer arrived at the court of Kamehameha I and became enchanted with the possibilities for exploitation of the islands, not the first or last adventurer to do so. He persuaded Kamehameha to give the Russians property on Oahu for storehouse space and perhaps construction sites for buildings. The doctor also persuaded Kamehameha's principal wife, Kaahumanu, to grant the company large tracts of land on Oahu.

Schaffer was doing well, but in his machinations he feared the Americans in Hawaii were plotting to kill him. He sailed off to Kauai and became friendly with the discontented king, Kaumualii, who had acknowledged Kamehameha's sovereignty over his island but was none too happy about it. Schaffer and Kaumualii concluded a deal whereby the Russian company would have a monopoly on the sandalwood trade on Kauai. The king of Kauai also pledged allegiance to Alexander I of Russia, and promised to allow the company to establish factories on Kauai. Further, Kaumualii promised manpower to erect buildings and to provide supplies for Russian ships.

Kaumualii, in exchange, was to receive the protection of the Russian Empire, and Schaffer gave the king a medal and made him an officer in the Russian Navy. Schaffer started construction of a house in Waimea, Kauai. Kaumualii, still plotting, told Schaffer he would give the company half of Oahu if it would help him wrest the other islands from Kamehameha's control. Schaffer sailed back to Oahu, his head spinning with ideas.

In Honolulu he ran up against Kamehameha's advisor, the Englishman John Young, and a group of American traders who harassed him to the point that he fled back to Kauai. On friendlier turf, he spent his time renaming the island's scenic spots in behalf of Russia, except for the most beautiful valley of Hanalei, which he immodestly

renamed Schafferthal.

Meanwhile, Baranov, back in Alaska, learned of Schaffer's plots and disavowed them, noting angrily that he had not authorized the use of force or threats of force to gain property in the islands. When Baranov's envoy Lieutenant Otto von Kotzebue visited Hawaii, he snubbed Schaffer deliberately. This insult, combined with Kamehameha's discovery of the Schaffer-Kaumualii plot, proved too much for Schaffer to overcome. Additionally, the Americans were spreading a rumor that war was imminent between Russia and the United States.

When Schaffer hurried to Kauai again he found the Russian flag still flying at Waimea, but Kaumualii was cool—either he had been warned by Kamehameha, or he realized the plot had little chance of success.

Finally Schaffer was hustled into a boat offshore of Kauai and told to leave the islands forever. He got as far as Honolulu in a very leaky ship, and with the help of another sea captain, got passage to Canton. He spent the time at sea writing denunciations of the perfidious Americans.

For the next few years the Russians carried on a desultory correspondence about their Hawaiian properties, then let it drop, showing no real interest in the Hawaiian Islands. What might have happened to Hawaii if the Russians had decided to back Schaffer makes interesting speculation.

As for Schaffer, he reportedly ended up in Brazil where he bought a title from the emperor and spent the rest of his days as Count von Frankenthal.

Some 160 years later, another Russian gave his views on Schaffer's efforts in Hawaii. He was Soviet Fleet Admiral Sergei Gorshkov, whose 25-plus years in the Russian hierarchy is exceptional, and who built the Soviet fleet into a wide-ranging and formidable force. Of the Hawaiian adventures, Gorshkov wrote:

"Not everyone knows that on 21 May 1816, the king of one of the Hawaiian Islands (the king of Kauai) became a Russian citizen. Moreover, he also turned the Island of Oahu over to Russia. Three Russian fortresses were established on that Island; Aleksandrovskaya, Yelizavetinskaya and Barklaya (true, they had to be abandoned later due to counter-action by the Americans)."

Meeting of Kamehameha I and Vancouver at "Village of Macacopah, Owyhee" is the subject of 1794 Thomas Heddington work (above); the chief's heiau, *next to his residence, was drawn by Louis Choris at the turn of this century (below).*

Crepin's engraving of Kalanimoku's baptism on board a French ship following Kamehameha I's death in 1819 (above). Already Western influence is evident in the table, chair, door on the house, in Pellion's 1819 engraving of Chief Kalanimoku's houses (below).

Liholiho, Kamehameha II, and his queen contracted measles and died on an uninvited trip to London in 1824.

Litho de C Motte

31

away. He whispered something to his brother, then the elderly John Young leaned over and kissed him. At two o'clock in the morning he died, and the ritual mourning began. At last, two of Kamehameha's oldest allies and friends took his bones away for burial in secret. The secret endures; to this day no one knows the location of the bones of the man who, through stratagem and savagery, founded an island kingdom.

THE END OF THE KAPUS

No one could have foreseen how quickly one of Kamehameha's wishes would be swept aside, certainly no one who stood among the *alii* at Kailua on the Kona coast a week after the king's death. There, with the gentle surf in the background, the assemblage heard Kaahumanu, the king's favorite wife, proclaim Kamehameha's son, Liholiho, as the successor to the king and one who would possess the land. But, she said, she would jointly rule with Liholiho.

Acceptance of Liholiho was immediate; Kamehameha had ordained it when his son was still a child. Acceptance of Kaahumanu was not as quick nor as wide, but it did take place. She settled into her job as queen regent—and quickly made it a powerful post.

Kaahumanu was strong-willed, one of the few who could face Kamehameha with equanimity. Early in their marriage she had reportedly committed adultery with one of Kamehameha's allies and was forced to hide from the king's wrath under a great rock in a place of refuge farther south on the Kona coast. Later she and the king were tearfully reunited by a *haole* sea captain, George Vancouver (who subsequently made other long-lasting contributions to the islands).

As queen regent, Kaahumanu began to pressure Liholiho for a change he was reluctant to make—an overthrow of the *kapu* system. It had happened in Tahiti and she wanted it to happen in Hawaii to break the bonds in which women were held. Her power was great, and Liholiho was new at the business of being king. Additionally, other events were weakening Liholiho's resolve. The war god Kukailimoku had been passed on to Kamehameha's nephew instead of to him, and the chiefs had forced him to surrender the monopoly in sandalwood trade which Kamehameha had enjoyed.

The stage was set for Kaahumanu. She had secretly broken some of the *kapus* by eating pork and shark's meat, and she was fond of the *haole's* liquor. Feeling she had nothing to fear from the gods for breaking the *kapus,* she now wanted to fear nothing from man, and she knew her vehicle had to be the king. In the end, she won.

Liholiho went to sea with a boatload of liquor; some say he drank rum for two days before coming ashore again where Kaahumanu had prepared a feast. In defiance of the *kapus,* the young king walked by the eatingplaces of the men, sat down with the women and began to eat. Afterwards he sent messengers to all sectors of Hawaii— the *kapu* system was broken. Kamehameha had been dead a mere six months.

The chiefs were divided in their opinions about the overthrow of the system that had kept society constricted but orderly for so long. Some of them had been breaking the *kapus* in secret anyway. But now they saw the *heiaus* desecrated, the images of the gods destroyed, and it gave them pause. Many of them feared for the future of the islands, correctly as it turned out. The end of the *kapus* and the opening of Hawaii to the West were about to bring to a close the era of the Hawaiians. What would follow would be exciting, turbulent and dramatic—but it would be only partially Hawaiian.

Queen Kaahumanu, Kamehameha I's favorite wife, ruled the kingdom as high chiefess after her husband's death.

CHAPTER TWO

IN THE
SHADOW
OF
LAHAINA

The exact date is unknown, but at some moment before March 1783, while Kamehameha was maneuvering for control of an island empire, another Englishman made an important discovery in the Hawaiian Islands. He was William Brown, who sold guns as well as furs. The furs were a lucrative trade; pelts gathered in the Pacific Northwest could be sold for as much as $100 each in Canton, and because Hawaii was a convenient port of call, the fur ships made frequent stops as daring English and American sea captains risked all to get the precious furs to China. Sailing ships soon became commonplace in the eyes of the Hawaiians.

Such a trader was Brown, and one day he found what other Westerners had missed—a passage through the reef into a fine harbor near an insignificant village called Honolulu.

Staring inland from the shore, Brown could not have been overly impressed. The harbor was promising, but the area itself left much to be desired. The weather was hot, the shore relatively unpopulated. He could see mud flats and there was, of course, the reef to contend with.

Despite these drawbacks, Brown calculated that the harbor had a future and that it would play an important role in the development of the Island of Oahu and the Hawaiian Islands in general. Certainly he saw himself as part of that future, and he hatched a plan to make sure of it.

The king of Oahu at the time was Kahekili, who had challenged Kamehameha in *Kepuwahaulaula,* the battle of the red-mouthed gun. That great sea battle had been inconclusive, but Kahekili looked longingly at Brown's ship, the *Butterworth.* The 30-gun frigate was the largest ship in Hawaii and Brown was prepared to put it at Kahekili's disposal in return for the use of Honolulu harbor. But within months Kahekili was dead, and his heirs began attacking one another—one faction using guns supplied by Brown. Retribution was swift; Brown and some of his crew were attacked and killed in Honolulu by dissident Hawaiians on the first day of the new year of 1795. Brown's body was stripped and hung on a pole on the shore. By year's end, Kamehameha had conquered Oahu and consolidated his kingdom, and Brown passed into history.

For a time, so did Honolulu. Events taking place on other of the islands eclipsed the importance of Brown's discovery, for those events would affect not only Honolulu but all the islands. New waves of strangers were arriving and the course of Hawaii's history would change dramatically. Some came to plunder, some to preach, and their clash would reverberate throughout the island chain.

Kalanimoku's palace at Pohukaina (Punchbowl) was lithographed by de Sainson based on a drawing by an unknown artist (below). C.R. Malden's 1825 sketch of Honolulu (right) shows a trail in dotted line leading to gun emplacements at Punchbowl fort.

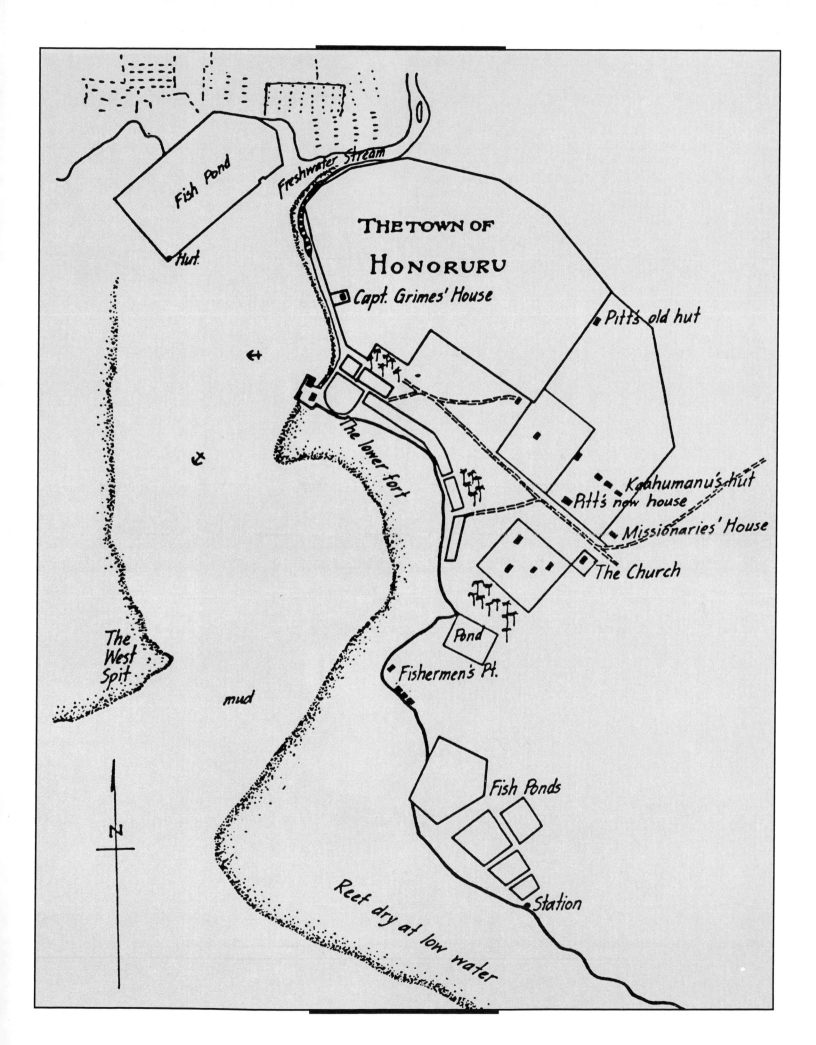

THE TOWN OF

HONORURU

Fish Pond

Hut.

Freshwater Stream

Capt. Grimes' House

Pitt's old hut

The lower fort

Koahumanu's hut

Pitt's new house

Missionaries' House

The Church

Pond

The West Spit

mud

Fishermen's Pt.

Fish Ponds

Station

Reef dry at low water

N

Louis Choris' 1816 lithographs (insets and left) show splendid detail of the dance, dress, ornament and hairstyles. The tattooed dancers' wrap-around garments are of bark cloth.

"NO GOD WEST OF THE HORN"

By 1819, the Atlantic whale had been hunted extensively and was growing scarce; the whaling industry was galvanized by news that a rich new whaling ground had been found off Japan. All eyes—most of them greedy—turned to the Pacific whaling grounds.

Hawaii now assumed a new importance. The tall ships and their hard-driving captains began to call in greater numbers, putting into both Lahaina, on Maui, and Honolulu. Both had natural sanctuaries and both had factoring industries that sprang up overnight to help resupply and reprovision the whaling ships. And like the rest of the islands, both locales had willing *wahines*. The whaling ships came with a vengeance, and with a vengeance the whalingmen wrote their own turbulent history. After 1822, when 60 whaling ships were counted in Honolulu, the floodgates opened. As the years passed, the two harbors were studded with masts, with several hundred ships per year at rest and their crews ashore roistering day and night. There was, as they put it, "no God west of the Horn," and the crews behaved accordingly. Drunkenness and fistfights were frequent; shops and dance halls were wide open and drunken sailors on the streets of Lahaina or Honolulu were commonplace. Nubile *wahines* were drawn to the ports like moths to a flame, and few of them returned to their homes.

There was some justification for the sailors' boisterousness. Their voyages lasted from three to four years at a time and port calls were infrequent. Their work was dangerous, their pay determined by the amount of whale oil they could bring home in the holds of their cramped ships. It was neither an easy life nor a predictable one, and few whalingmen ignored the chance to escape into a wild time ashore.

The whalers' impact on the native populations around Lahaina and Honolulu was deep and lasting. They came into a land already feeling the effects of contact with the West. At the time of Cook's

discovery, the native Hawaiians numbered at least 300,000. By the time the whalingmen arrived, it was down to about 135,000. Measles, smallpox, venereal diseases—their decimation of the Hawaiian population was more severe than any of the battles of the *alii* or the inter-island warfare. The whalingmen took some Hawaiians off on the long whaling voyages as replacements for dead *haole* crewmen, but this loss was negligible compared to the strangers' effect on Hawaiian health.

The ships were supplied by farmers who grew their products in outlying farms and brought them into Lahaina and Honolulu. To satisfy the demand for beef, cattle were driven through the streets of the town—to the complaints of the residents—and slaughtered as necessary in the ports. Economic choices wreaked havoc on the delicate environment of the Hawaiian shoreline and also on the Hawaiian sensibilities. Dust clouds hung over the paths into the ports; the stench of slaughtered beef was in the air, blending with the scent of greed.

Whaling meant money and industry. Goods were transshipped in Hawaii, and because the whaling ships required repair facilities, other merchant vessels called as well to make needed repairs.

In this boom-town atmosphere the *makaainanas,* the common people, were bewildered and confused. As *keiki O ka aina,* a child of the land, the average Hawaiian saw his values crumbling, saw the introduction of foreign goods, watched the excesses of the whalingmen ashore and calculated the worth of the goods flowing in and out of the ports. Already less numerous, already seeing more of his land taken in various enterprises, already having lost the *kapu* system that helped locate his life in the order of things, the Hawaiian was hard pressed to make sense of his life and times.

And if he looked in another direction, a second set of *haoles* confused him just as much. They came with a pitiful handful of possessions and tales of a thundering, vengeful god who was everywhere, but who would save the souls of his Hawaiian children. In their own way, the missionaries would exert more influence in Hawaii than the whalingmen. At least they would outlast them.

The port of Honolulu in 1816, as depicted by Louis Choris.

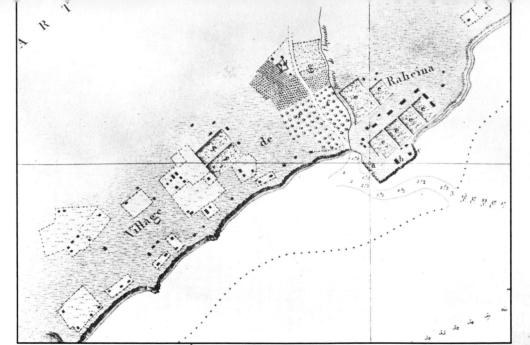

The 1819 map of Lahaina (left) was drawn by an artist on the French ship L'Uranie. The famous Roach fleet (Enterprise, William Roach, Pocahontas and Honqua) floats among a school of sperm whales off the Hawaiian coast (right). The fort at Honolulu (below) took director John Young one year to build.

BANNERS IN A HEATHEN LAND

In one respect the missionaries were fortunate—the stage had been set for them by events in Hawaii. Had they landed at some other moment, instead of appearing off the coast of the Island of Hawaii on March 30, 1820, they might have been rebuffed.

But despite the terrible consequences of the foreigners' intervention in Hawaii, there had been some enrichments that caused the *alii* to listen to the Bible-bearing newcomers. The fur trade had brought a measure of prosperity to the islands. So had the sandalwood trade, which in the early 1800s became a royal monopoly, with the islands' sandalwood trees selling briskly to Chinese artisans. On Hawaii Island, the English naval officer George Vancouver had introduced horses, on which Kamehameha I had placed a *kapu* which protected them for ten years.

So here were imported ideas; they would, perhaps, fill a void created by the end of the *kapu* system.

The impetus for the missionaries was the interdenominational American Board of Commissioners for Foreign Missions, founded June 29, 1810, in Bradford, Massachusetts. The board was inspired by the life and death of a young Hawaiian, Henry Opukahaia, who showed great promise as a scholar and who lived for a time with the president of Yale University. Opukahaia was being groomed as the first Hawaiian educated in the Western sense to return to the islands and preach the gospel, but he died at 26 of typhus while still in school in Connecticut. The tales of his death, in which he anguished about the spiritual future of his countrymen, stirred missionary fervor and spurred missionary activity. Stirring, too, was the sermon delivered by the Reverend Heman Humphrey in Goshen, Connecticut, late in 1819. The Reverend intoned, among other things, that "Christendom now possesses ample resources and ability, she is solemnly bound in the name of God, and with the least possible delay to set up her banners in every heathen land . . ."

On the afternoon of October 23, 1819, the Reverend Hiram Bingham, 30 years old, stood on a dock in Boston, and with his wife stared out at the brig *Thaddeus*. With them were the Reverend Asa Thurston and his wife, Mr. and Mrs. Samuel Whitney, Dr. and Mrs. Thomas Holman, Mr. and Mrs. Samuel Ruggles, Mr. and Mrs. Elisha Loomis and the Daniel Chamberlains with their five children. There also were three Western-educated Hawaiians. After a short ceremony, the passengers rowed out to the *Thaddeus* to begin the voyage to a strange and pagan land.

It was by any standard a hardship.

Packed into tiny cabins, ravaged by seasickness, buffeted by storms, but consistent in their morning and evening devotions, the weary missionaries counted the days with a quiet desperation. The children fared better, dancing about the ship's deck and absorbing Hawaiian words from the three Hawaiians returning to their home. Some dissension developed in the little missionary band, with arguments between Bingham and Dr. Holman, but in general their common purpose helped maintain good relations.

One hundred and sixty-four days out of Boston, the *Thaddeus* came in sight of the Island of Hawaii and the crew prepared for the worst. Not knowing the situation in the islands, the cannons were readied to repulse boarders. But the crew and the missionaries were shortly to receive news that electrified them. A party went ashore and returned with word that Kamehameha I was dead and the *kapu* system overthrown. The end of the system was, in the eyes of the missionaries, the beginning of the Lord's work in Hawaii.

They went ashore in Kailua, Hawaii Island, on April 4, 1820, pre-

The stately portrait of the scholar Henry Opukahaia (above) contrasts with the strong, athletic Hawaiians near the pali (opposite), beasts of burden themselves before the horse's introduction, and early surfers (inset) whose water sport was discouraged by the missionaries.

sented themselves to Liholiho, Kamehameha II, and asked permission to stay and teach Christianity; he demurred. Four days later, he granted their request, whereupon the missionaries then asked if they could establish themselves in Honolulu as well. Four more days passed, and the second request was granted. The Thurstons and the Holmans remained in Kailua, and the rest of the missionary party sailed on to Honolulu. On Oahu, they were granted the use of property lying on an arid plain between the mountains and the ocean and adjacent to a path that led into Waikiki. Oahu's governor Boki had thatched huts built for them on the dusty plain, and they ventured out from this small enclave of Christianity to do God's work.

Regarding Liholiho as a friend, the missionaries set about converting the royalty. Keopuolani, the queen-mother, was an early convert, as was the powerful chieftess Kapiolani. Within two years, the missionaries had standardized the written form of the Hawaiian language and produced Bibles. They founded schools. They began to evolve into a dominant force in island affairs.

Meanwhile, four years after the missionaries arrived, Liholiho decided to visit England. His kingdom had been influenced by French and English visitors and he wished to call on England's monarch, George IV. Liholiho and his wife, Kamamalu, sailed for England aboard the whalingship *L'Aigle* with an assortment of friends and strongboxes crammed with money. There was a stop in Rio de Janeiro, and then the royal couple turned up in London to the sur-

prise of the British government—they had neglected to inform them of their impeding visit. The government reacted well, and Liholiho and Kamamalu were grandly entertained even as an audience with the king was being scheduled. They were never to meet him, however, for every person in the visiting party was stricken with measles. Treated by the best physicians, they began to recover except for Queen Kamamalu, who grew steadily worse. On July 8, 1824, Kamamalu died in the approaching evening. Liholiho, devastated, lost his own will to live and died six days later.

Under Kauikeaouli, brother of Liholiho, who ascended the throne of Hawaii as Kamehameha III, the missionary forces continued their work. An important step was the conversion of Kaahumanu, who had been such a power in the islands for so many years. As the wife of Kamehameha I, she had been a behind-the-scenes advisor of considerable acumen and boldness. As Liholiho's advisor, she had caused him to overthrow the *kapus.* She had later married the ruler of Kauai, Kaumualii, taking both the island and the chief into her ample embrace; to further consolidate these gains, Kaahumanu also married Kaumualii's seven-foot-tall son.

Despite this deplorable—to the missionaries—situation, Kaahumanu was their friend, being a convert and also the type of person who couldn't resist lavishing affection on the missionary women. Under her care and protection, the missionaries in Honolulu began to expand their activities and steadily made progress, not only in the numbers of Hawaiians converted to Christianity, but in other educational ways. When Kaahumanu died at her home in Honolulu in 1832, the missionaries lost a protector, advisor and friend.

The missionaries had their share of enemies, not primarily among the native Hawaiians who more often regarded them as a curiosity, but among the *haoles,* the white settlers, who viewed them as upstart newcomers out to destroy a lifestyle and an island paradise. To some extent they were right—the missionaries wanted an end to what they considered the licentiousness of the population, brown *and* white, and the whites, especially, wanted the status quo. One British sea captain was so incensed by the changes proposed by the missionaries that he stood his ship off Lahaina and lobbed cannonballs toward

Namahana (above), one of Kamehameha I's widows, was an intelligent, Christian convert. Kaahumanu, who worked avidly for the Christian cause, preached with the Reverend Hiram Bingham at Waimea on a tour of Oahu in 1826 (below).

the home of the Reverend Richard Williams. In Honolulu, Hiram Bingham was attached by a mob of sailors. Still the missionaries kept preaching that to work on the Sabbath, to drink excessively and to engage in unrestrained sexual activity were deadly sins that the Lord would punish.

Such clashes were inevitable and might have been worse. The coolest heads, it developed, belonged to the Hawaiians. Although torn by the two opposing points of view, the Hawaiian leadership recognized that steps had to be taken to preserve the peace. In a series of meetings they found out just how far apart the two factions were—the missionaries wanted the Ten Commandments as the law of the land, and the opposition wanted no restrictions at all. Kamehameha III, still a child, tried to defer a decision as long as possible.

The missionaries stretched their orders not to interfere in local politics—and did so more than once. Justifying their role by citing the necessity to secure the islands from the tender mercies of the visiting ships, the missionaries became as militant in the cause of morality as the sailors were in the cause of hedonism. Elisha Loomis set up a printing press and produced a tome on the proper behavior of Christian people; Hiram Bingham, in service after service, invoked God's patience but also His wrath, and the conflict continued. Every visiting whaling ship posed a new problem for the missionaries, just as every Sunday morning service was greeted with scorn by the sailors and a good percentage of the resident *haoles*.

In their first few, faltering years, the missionaries evidenced their personal strengths as well as their personal prejudices. Of the original pioneers from the brig *Thaddeus,* Dr. Holman and his family seemed more at ease with the Hawaiians, but also became the first casualties. Drawing further away from the strict missionary milieu, the Holmans seemed to like Hawaii but to dislike the missionary zeal of Hiram

King Liholiho (Kamehameha II) and Queen Kamahala enjoy the theater in London shortly before their deaths (above). Their bodies were returned to Honolulu, where they were interred at the royal mausoleum at the sacred enclosure of Honaunau (below).

Elisabeta Kinau, daughter of Kamehameha I, who became kahina nui in 1832, comes home from church in a scene that contrasts the old and new architecture and dress of early Honolulu, while Boki and Liliha retain their authentic Hawaiian look for an 1824 London portrait (inset).

Nahienaena (inset), royal princess, sister and
great love of Kamehameha III (below).

Bingham. After little more than a year in the islands, they sailed away. Bingham, whose forceful personality was to be both an advantage and a liability, depending on the occasion, was the unflagging leader of the little band which for more than six years battled extreme odds to establish its Protestant views.

In their seventh year in Hawaii, the missionaries faced a new threat—the arrival of two French Catholic priests to set up a mission in the islands.

For four turbulent years, the Catholics tried valiantly to gain a foothold. They ran afoul not only of the Hawaiian leadership, who were not happy at any new religious complications, but also the Protestants who saw the Catholics as rivals, and finally the sailors and other resident whites who saw the priests simply as new interlopers. The Catholics' most notable protector was the governor of Oahu, Boki. As the priests soon learned, having Boki as a friend was worse than having him as an enemy. Mercurial, quixotic and fun-loving, Boki had visited England himself and had his own ideas of how the islands should be governed. He was, by any account, highly political, and by championing the Catholics he removed himself from the circle of missionaries and the current Hawaiian leadership. Unfortunately, Boki drank to excess, was a poor businessman and an incorrigible gambler. When life finally became unbearable, he outfitted two ships and sailed on December 3, 1829, for the New Hebrides in search of an island said to be laden with sandalwood trees. There is evidence that sandalwood was merely an excuse; Boki, thwarted at home, may have had ideas of colonization. Six months later, one of the ships returned with most of its crew dead of a mysterious illness. The other, bearing Boki, was never seen again.

With Boki out of the picture, the Hawaiian chiefs decided the time had come to send the priests away. Late in 1831, the two Catholic priests were put aboard a government schooner and sent to California, leaving only a few score converts.

Protestantism had carried the day, and the missionaries were pleased. They had other reasons to be pleased as well. The churches were filled, and the schools were using textbooks in Hawaiian printed by the missionaries. Many of the teachers were Christians, and the missionaries were justly proud that they had found an effective way to spread their influence—and the Word.

Seven years after their expulsion, the two priests returned to Hawaii but were prevented from preaching or attempting to convert the Hawaiians. Two more priests joined them, and finally their presence brought down harsh edicts against the islands' relatively few Catholics. Mass was forbidden, and native police tried to surprise Catholics at prayer so they could be arrested; some were, in fact, arrested and forced marched to jails. It was to be years before Catholics could openly practice their religion in the islands.

A "formal entertainment" at Kamehameha III's country place included one female hula dancer.

NAHIENAENA

The new king, meanwhile, was showing disturbing tendencies toward self-indulgence in the extreme. Kamehameha III was a teenage tavern owner and an accomplished seducer whose affairs disgusted the missionaries and caused no little political entanglement. His example caused the common people who had become converts to revert to their old ways. Attendance at church and school dropped off, and the missionaries braced themselves for a general and unchecked rejection of all their efforts.

That it did not come, that the king himself underwent a change, resulted from a tragic occurrence in which the missionaries' teachings and the customs of old Hawaii came into a direct and terrible confrontation.

In June 1834, Bingham and an influential medical missionary, Dr. Gerrit Judd, rushed to Kauikeaouli's side in response to reports that he had tried to kill himself. The reports were true. The king had tried to end his life because of his great love for his sister, Nahienaena, who had rejected him out of fear of the Christian governor of her home island, Maui. Six weeks later, the king did, indeed, sleep with his sister. Incest was not frowned upon among the royalty of old Hawaii; in fact, the union of the king and Nahienaena was favored by some chiefs as an ideal union, preserving the inherent characteristics of their respective ranks. Such a concept horrified the missionaries, and afterwards the king tried to spirit Nahienaena away to Waianae, home of the wastrel Boki, but she was sent home to Maui instead. The Christian chiefs among the Hawaiians had prevailed. Nahienaena was disciplined severely by the church.

Outwardly, Kamehameha III made concessions to the Christian influences now rooted strongly in his islands. He approved a tough new code of conduct with hard penalties for murder, theft, adultery and other crimes, but he also neglected many of the affairs of state. Nahienaena, meanwhile, suffered a final hard punishment from the church—she was excommunicated in May 1835. Now she began to visit the king again, and before the year was out had become pregnant. A marriage was arranged with a young chief, and her son was born the following August but lived less than a day. Nahienaena herself, tortured and dejected, died before the year ended, a tragic figure who haunts Hawaii's history as an example of the clash between old customs and new moralities in an isolated civilization.

Kamehameha III, devastated by the death of his great love, took a more serious approach to life but spent more and more time on Maui. Honolulu was still a magnet for the whaling ships, but Lahaina was more so, and Maui seemed to be somehow livelier and more colorful. Honolulu was still the arid plain, although beginning to grow and spread. The king obviously enjoyed Maui for its easy ways, and Honolulu suffered by comparison.

Meanwhile, political events were casting shadows across the Pacific. Warships of France, England and the United States were prowling the waters literally and testing the waters figuratively. Kamehameha III got a taste of power politics in the affair of the Catholic priests.

In April 1837, the two priests who had been banished in 1831 reappeared in Hawaii and were once again ordered to leave. French and British sea captains intervened and the priests were allowed to stay,

Kamehameha III, Hiram Bingham, Kinau, Captain de Petit Thouars and Captain E. Belcher were among the negotiators for French Catholic priests' rights at an assembly at Halekauwila Palace in 1837.

with the provision that they not attempt to make converts. In November more priests arrived, and the situation grew tense. Word got back to France that the priests were being denied their rights, and the French government decided that steps had to be taken. On July 9, 1839, a no-nonsense French naval officer, Captain C.P.T. Laplace, arrived aboard his frigate *L'Artémise;* the next day he issued his ultimatum—there was to be freedom of worship for Catholics, a parcel of land for a church and the Roman Catholic Church in the Hawaiian Islands was to be ministered by French priests. Laplace also demanded $20,000 as a deposit to the French government in recognition that the demands were valid and would be met. Kamehameha III was, as usual, in Lahaina; the demands were acceded to by the governor of Oahu who borrowed the $20,000 from local merchants. Laplace then turned up with additional demands—French citizens could be held accountable only to a jury of foreigners selected by the French consul, and there would be no prohibition of French wines.

In the wake of the *L'Artémise* came a sober realization. Hawaii was sovereign and independent but also weak; hardly a match for any major foreign power who threatened war if demands were not met.

The Protestant missionaries, who were not noticably upset at the expulsion of the Catholics in the first place, continued their efforts throughout the reign of Kamehameha III. New arrivals brought fresh initiatives, and the departure of the autocratic Hiram Bingham in 1840 marked the end of an era—or at least the end of the beginning. Bingham had dominated much more than his fellow missionaries in his years in the islands, being firmly convinced that he and God were in partnership. Few denied that his unyielding, often imperious manner worked both for him and against him as he attempted to bring God to the heathen. The mission program in the islands had evolved. No longer was it a new and exotic religion. Diligence and hard work—often at a terrible price—had so infused Christianity into everyday life of the islands that the *haoles'* faith became widespread and permanent. The missionaries had endured the bad old days when any moment could see their expulsion and now were secure in their accomplishment.

Not so the whalers. Having arrived before the missionaries, the whalers initially appeared stronger and more likely to last. Their great ships darkened the harbors of Lahaina and Honolulu for decades, but they were not to endure as the missionaries endured. In the 1820s, there were more than 100 ships a year in Lahaina and Honolulu; in the next two decades the numbers doubled twice; and in 1846 there were nearly 600 ships calling at Hawaiian ports. No one would have forecast their end.

But in 1859, an oil well went into production in Pennsylvania and the end of the whaling industry was in sight. The Civil War hastened its demise when many of the ships out of New England were pressed into service as merchantmen. Finally, in the fall of 1871, 33 whaling ships were caught by ice in the Arctic waters north of the Bering Strait. Although the crews escaped, the ships were ground to pieces by the remorseless ice, finishing what a war and a new industry had begun. The whalers never again were numerous or powerful in the Hawaiian Islands.

Of the two groups—whalers and missionaries—the whalers were in most ways more interesting, more colorful and certainly more exciting, but it was the missionaries who had the deepest influence. They had brought a powerful religion to a new land; they raised families which in the ensuing years would be the most influential of all the *haoles.* Their descendants amassed fortunes, led political parties, and set the style and tone in certain social circles throughout the years. Historians today can judge the impact of the whalers and of many other events and situations in the islands, but the question of the missionaries' activities always gives pause. Would the islands have been better off, or worse, without the missionaries? The question is hypothetical—and unanswerable.

Bark cloth (tapa) *was adapted to the transitional garment introduced by Western missionaries.*

CHAPTER THREE

THE
GATHERING
PLACE

Honolulu, Oahu, Nov. 1840. J. W. Dana, from shipboard.

The more-than-30-year reign of Kamehameha III was the longest of any Hawaiian monarch, but that was no indication of stability. The period was marked by growth and depressions, advances and declines. The king fluctuated between drunkenness and intense sobriety, between a great concern for his people and total disregard of their situation. Honolulu had been growing and changing rapidly and the islands in general were taking on a new look. The Hawaiian population continued its decline and superpowers were eyeing the islands with growing interest.

As is usually the case, strong personalities emerged. Dr. Gerrit P. Judd, the medical missionary, became a strong, some said despotic, advisor, holding several government posts at once and making his presence felt in all great affairs. The Hawaiian community produced perhaps its first genuine intellectual in David Malo, a brilliant scholar and a strong supporter of the missionaries in the islands. He was mistrustful of all other *haoles,* and he accurately forecast the domination of the islands by outside forces. An urbane Scotsman, Robert Wyllie, became head of the Foreign Office and a strong influence on the monarchy. Young John Ricord of Oregon became Hawaii's first attorney general.

Honolulu now was changing shape almost daily. The thatched huts were giving way to more permanent structures. Paths that had led from the "arid plain" to all parts of Oahu—"the gathering place" in the Hawaiian language—had become streets, and the streets were filling with carriages. The population grew from a few hundred at the time of the missionaries' arrival to upwards of 3,000 by 1823. The missionary houses, built with lumber brought around Cape Horn from Boston in the early 1820s, were among the earliest permanent "modern" structures. At a time when most of the area west of the Rockies was still hostile territory, a printing press was shipped around the Horn and housed in a structure of coral in what was becoming downtown Honolulu. The islands then had the oldest printing house west of the Rockies. In 1841, the imposing coral-block Kawaiahao Church was built and served as the royal chapel during the life of the monarchy. Kings and queens were crowned here, and in it were held some early legislative sessions.

As Honolulu grew it attracted more foreigners—not only American but British, French, German, Scots and others. David Malo, growing embittered, watched the "white tide" rolling across the islands and feared for the future of his nation. It seemed that *haoles* were, at last, discovering the Pacific in earnest. By the end of the 1840s, Tahiti and the Marquesas Islands belonged to the French and New Zealand to the British. As nationalism flourished in other climes and foreign war-

Kamehameha III, a tall, handsome man, reigned for 30 years over a turbulent, changing Hawaii. Original pencil and watercolor portrait by August Plum is in Bishop Museum.

A shipboard view of 1840 Honolulu includes James Dwight Dana's sketches of the fort and harbor (above, left), Punchbowl backdropping the Kawaiahao Church at right (above, center) and Diamond Head overshadowing grass houses at Waikiki (above, right). The 1840 village (below) is probably near Waikiki, and Pa'u riders gallop away from Punchbowl (inset).

ships called at Honolulu, the people of Hawaii wondered how long their small nation could continue to be independent.

As the 1840s opened, the British consul general in Hawaii, Richard Charlton, fell into disagreement with the government over his claim to certain properties. Rebuffed, Charlton left the islands in a rage, vowing to seek justice. He was succeeded by Alexander Simpson, a rabid imperialist who immediately began to plot Hawaii's annexation by Great Britain. Simpson unsuccessfully argued Charlton's case in Hawaii, and failing to persuade the government to release the lands Charlton claimed, wrote the commander of the British fleet in the Pacific seeking redress.

The message reached Admiral Sir Richard Thomas in San Blas, Mexico. The admiral promptly dispatched the frigate *Carysfort*, commanded by Lord George Paulet, under orders to see justice done and protect British interests. On February 10, 1843, the *Carysfort* anchored in Honolulu, and Paulet let it be known that he would talk with no one but the king himself. The threat of the *Carysfort's* guns underscored Paulet's forcefulness. All over Honolulu the resident foreigners were filling carts with valuables to get them out of the city before the storm broke.

On February 18, the king capitulated. Paulet won Charlton's lands for him, won recognition for Simpson (who had been unofficial as far as the monarchy was concerned) as consul general of England, won new court hearings for local Britishers in several commercial cases and won a concession that Britishers could be held in jail only in cases of felony as approved by British court systems. Paulet's presence and Simpson's pressing claims also convinced the king that Great Britain was seeking nothing less than annexation of Hawaii. To forestall such an event, the king met with agents of the United States and France in efforts to offer Hawaii jointly to both nations under terms favorable to Hawaii. It was, in the view of Kamehameha III, the lesser of two evils. Papers were readied.

On the morning of February 24, the autocratic Dr. Judd changed his mind and refused to sign the papers. As prime minister (and not-

Kamehameha III's The Mahele Book *(below); the left page lists the king's lands, those on right are lands granted to the chiefs. Lord George Paulet (opposite) and Admiral Sir Richard Thomas (inset), both circa 1843.*

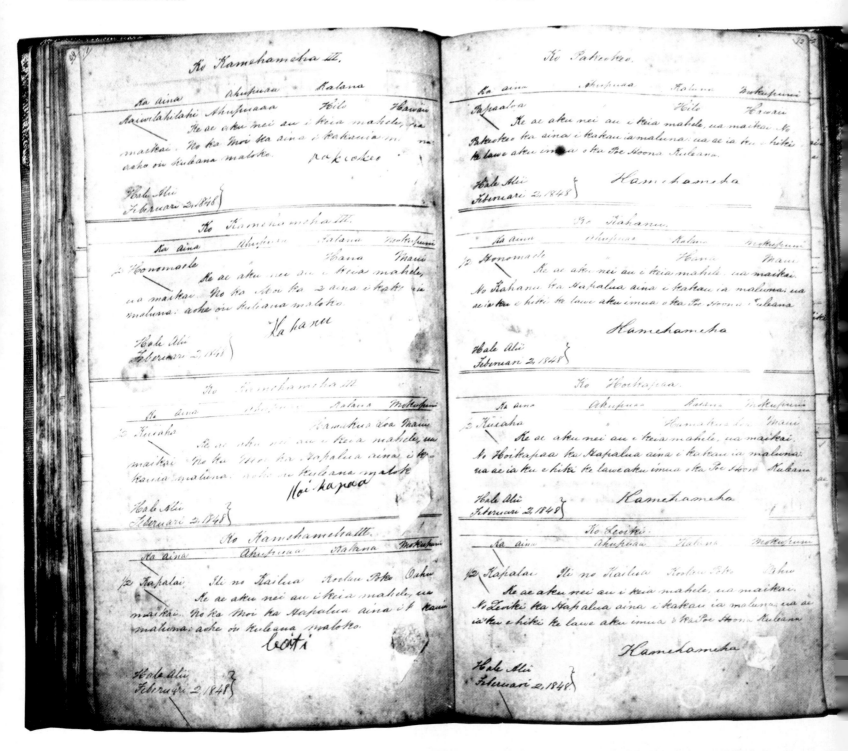

so-silent partner in most other offices), Judd's affirmation was necessary for the legality of the cession to the United States and France. When he refused to sign, the king knew the end was in sight.

On the following day, Kamehameha III relinquished his nation to Great Britain (represented by Paulet). At a small fort near the Honolulu waterfront, the deed of cession was read, the Hawaiian flag lowered and the flag of Great Britain raised.

Under terms of the agreement, Kauikeaouli and his advisers would continue to administer internal affairs. For business affecting foreigners, Paulet, the king or his deputy and two officers from the *Carysfort* would serve as a commission; Dr. Judd agreed to join them as the Hawaiian representative. Almost at once, Paulet went beyond the understanding and began to assess new taxes on the Hawaiian population. Liquor laws were relaxed and laws against fornication repealed altogether. Paulet and Dr. Judd engaged in behind-the-scenes combat,

with Judd attempting to frustrate Paulet's actions in hopes that the whole affair would be, somehow, undone.

At the same time, a new directive from the British Foreign Office reached the British Pacific fleet commander, Admiral Thomas. It advised that native governments should be treated with dignity and courtesy, and that they should be given a sense of their own independence. In other words, the directive contradicted Paulet's actions in Honolulu in no uncertain terms. Thomas was spurred into action.

Sailing at once in his flagship, the HMS *Dublin,* Thomas reached Honolulu on July 26 and had an immediate conference with Paulet. Thomas then met with the king and worked out agreements on the treatment of British subjects in the islands. Subsequently, Thomas announced that the independence of Hawaii would be restored immediately.

Paulet, downcast, nevertheless turned up with everyone else on the

---

DAVID MALO
ABOVE THE WHITE TIDE

*E*very culture produces its intellectuals, and Hawaii has had its share. One of the earliest to be recognized was David Malo.

Born in 1795 on the Island of Hawaii, Malo was placed in the household of a high-ranking Hawaiian chieftain, Kuakini, brother of Queen Kaahumanu, who was the principal wife of Kamehameha I. From this vantage point, Malo was steeped in the lore of ancient Hawaii's mythic and historical past.

Malo became a Christian under the influence of the missionaries, but carried a sense of foreboding about the presence of foreigners in the islands. Nevertheless, he was an avid reader of everything produced by the mission presses. In 1831 he entered the Lahainaluna school on Maui, and ten years later was one of the members of the Royal History Society formed in Lahainaluna.

In 1837 the sensitive and thoughtful Malo wrote to the queen regent, Kinau, a passage that has often been quoted by historians, reflecting his maturing feelings about the presence of the foreigners:

> . . . If a big wave comes in large fishes will come from the dark ocean which you never saw before, and when they see the small fishes they will eat them up; such also is the case with large animals, they will prey on the smaller ones; the ships of the whitemen have come, and smart people have arrived from the Great Countries which you have never seen before, they know our people are few in number and living in a small country; they will eat us up, such has always been the case with large countries, the small ones have been gobbled up.

Malo became a successful businessman, producing molasses and growing cotton. In 1841 he became the first superintendent of schools, and the following year he was elected a member of the first house of representatives. Despite his doubts about the benefits of having foreigners in the islands, the missionaries licensed Malo to preach and he did so.

David Malo

His contribution to Hawaiian literature came in 1840 with Hawaiian Antiquities, *a book which historians consider flawed by its subjectivity but extremely valuable for its data regarding ancient culture in Hawaii.*

In October 1853, Malo was in ill health and asked to be taken to Lahaina to be buried in the hills behind the town "above the white tide." He was afraid the cemetery lands in Lahaina would one day be covered by the developments of waves of white settlers. After his death his wishes were carried out.

Malo was considered a radical by some factions of the government in Hawaii, but a reappraisal indicates he was simply ahead of his time. His great desire was to keep Hawaii for the Hawaiians, and it was a losing struggle. Intense, sensitive and intelligent, Malo was not easily dismissed by either Hawaiians or missionaries. He was, all at the same time, smart, articulate and troublesome—a man more in touch with the future than the present.

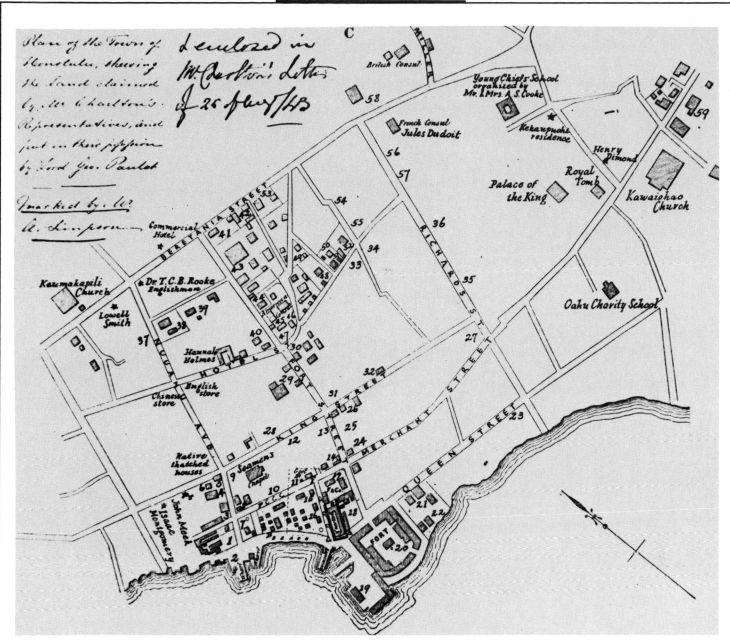

Map of Honolulu City—August 25, 1843

(Copy of photostat in Public Archives: original in British Consulate)

Map showing tract of land (rectangular piece near wharf, marked off with dotted lines), which Captain Richard Charlton, British consul general, claimed had been given to him by Kalaimoku, high chief and right hand man of Kamehameha I. Original in the British Consulate, Honolulu.

1. Brinsmade, Ladd & Co.
2. Brinsmade, Ladd & Co. wharf
3. Grimes Store, American
4. Hudson Bay Co.
5. Joe Booth's saloon
6. Native houses
7. Straw houses used as fish market
8. Stephen Reynolds' Store, American
9. Native thatched houses
10. Mr. and Mrs. John Paty
11. Two-story building with lookout
12. Seamen's chapel
13. Pierce & Brewer
14. Small wooden buildings
15. Empty lot 16. Sheds 17. French & Co.
18. Henry Skinner & Co.
19. James Robinson & Co.
20. Old fort and residence Governor Kekuanoa
21. Hale Kauwila, Government House
22. Mauna Kilika, Government House
23. Residence, Kekauouli
24. John Cummins Store
25. Sung & Co. bakery

26. Store   27. Anton Silva
28. C. H. Nicholson, tailor
29. E. C. Webster Store
30. Robert Davis, American
31. Residence, High Chiefs Paki and Kona
32. Residence, High Chiefs Paki and Kona
33. Judge Robertson's residence
34. James Jackson Jarvis
35. Residence, Princess Victoria
36. Residence, William Sumner
37. Scattered native houses
38. Residence, Mr. Skinner, Englishman
39. Father Damon
40. John Colcord, blacksmith
41. Residence, Charles Brewer
42. Mr. Jones
43. Roman Catholic Church
44. Captain John O. Dominis
45. French Hotel
46. Dr. R. W. Wood ..47. Stove
48. Alexander Adams, Englishman
49. Captain Dowsett, Englishman
50. Odd Fellows Hall
51. George Pelly   52. William Wond
53. Captain and Mrs. J. O. Carter
54. William French residence
55. Hawaii Theater
56. Residence, Chief Kaeo and Lahilahi
57. Residence, Chief Haalelea
58. Captain Dominis residence: now Washington Place (residence, governors of Hawaii)
59. American missionary houses

A Kamehameha royal family portrait includes the rare image of one reigning and two future kings, circa 1852.

flat plains east of Honolulu on July 31. It was a fine morning and a huge crowd had gathered. The king arrived with his retinue to the cheers of the crowd. Gun batteries fired, not only on the plain itself but from batteries on the volcanic tuff cone called Puowaina, later Punchbowl, near the heart of the city and from the fort in downtown Honolulu. Ships in the harbor fired salutes as well, and a contingent of British Marines paraded. The Hawaiian flag was raised and the king, his adviser and an escort of royal guards walked in a stately but joyous procession to Kawaiahao Church, where Judd read the proclamation that restored Hawaiian independence. The king made a speech, using for the first time the words that would become the motto of Hawaii: *"Ua mau ke ea o ka aina i ka pono,"* which Judd translated to the rapt congregation as, "the life of the land is preserved in righteousness."

Hawaiian independence seemed secure, at least for the time being. The United States, following talks between Hawaiian envoys and U.S. Secretary of State Daniel Webster, had indicated that it would look with displeasure on any attempts to annex Hawaii by another power; France and Great Britain signed a dual agreement in 1843 that recognized Hawaii's independent status. It is doubtful that at that moment, anyone, anywhere, thought of Hawaii's future as anything but as the kingdom it had become. Certainly no one thought that by the end of the century the Hawaiian flag would be lowered once more, never to be raised again over an independent kingdom.

GROWING PAINS

By 1840, Honolulu was growing and diversifying. Whaling was still the most important industry to the islands as a whole. However, even at this early date some far-sighted businessmen were looking to industries that were less seasonal, more secure and which did not wreak havoc on the local environment and sensibilities. It also became clear that some sense had to be made of the use of the land and some arrangement made between chiefs and commoners concerning the available lands. The missionaries hoped that if the Hawaiians became small landowners, it would contribute to their stability and, ultimately, to their virtue.

Traditionally, the chiefs enjoyed the use of lands in parcels called *ahupuaas,* which were often—but not always—wedge-shaped areas reaching from the mountains to the sea. Within such a parcel could be found all or most of the resources necessary for support. The common people were required to provide labor to work the chiefs' lands, but were allowed to claim their *kuleana.* In a system that was already complex, land use in post-Cook Hawaii, especially Honolulu, made old systems outmoded. The concept of small landowners found favor with the king, and his advisers and ranking chiefs agreed to study the situation with an open mind.

The resulting land division created as much confusion as it was designed to alleviate. The king gave up his rights to all lands except certain estates, to be known as crown lands. Chiefs were allowed to take out titles to the lands they had previously held. Commoners were permitted to buy, in fee simple, *kuleanas.* Aliens could lease land for 50 years (eventually a law was passed to allow them rights of purchase). The *haoles,* having come from civilizations that prized titles to property, reached for as much land as they could get. But it took some of the chiefs years to establish their property rights, and the common people often got horribly confused in the bureaucracy surrounding their claims. Part of the problem was government itself, whose surveyors seldom agreed on what a *kuleana* consisted of—

with the result that the *kuleanas,* instead of being a uniform size, varied from a spot of ground to upwards of 40 acres.

The land division was called The Great Mahele, and for better or worse it changed the way land was regarded in Hawaii. On the one hand it gave small landowners rights they had never before possessed —rights to sell, lease or cultivate their lands in whatever manner they saw fit. On the other hand, it liberated the small landowners from the necessity of making their lands pay taxes, and a lot of them simply decided that cultivation was too much work. They found other things to do. The Great Mahele, instead of insuring that the small landowner develop a deep love and respect for his property, made it possible for him to sell it—and sell he did. By the end of the nineteenth century, foreigners owned four acres of land for every acre owned by a native, including the chiefs. The movement that began as an attempt to tie the Hawaiians closer to the *aina,* the land, caused them to lose it in great quantities.

Honolulu had another industry that enjoyed a period of steady and reliable growth. The whalers and their money attracted women from the countryside, and prostitution—of a sort—flourished. It was initially a sort of happy trade-off; not until later would it be put on a more businesslike basis. At any rate, up to $100,000 a year passed through the hands of the women of the ports, a sum equal to the government's annual revenue. A dark side of the picture was the proliferation of diseases—not only venereal but the diseases to which the West was more or less immune and to which the Hawaiians continued to succumb—influenza, measles and smallpox. By 1850, the Hawaiian population was estimated at fewer than 100,000, or about a third of the numbers in the islands at the time of Captain Cook's "discovery" for the West.

GOLD FEVER

The Great Mahele had induced foreigners who bought native lands to begin producing; rice, sugar and coffee farms sprang up beyond Honolulu and on the other islands. Farmers also tried wheat and silk. The white potato so favored by itinerant whaling fleets caught on well on both Maui and Oahu, and its development and marketing in the late 1840s helped Honolulu parallel and then exceed Lahaina as a favored stopover port. Some sober businessmen tried to look beyond the whaling industry, believing that the islands needed other, less seasonal sources of revenue, and the farming was encouraged.

The idea of developing agriculture was spreading and finding favor when another event more than 2,000 miles away seized the islands' imagination and sent the populace into a frenzy of activity. The schooner *Louise* anchored in Honolulu harbor, bringing the electrifying news that gold had been discovered in California. The gold, it was reported, was simply lying there. Anyone could have it by digging and washing.

In the next few months, hundreds of people left Hawaii for the California gold fields, among the first to descend on the Sacramento Valley. Citizens by the scores filed "intention to depart from the Kingdom" notices, and merchants promptly shipped most of their stocked-up foreign goods to California. Anything that conceivably could be of use in the gold fields was taken from the shelves and packed onto

Sugar is being loaded off Lahaina.

departing schooners, barks and whaling ships headed for California. The supply of goods in Honolulu markets suddenly was very low.

And then the exodus was reversed.

Miners thronged to Hawaii during the winter months to escape the cold and squalor of the mountain camps. They created a sensation. It wasn't just that they were strange looking—wearing bushy beards, hats and occasional swatches of Chinese silk—but also their willingness to spend up to three times the normal prices for whatever they wanted that Hawaii could provide.

For the next few years there was a more-or-less steady flow of persons between Hawaii and California. California ports were two weeks away compared to the 80 or more days to the East Coast. The Hawaiian monarchy, which traditionally had looked to England and Europe for examples of how to conduct themselves and the affairs of state, now looked commercially and realistically at the nearest market—the United States. In 1850, California became a state of the Union. All at once the destinies of Hawaii and the United States seemed to be increasingly linked, and in the minds of some people in Hawaii, becoming a part of the United States was not the least desirable future they could envision. Many remembered their emotions in the Paulet affair when the flag of Great Britain soared in the clean blue sky over Honolulu. Perhaps the United States would be the answer, or at least a better answer than some European power.

The United States had exercised a certain influence in the islands through the missionary movement and through able ministers and advisers to the monarchy. The monarchy, as noted, continued to lean toward European styles of pomp and circumstance—a natural inclination since the United States itself lacked a monarchy. In most areas, however, American concepts and ideals were at work in the islands. The year 1839 had seen a law code; the following year a written constitution had emerged which created an executive branch of king and chiefs, as well as a legislative branch of two houses, a council of chiefs and an elected lower house. A supreme court was created. Eleven years later it was an American, William Little Lee, who wrote most of the new constitution.

Hawaii, especially Honolulu, was struggling to escape the grip of the whaling industry, and Honolulu was eager to prove itself an urban center. In 1850, having looked toward California for markets and having acknowledged the growing commerce between California and Honolulu, the king declared Honolulu to be a city and the capital of his kingdom. In the wake of that declaration came the formation of several important groups—the Royal Hawaiian Agricultural Society, Honolulu's first volunteer fire department, an official postal service, a board of health and a chamber of commerce. Aboard the *Charles* out of Boston were the first pipes for a public water system.

There were setbacks. Merchants in the booming city of San Francisco began ordering goods direct instead of having them transshipped from Honolulu. Another outbreak of smallpox was a serious problem. Hawaii's exports fell but continued at a lower level, and the gold rush boom ended as abruptly as it had begun. But none of these things permanently disoriented the business community in Honolulu, and their enterprising efforts kept both themselves and the island kingdom moving toward a stabilized economy—a stability that would be achieved by diversification.

As once the sea had provided a major source of revenue, it now was to be the land. Sugarcane had grown wild in the islands and there had been some abortive attempts to market it. It was being sold on the West Coast, but harvesting efforts were primitive, labor was scarce and the smaller sugar growers were declaring bankruptcies. Sugar, however, had enormous potential, and everyone knew it. What couldn't be foreseen was the incredible social changes which the rise of sugar would bring throughout the islands.

Our Lady of Peace Roman Catholic Church on Fort Street was dedicated in 1843.

CHAPTER FOUR

CAPITAL
OF A
KINGDOM

In the 1850s frame buildings were replacing the grass huts of Honolulu, the paths had become streets and the streets were formed into patterns. As the arid plain was being transformed physically, there was a corresponding development in the psyche of the city. Decisions were being made in downtown headquarters by men wearing business suits. Men walked the streets of Honolulu who had also walked the streets of London, New York and Paris; arriving ships brought new blood and new outlooks, and all the while the descendants of the missionaries and other early *haoles* were assuming leadership roles in the islands. The Hawaiians continued to recede, both in numbers and in influence. Because of their diminishing role in Hawaii, the time came when they were not considered adequate even to work the plantations.

It was a stereotyping both curious and persistent. The first contact between Hawaiians and Westerners found the Hawaiians marveling at the laziness of the *haoles*. In less than a century the outlook was reversed, and the *haoles* felt the Hawaiians had little ambition. The white men saw them idle when others were working, and the criticism grew that the Hawaiians were shiftless. The Hawaiians, in turn, regarded most methods of the *haoles* as ridiculous and refused to get involved in some types of labor.

So if the Hawaiians were not suitable, neither were they numerous, and certainly they were not always willing—they kept their own calendars, moved through life without clocks. This was not lost on the men downtown who stood at mid-century in Hawaii and looked to the future.

Sugar was the crop of the future. It would have to be sold in the United States, hence everything possible must be done to work out continuing agreements with the U.S. government. At the same time, there was not enough labor in the islands to produce it, therefore everything possible must be done to get good, cheap labor from somewhere else. The solution seemed clear and there was a consensus—get labor from China, sell sugar to America.

Although there had been a scattering of Chinese in Hawaii dating back to 1794, the first shipment of "coolies" arrived in January 1852 to work on the fledgling sugar plantations. Their arrival was hailed

The port of Honolulu in 1857. The three-story Custom House is at far left. The large two-story building center was built as a public market, later occupied by C. Brewer & Co.

as the beginning of a new era. Within a year there were problems. Some of the Chinese laborers showed no more inclination to work forever in the fields than the Hawaiians had shown, ending up from time to time in Honolulu prisons on bread and water for refusing orders. The majority of the Chinese worked out their five-year contracts and then got out of the fields—they went into Honolulu, preferring the city life. The more adaptable went into small business ventures and prospered. The ones who prospered indeed were those who followed the traditional Chinese route to wealth and began working on plans to buy land. The less adaptable Chinese committed criminal acts and brought the wrath of the Hawaiian government down on them. All in all, reflected the downtown Honolulu businessmen, the first attempt at cheap labor was not an unqualified success.

Still, sugar looked hopeful. There were now at least a dozen plantations in Hawaii and some technical advances in refining which gave impetus to the already high hopes. The government was solidly behind the industry, and despite minor setbacks the future was promising.

Kamehameha III died on December 15, 1854, leaving no legal heir. It had been an eventful reign, the last nine years of it from a one-story building in downtown Honolulu later called, somewhat grandiosely, Iolani Palace. The king was succeeded by Alexander Liholiho, from another part of the Kamehameha dynasty, who took office as Kamehameha IV and lost little time establishing an anti-American outlook. It stemmed, some said, from his travels in America where on one occasion he was ordered out of a train compartment by a conductor who thought he was a black. In other places, especially in France and England, Liholiho and his brother Lot were warmly received. The travels came about in the first place because of the tireless Dr. Gerrit Judd, then minister of finance, who thought the young princes should see something of the world. Judd may have regretted his decision.

Missionaries were largely excluded from the government of Kamehameha IV. Liholiho and his queen, Emma, maintained a court that was elegant and artistic. Liholiho himself was as mercurial as he was aristocratic and once shot his private secretary, Henry Neilson, under

King Kamehameha IV, circa 1860.

the false suspicion that Neilson was having an affair with Queen Emma. Neilson was seriously wounded and never really recovered, dying two years later. Unhappiness was to dog Liholiho despite his brilliance; he was broken by the death of his 4-year-old son, Prince Albert. Fifteen months later Liholiho himself died and was succeeded by his older brother Lot, who became Kamehameha V, and in many ways was more like the original Kamehameha than any of the other monarchs of Hawaii.

Throughout these changes, the sugar industry looked to America for a treaty of reciprocity. Kamehameha IV, the anti-American, and Kamehameha V, the ardent monarchist, both abhorred the thought of Hawaii's annexation by the United States, but they went along with the desire for such a treaty. In the first year of the reign of Kamehameha IV, a delegation left Honolulu for Washington, D.C., and negotiated a treaty, but it languished in the U.S. Senate for more than a year and finally died. Something more momentous was about to take place in America.

War broke out between the Union and the Confederacy. In Honolulu, the sentiment was for the Union, and downtown buildings were strung with red, white and blue bunting across their facades and across the streets to other buildings. Islanders enlisted in the Union cause and saw action. Honolulu businessmen accurately forecast the outcome of the war and what it might mean to Hawaii—the Union would prevail and the treaty of commercial reciprocity, which would benefit Hawaiian sugar, would become a reality.

The war, meanwhile, was emphasizing the importance of the sugar industry in Hawaii because it marked the beginning of the end for the whalers. Already shrinking because of the discovery of petroleum, the industry lost many ships which were pressed into service on

Queen Emma (above) and Kamehameha IV founded The Queen's Hospital (below), completed in 1860.

one side or the other. By war's end, sugar loomed even larger as Hawaii's primary industry.

Sugar on the Southern plantations languished because of the war; the misfortune of the Southerners allowed more Hawaiian sugar to find its way to U.S. markets. The end of the war, however, also meant the reemergence of Southern sugar, and the policy of the Hawaiian government and business leaders now became that of achieving the treaty of reciprocity. Under such a treaty, Hawaiian sugar would go duty-free into U.S. markets while certain American products would have the same consideration in Hawaii.

Americans living in the islands pushed the reciprocity idea with considerable vigor. As early as the 1850s, the idea of annexation by the United States had become a topic, and a controversial topic at that. Most agreed that a reciprocity treaty binding Hawaii and America closer economically was a good thing, and necessary. On the other hand, there were those who feared that the United States had designs on the islands, and that such a treaty would weave the destinies of the two countries into one whole cloth.

Meanwhile, the king, the last of the Kamehamehas, had been ill and died on December 11, 1872, on his 40th birthday. He was a bachelor and left no heirs; the legislature was left with the responsibility of selecting a new ruler. Two men—David Kalakaua and William Lunalilo—campaigned vigorously, outdistancing the handful of others. Lunalilo was known as "Whisky Bill," with good reason; he

Like some other missionaries, the Levi Tenney family (opposite, above), put down roots in Hawaii. Princess Victoria Kamamalu (opposite, below), sister to Kamehameha IV and V and heir to the throne, died in 1865, the year following this photograph. Prince Lot, seated left, and Prince Alexander Liholiho accompanied former missionary Dr. Gerrit P. Judd on a diplomatic mission to Europe in 1850 (above).

King William Lunalilo (left) founded the Lunalilo Home (above) for older, infirm and poor people of Hawaiian blood or extraction.

nevertheless won an overwhelming victory in a popular vote and a few days later was elected by the legislature.

Lunalilo's reign was brief but interesting. He was educated, musical, charming and undoubtedly a drunk. He also was beloved and respected. Reversing the somewhat draconian decrees of Kamehameha V, Lunalilo liberalized the constitution and made possible a home for the aged that was a model of its kind. In a more controversial move, he ordered the segregation of lepers, sending these unfortunates to a colony on Molokai where conditions quickly became so deplorable that Lunalilo lost the respect of many of his people. One man who went to Molokai was Father Damien Joseph de Veuster, a Belgian priest whose work among the lepers—and his death from the disease after sixteen years of incredible devotion—would make Father Damien of Molokai world famous.

A second event cost Lunalilo much of his popularity. Resentful of the rigid discipline ordered by its senior officers, the king's Household Troops mutinied, seized three six-pound cannons and trained them on Iolani Barracks opposite the royal residence. Their demands were simple, but their methods brought a complete breakdown of discipline and threw Honolulu into confusion for a week. Foreign residents contemplated seeking outside help as more and more Hawaiians joined the rebels. Lunalilo, lying ill in bed, offered clemency and it was accepted. At the end of the week, the Household Troops were disbanded, but the government had been humiliated.

Lunalilo had another nagging problem. The treaty of reciprocity, which everyone wanted, now was coupled in the public mind with an idea floated by Henry M. Whitney, editor of the English-language *Pacific Commercial Advertiser.* He urged the government to give the Americans a 50-year lease on Pearl Harbor in exchange for a treaty of reciprocity.

The very idea prompted a hue and cry among the native Hawaiians, who had no desire to turn over the site, known as Puuloa, to the American government. They found a champion in a clever political maverick (with a comparably stormy personal life), Walter Murray Gibson, who started his own newspaper to protest the idea. Lunalilo vacillated on the question for weeks, finally saying that he couldn't

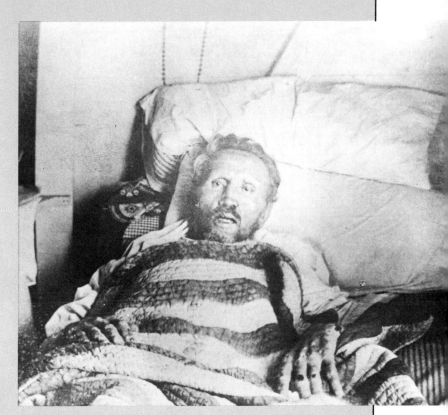

Father Damien, a young man (left) and two days before his death (right).

FATHER DAMIEN THE LEPER

*I*n 1830 a new and terrible disease was noted in the Hawaiian kingdom. By 1866 government ships were carrying its victims into isolation, to a remote peninsula on the Island of Molokai.

The disease was caused by a bacillus, leprae, but no one knew how it was transmitted. The Hawaiians called it mai pake—the Chinese disease—but no one knew how it had come to the islands; everyone knew there was no cure for it.

Leprosy was the historic, terrible scourge, a particularly ugly and wasteful disease, and most men avoided any contact with suspected lepers. To be condemned to Kalaupapa, the leper settlement on Molokai, was to be sentenced to death, for there was no return from Kalaupapa for most victims. Thus it was astonishing that a young man would choose to live his life there among the rejected of mankind.

He was Father Damien Joseph de Veuster, a member of the Hawaiian mission of the Sacred Hearts. Born in Belgium, his life had been filled with dreams of service—and, perhaps, martyrdom.

For sixteen years Father Damien lived at Kalaupapa, never shirking his duties and never shrinking from contact with the lepers. His critics claimed he could have been more careful, that he sought out the lepers to fill some need within himself. Whatever his reasons, Father Damien of Molokai was a source of comfort to the lepers, and a positive force for good in the administration of the unfortunate colony.

Inevitably, he became known as Father Damien the Leper. He had known for some time that he had contracted the disease, but had kept it to himself until its ravages on his face and body became apparent to all. He continued to work at Kalaupapa until his death from the disease in 1889. He was buried near a small frame church on the peninsula at Molokai, near the lepers he had tended all his adult life.

He has since been honored. A statue of Father Damien appears, along with Kamehameha I, in the Statuary Hall of the nation's Capitol. He was chosen with Kamehameha to represent Hawaii before the world.

In Honolulu, a replica of the same statue of Father Damien stands on the north side of the courtyard of the State Capitol Building. At the other end of the courtyard is a statue of the Hawaiian monarch perhaps most revered of all Hawaii's rulers, Queen Liliuokalani. Father Damien of Molokai would have smiled to find himself in such good company.

support the idea wholeheartedly. The king's physicians and the Hawaiian *kahunas* who had seen him knew Lunalilo was unable to do *anything* wholeheartedly, for he had caught a cold that was turning into something much more serious. Lunalilo went to the island of Hawaii for a rest, but was brought back to Honolulu in a weakened condition and died on the evening of February 3, 1874. His death paved the way for the election of the man who had been his chief rival, David Kalakaua.

Kalakaua, in the tradition of Hawaiian monarchs, was to prove both charming and capricious, but he began his reign by pushing hard for the treaty of reciprocity which promised to bring so much prosperity. He sent a small delegation to Washington to promote the idea, and on November 17, 1874, set sail himself for the United States, thus becoming the first foreign monarch to visit America. He spent eleven days in Washington, meeting President Ulysses S. Grant, appearing before a joint session of Congress and attending social events planned in his honor. The king returned home and waited. On March 18, 1875, the U.S. Senate voted for a treaty, but complications arose. It was not until September 9, 1876, that the treaty was a fact. The cession of Pearl Harbor had not been mentioned.

And now the need for laborers was even more acute.

David Kalakaua (left) was the first foreign monarch to visit America. The "English Church" (right), built in 1866 adjacent to Washington Place, was the predecessor to St. Andrew's Cathedral. A Mormon settlement at Laie in the late 1870s (below).

An 1875 Reciprocity Commission in San Francisco (above) included Governor John Dominis Jr., seated left, King David Kalakaua, center, and Governor John M. Kaupena of Maui, right; standing left to right, Henry A. Pierce, U.S. Minister to Hawaii, and Luther Severance. King Kalakaua's boat crew (below) were members of the Iolani Boat Club.

Lock boxes installed across entire face of lanai sidewalk were a feature of the Post Office on then unpaved (1870s) Merchant and Bethel streets (top, left). The Old Royal Hawaiian Hotel in downtown Honolulu (top, right), was remodeled in 1917 to become an Army and Navy YMCA. King Kalakaua named the Judiciary Building on King Street "Aliiolani Hale" in honor of Kamehameha V (bottom).

For a quarter of a century the merchants of Honolulu had been pushing for reciprocity, and now they had it. For another quarter of a century the treaty was in force. The sugar acreage in the islands increased 1,000 percent to 125,000 acres by 1889; the export crop increased from 25 million pounds a year to 250 million and by 1897 to 500 million pounds.

In Honolulu the sugar plantation agents were accustomed to handling large statistics. They brought in supplies, negotiated to sell crops and kept up a steady public relations program with the government and the banks on behalf of the planters. Beautiful homes were springing up in Honolulu and elsewhere as sugar money poured into the islands. The problem now was maintaining a steady labor supply.

The planters who had been less than enthusiastic about the Chinese were vocal about their choice of northern Europeans as laborers, but the northern Europeans had other ideas. They wanted much more money and much better working conditions than the planters were willing to provide. The planters again turned to the Orient, this time speculating on the advisability of using Japanese labor. And speculation it was, for Japan remained virtually a closed society; little was known in the West about the Japanese manner of doing things. To find out what was possible, Hawaii had sent Eugene Van Reed, an American who had lived in Japan, off to Tokyo as the Hawaiian consul general to Japan.

Van Reed was able to sign about 400 Japanese laborers, but due to confusion and a power shift in the Japanese government, fewer than half of them actually sailed on the first voyage aboard the *Scioto* on May 17, 1868. When they did arrive in Honolulu, Kamehameha V sent them a barrel of fish by way of greeting, and local newspapers admonished the planters to respect the Japanese customs and treat the new laborers well. It was not to be easy, however, and conflicts sprang up almost immediately.

The first Japanese came on three-year contracts at $4 a month, with food, housing and the voyage itself to be paid for by the planters. A promised $10 advance somehow did not materialize, communications became confusing and the Japanese suddenly discovered a whole range of rules set down by the planters but not made public. Tools that were lost or stolen had to be paid for by the laborers; visitors were limited and lights were to be out by 9 p.m. Any absence from work was an automatic fine. The planters appeared autocratic and exploitative to the Japanese laborers, and the Japanese appeared intransigent to the planters. After the first blush of happiness at their arrival, the relationships quickly cooled. It would be nearly twenty years before more Japanese came to put an indelible stamp on the cultural map of the islands.

So the planters were looking again. Portuguese from Madeira and the Azores arrived and were twice as ambitious as anyone suspected; from the start they regarded the plantations as a steppingstone to owning their own land. By a sort of racial default, the planters looked again to the Orient and decided that whatever the fault of the Chinese workforce, it was available. The Chinese arrived in varying numbers each year and they, too, put their cultural chop on the islands.

They came, often, in mean little ships, overcrowded, harassed and frightened. Some were more fortunate than others and enjoyed relatively comfortable voyages. All looked forward to life in the Sandwich Islands.

What they found was a type of racism that was unsubtle and direct. The planters, of European stock and outlook, had little sympa-

Chinese bound for Hawaii on S.S. China, circa 1901 (above, left), a Hawaiian father heads a "Chinese family" in 1893 (above, center) and a "Chinese Kau-Kau Man" sells food to plantation workers, circa 1912 (above, right). Laborers load cane into oxen-pulled carts in 1888 (below).

thy for the plight of the Oriental laborers. The king, Kalakaua, in turn had little sympathy for the *haoles*. But he recognized that sugar was the primary support of the kingdom, and his subsequent dealings with the planters veered between ambiguous and ambivalent. Kalakaua may even have felt some pity for the Oriental workers, but his concerns lay with the Hawaiian people and his own lifestyle, which had taken on a kind of opulence that the *haoles* considered frivolous and expensive.

While the planters continued to amass a degree of wealth, and the Oriental laborers continued to work the earth of Hawaii (and plant their own seed—many Chinese-Hawaiian marriages began to take place), Kalakaua decided to make a world tour to see for himself how things worked in other places.

In 1881, Kalakaua and his retinue sailed for San Francisco and enjoyed that city's considerable hospitality. His next stop was Tokyo, where he dropped a bombshell or two. To the dismay of his *haole* advisors, Kalakaua suggested to Emperor Mutsuhito that a federation of Asian nations be formed, with Hawaii to be included. Secondly, Kalakaua tried to arrange a marriage between a young Japanese prince and his own beautiful niece, Princess Kaiulani. Neither suggestion was acted upon, but the nervous advisors decided to keep a closer watch on the king who, as it turned out, was full of surprises.

Kalakaua and his party went on to China, Hong Kong and Southeast Asia. Progressing on to India and Egypt, Kalakaua made a good impression and finally arrived in Italy, where he met the king and Pope Leo XIII. In England he was welcomed with warmth by Queen Victoria and presented an Honorary Knight Grand Cross of the Order

of St. Michael and St. George. His sweep through much of the rest of Europe was a grand success. In America again, he met President Chester A. Arthur, then rode a train across the country, eventually reaching Honolulu on October 29, 1881. The city was wild with dancing and feasting his return; the king had been away for ten months.

What Kalakaua absorbed from his triumphal tour was not exactly what his advisors had in mind. The trip had given him a sense of grandeur, of the position of a king, and from his palace in Honolulu he determined to be a ruler in the great tradition, not just a figurehead. He decided upon a coronation, to be held in the new Iolani Palace at the heart of the city.

The palace was a grand setting. Brand new and large for its day, it had a full basement, two main floors, six towers, wide *lanais* (verandas) and furniture of gold and ebony. On the auspicious day, Kalakaua was invested with the feather cloak of Kamehameha I and a gold crown—which he placed on his head himself—handmade in England at a cost of thousands of dollars. As a reminder that the islands had not lost a sense of history, Kalakaua also wore a whale's tooth pendant of the type worn only by the ancient *alii*. Despite his elaborate preparations, the coronation was not a huge success, and the fact that he had ordered performances of the *hula* shocked some of the more staid members of the community and a newspaper or two. Kalakaua was unabashed. In the months that ensued, he continued to stress the rights of the monarchy and the necessity to maintain strong Hawaiian traditions and customs. In both instances, he incurred the enmity of many leading businessmen. It didn't seem to bother him at all.

A group of children gather behind a Portuguese bread lady, circa 1900 (opposite), while a slightly older group surrounds the "king" of Hawaiian sugar, Claus Spreckels, on board a steamer (above). Kalakaua, seated center (below), visited Japan during his trip around the world in 1881.

Princess Keelikolani (above), while of high chiefly rank, was never considered a candidate for the throne. She created her own Victorian "palace," Keoua Hale (top right) within sight of Iolani Palace (below). She returned to her birthplace, a grasshouse in Kailua, Hawaii (bottom, right) where she died in 1883.

*King David Kalakaua stands with his retinue in front of Iolani Palace
in 1882 (above) and joins in his birthday Jubilee Festivities on the
palace grounds four years later (below).*

The Kaimiloa, flagship (indeed, only ship) of the Hawaiian Navy, in 1887. Kalakaua stands on the ship's bridge (inset).

DREAMS OF EMPIRE

Kalakaua began to have visions of a grand oceanic empire, visions that were fed by the ambitious dreams of Walter Murray Gibson, now premier and foreign minister. From his handsome new palace, the king looked out over a city that was growing up as well as out. There were now a number of multi-storied structures and the city had taken on a character, a kind of atmosphere that seemed to meld a maritime community with an American accent, a touch of Old World charm and the whiff of joss sticks. It was cosmopolitan and interesting. Kalakaua's mistake was that he considered it to be the seat of a potential Polynesian confederacy, and in this delusion he was supported by Gibson. The two men were comfortable with the progress of Honolulu and Hawaii in general, but they erred in underestimating the interest of other, more powerful nations in Pacific affairs.

A civil war was brewing in Samoa with two rival chiefs, Malietoa and Tamasese, preparing for battle. The situation was being watched closely by Germany, which considered annexing the entire island chain, and by the United States and Britain, which were nervous about the Germans' overt desires for Samoa.

Ignoring the larger powers, Kalakaua and Gibson sent an envoy to Samoa who suggested to Malietoa that a federation be formed that would link Hawaii and Samoa. Inspired by his own experience in England, Kalakaua offered to present Malietoa the Grand Cross of the Royal Order of the Star of Oceania, and Malietoa leaned toward the idea of confederacy.

The Germans were incensed, the Americans bemused and the British disgusted with the Hawaiian initiative. What followed next would exacerbate the situation—Kalakaua and Gibson emphasized their ideals by sending to Samoa the new Hawaiian navy.

The navy consisted of a former guano trader converted into a training ship and carrying four cannon and two Gatling guns. Called the *Kaimiloa,* it was commanded by George E.G. Jackson, a British ex-lieutenant of the Royal Navy with a strong penchant for alcohol, currently the principal of a boy's reform school; two dozen of the boys, in fact, comprised a third of the *Kaimiloa's* crew. The ship sailed in mid-May 1887, and for the next eleven days Captain Jackson was too drunk to navigate. When she finally reached Samoa and began cruising among the islands to show the flag, the *Kaimiloa* was shadowed by a German gunboat.

Now the mission took on more comic-opera overtones. Kalakaua's delegation to Samoa fell into disfavor for what the Samoans told Kalakaua were "intemperate" habits, with the envoy described as a most dissipated man. Kalakaua and Gibson recalled the delegation, but their letter took more than a month to reach Samoa. Meanwhile, a group of *Kaimiloa* crewmen mutinied and would have blown up the ship except for the intervention of the captain of the German gunboat. These events alone may well have spelled the end of the confederacy concept, but it was the possibility that Germany would declare war on Hawaii that give Kalakaua and Gibson pause. In the end, they bowed to the obvious balance of power and abandoned the idea of a Polynesian confederacy.

The confederacy fiasco was merely one of the ventures that irritated the local businessmen about Kalakaua. They were appalled at his capacity to spend money, annoyed by his inclination to do as he pleased despite the legislature, and privately upset by his lifestyle, which was more regal than routine. What annoyed them further was the fact that Kalakaua always seemed to have the votes he needed for whatever he wanted, in spite of his excesses. But the storm would break; Kalakaua came under fire for apparently accepting bribes to allow the sale of opium in Hawaii—it had been sold under government control earlier, then declared illegal—and finally the king was forced to dismiss Gibson and other supporters. A reform-minded group forced Kalakaua to sign a new constitution which greatly curtailed his powers. Soon afterwards, Gibson died of tuberculosis, and Kalakaua watched his powers erode.

WAVES FROM JAPAN

The islands' *kamaainas* (old-timers) must have had a sense of *deja vu* in 1886, for the old problem of labor for the plantations resurfaced. Again it was the Japanese who loomed as the best hope of the planters. The need for them was intensified by the U.S. Congress, which in 1894 restored Hawaiian sugar to a privileged place in the American market. There was suddenly a new demand for immigrants who would work in the canefields. The Japanese were seen also as a counterbalance to the influx of Chinese, who were pouring into Honolulu in greater numbers.

The Honolulu they were pouring into was taking on a much more cosmopolitan air. In addition to Iolani Palace there was the impressive Opera House in what would become the capitol complex. Paths leading over the mountain ranges had become rough roads, passable

by horse. Out in the hinterlands of Waikiki to the east of Honolulu there were as many as 25 or 30 buildings amid the coconut groves, and in downtown Honolulu there were emporiums, mercantile establishments, ship chandlers and business offices handling the affairs of the outlying plantations. Kalakaua himself had a beach cottage in Waikiki. Iolani Barracks, built along the order of a medieval castle, housed the Royal Hawaiian Guard in an area not far from the palace. Nearby was the imposing home built by New Englander John O. Dominis. After Dominis disappeared at sea in the 1840s en route to China aboard the brig *William Neilson,* his widow took in boarders, one of whom was U.S. Commissioner Anthony TenEyck. TenEyck gave the home its name—Washington Place, in honor of the first American president. In time, Captain Dominis' son, John Owen Dominis, married Lydia Kapaakea, who was to ascend to the throne as Queen Liliuokalani. Washington Place became her private residence after her husband's death in 1891.

(After the queen's death, one of her heirs, Prince Kuhio, suggested the territory acquire Washington Place as the executive mansion. It did so in May 1921, and Washington Place became the official home of the governor of Hawaii when it was opened formally on April 21, 1922, by Governor Wallace Rider Farrington. It continues to be the home of the governor of Hawaii.)

Downtown Honolulu also was taking on identifiable names. Beretania Street was the Hawaiian equivalent of "Britain." Fort Street,

Devastation after the 1886 Chinatown Fire (above), undoubtedly battled by Volunteer Engine Company Number Two, the steam pumper, fire chief and his assistant (right).

Kawaiahao Church, as viewed from the Judiciary Building, had recently lost its steeple in 1887; Diamond Head and the undrained swamps of Ala Moana, Kewalo and Ala Wai are in the distance.

Charles Reed Bishop.   Bernice Pauahi Bishop.

A LEGACY OF LOVE

*B*ernice Pauahi Paki, Hawaiian princess and great-grand-daughter of Kamehameha I, was born in 1881 and grew into a slender, beautiful and amiable lady who was to have a profound effect on the islands she loved.

She upset her parents only once—when she renounced her be-trothal to Prince Lot, who would become King Kamehameha V, to marry a man with three strikes against him. Charles Reed Bishop was a newcomer, a commoner and a haole.

But Bishop was in Hawaii to stay and soon gave evidence of his ambition and his energy. He became a powerful banker, a collec-tor of customs and eventually minister of foreign affairs of the Hawaiian kingdom (and accepted by his in-laws).

The Bishops had no children. Mrs. Bishop, however, had a vast inheritance and an inclination to do something for Hawaii's chil-dren, so she willed that her estate be set aside for the establishment and maintenance of two schools for Hawaiian youth—the Kame-hameha Schools.

She also inherited and acquired artifacts that proved to be the start of a museum eventually to become one of the most famous in the Pacific. Today the Bishop Museum, an independent organi-zation founded in her honor, is world famous for its collection of Polynesian art and artifacts.

Over the years the Bishop Estate trustees have administered the complex holdings that now make the estate the largest landowner in the islands, surpassing even the federal government. Amount-ing to about one out of every twelve acres in Hawaii, a total of 341,546 acres, or slightly smaller than the Island of Oahu, the estate's assets are well over a billion dollars. More than 95 percent of the land is in agriculture or conservation; the remaining few percent contains hotels, apartments, and commercial and indus-trial operations and produces more than half the estate's income.

As Kamehameha V lay dying, he pleaded with Bernice Pauahi Bishop to succeed him as monarch, but she turned away. She never turned away from her love of the land and its people, how-ever, and today her legacy is appreciated by Hawaiian children.

which ran down to the waterfront, had been the site of an old fort. Nuuanu Avenue grew along the path that led from Honolulu through magnificent Nuuanu Valley just above the town. In Nuuanu, Queen Emma, wife of Kamehameha IV, built a classically simple home that became her escape from the rigors of the city and its court life. Also in Nuuanu, a royal mausoleum was started in 1865 and improved as the years went by; the Kamehameha dynasty, with the exception of Kamehameha I and Lunalilo, are entombed there. (Kamehameha's bones are hidden to this day, in keeping with ancient tradition. Lunalilo is entombed on the grounds of historic Kawaiahao Church, on Punchbowl Street.)

Rising above the capitol area was Puowaina, the Hill of Sacrifice, a volcanic cone on which ancient sacrifices had been performed. The street leading from it to the city was called Punchbowl, as Puowaina itself gradually came to be called. Paralleling Beretania Street was King Street, and the main business street would be called Bishop Street, after Charles Reed Bishop, prominent banker and husband of a princess, Bernice Pauahi. The princess was a descendant of the Kamehamehas, and as a memorial after her death, Bishop endowed a museum to the west of the city to house relics of royalty. Bishop Museum grew into an historic storehouse and a center for research in the Pacific. Also crossing downtown were streets named for obvious reasons—Queen Street and Merchant Street.

The city that was a seaport with overtones of the Old West took on a new flavor with the influx of foreign labor. Some of the signs hanging over establishments now contained Chinese ideograms. There were mah jong parlors and herbal doctors and acupuncturists. As the Japanese immigrants began to pour into Honolulu, other types of establishments sprang up—Japanese bath houses and Shinto temples.

In 1876 there were 35 sugar plantations in the islands, a number that would double in a decade. In the rush to bring in foreign labor, the planters increased Hawaii's population by at least 300,000, and many more came on their own to work in the plantation fields. While the treaty of reciprocity in 1876 was a significant step in Hawaii's commercial life, it also brought about the infusion of foreign elements into Hawaiian society and changed it forever. More significant than the architecture of Honolulu, undergoing a subtle change with the addition of pagodas and temples; more important than the role of laborers in the canefields; and more important than any contribution

Hawaiian workers rest against the walls of Honolulu Iron Works, 1889, which hired native laborers exclusively. Skilled mechanics came from the mainland.

to a healthy economic base for a flourishing sugar industry—the arrival of the Oriental laborers and their ultimate assimilation into the mainstream of Hawaiian society would give Honolulu its sense of style, its unique melting-pot ambience.

Watching bemused were the remnants of a once-great Hawaiian people. Their numbers had shrunk from more than 300,000 a century earlier to an estimated 50,000, and they viewed the arrival of the foreigners with a curious equanimity. Their tradition always had been to welcome strangers, and the newcomers were taking jobs they didn't much care for anyway. A more pressing problem was the growing fear that the United States would move to annex Hawaii and bring down the monarchy forever. While the Hawaiians had little control over such events, they could worry about their consequences, even as the *haoles* seemed to be working to bring them about. The *haoles,* to be sure, were looking at the island kingdom from a different perspective, and annexation began to look like the most promising route to follow. The Oriental laborers, lacking the power to influence events one way or the other, bided their time.

It was a period of tensions in the islands, with no one knowing which way the winds would blow. Out in the canefields—populated now by not only Japanese and Chinese, but also Filipinos, Koreans and some Europeans—the laborers plunged their hands into the Hawaiian soil and dreamed of making a part of it theirs despite their current status as laborers. Not in their wildest dreams, however, could the Oriental workers foresee the dawning of one day in the islands when there would be Chinese millionaires and Orientals in every profession and trade, when the governor of Hawaii would be the son of a Japanese sumo wrestler, when the state legislature and many state and city offices would be dominated by persons of Japanese ancestry. Oriental words would find their way into the language; a distinctive pidgin English would be built around Japanese inflections and phrases. (Indeed, there are as many varieties of pidgin English in Hawaii today as there are races; the differences among them are subtle, often humorous and impossible for a newcomer to detect.)

This would come in time. But as the new century loomed, there was still a great deal of uncertainty in Hawaii—and downright suspicion. There were now many in the islands who looked to America as the best hope for Hawaii's future, despite what others in the islands might think. Over Honolulu there fell a gradual, but perceptible, air of watchful waiting.

The Mission School, circa 1878, was the first Protestant mission building in Honolulu.

Walter Murray Gibson, minister of foreign affairs, stands in 1886 in front of Kapiolani Home with Catholic nuns and leper children (top). Oahu Bethel, the forerunner of Central Union Church, represented the beginning of the haole *church (middle). The students wear white muumuus while their teachers wear black in front of the Kawaihao Seminary in 1869 (bottom).*

A Chinese man plows rice with water buffalo in the nineteenth century (far left), Diamond Head watches over workers in a rice field in the McCully district (left) and newly arrived Japanese plantation workers are guarded by lunas, field bosses, on horseback (below).

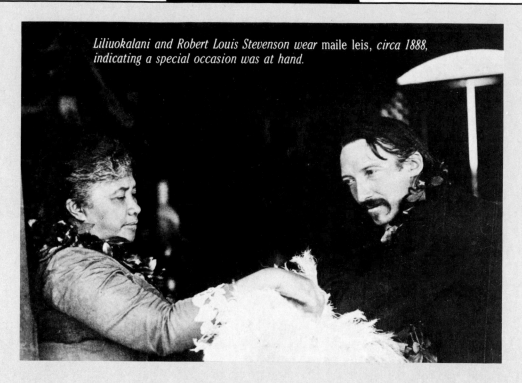

Liliuokalani and Robert Louis Stevenson wear maile leis, *circa 1888,* indicating a special occasion was at hand.

INSPIRING THE MUSE

Men *from distant places looked at a map and saw not just an outline of the islands, but blue lagoons and dusky maidens, tropic seas and sun-washed beaches. The spell of Hawaii was cast over a wide area, and none were less immune to the lure than writers.*

Some of the biggest "names" in the literary world took at least a cursory look at Honolulu and Hawaii. One of them was Herman Melville (one day to write Moby Dick*) who jumped ship in Hawaii in 1843, stayed about four months and left. He wrote very little about Hawaii, which he considered just another instance of white civilization sounding the death knell of the noble savage.*

A more prolific writer was Mark Twain, who arrived in Honolulu nearly a quarter-century after Melville and also stayed four months. Twain, however, reported at length on Hawaiian affairs for his California newspaper.

Robert Louis Stevenson came to Hawaii for his health in 1888 and took a beach cottage in Waikiki. He became a friend and confidant of King Kalakaua and enjoyed island living. Unlike some others he worked well in Hawaii; in addition to a number of highly literary letters, he completed work on The Master of Ballantrae *and wrote a fine short story,* The Bottle Imp. *Seeking still warmer climes, Stevenson moved to Samoa, where he died of a stroke at the age of 44.*

Jack London was already famous when he and his wife Charmian arrived in Honolulu in 1907 aboard their yacht and cut a swath through local society. Later, London annoyed some of his hosts by including tales of the leprosy settlement at Kalaupapa, Molokai, in his fiction. London often talked about making his home in Hawaii but died in California in November 1916.

Somerset Maugham, also famous by the time he arrived

in Honolulu in 1916, visited the famous red-light district of Iwilei in Honolulu and wrote a short story called Rain, *about a Honolulu prostitute. He hoped the story would enjoy a modest success. As it turned out, it became a small classic, heightened his literary reputation, and made him rich.*

A lesser-known but knowledgeable writer on Hawaii was Isabella Bird, a Yorkshire lass who wrote the classic Six Months in the Sandwich Islands, *an unabashed love letter about the islands she visited in 1873, and one of the finest accounts ever written of travel in remote places.*

A book that caused a sensation in the islands was James A. Michener's Hawaii, *a weaving of fact and fiction that had Honolulu residents busily trying to identify the characters in Michener's lively account of island families. Not all of the residents were pleased at his portrayal of local society, but the book enjoyed a huge success in Honolulu as elsewhere.*

One writer who found success in Honolulu was Earl Derr Biggers, hardly a household word but destined to become famous as the creator of one of the sensational detectives of modern times. Biggers came to Honolulu on vacation in 1919 and became entranced with newspaper accounts of a Honolulu Police Department detective of Chinese ancestry, Chang Apana. Six years later, Biggers published a book which signaled the appearance of a Chinese detective of engaging charms. The book was The House Without a Key, *and the detective was Charlie Chan.*

Numerous other writers, historians, correspondents— then filmmakers and television crews—visited the islands, turned out films both good and terrible and filed thousands of words on aspects of island life. They still do. For better or worse, Honolulu and Hawaii still attract and seldom disappoint.

CHAPTER FIVE

CAPITAL
OF A
REPUBLIC

I t was, in retrospect, a most unsettled time.

Avowed royalists in the islands supported not only the monarchy but the *concept* of a paternalistic monarch; others preferred a constitutional monarchy; and the annexationists wanted Hawaii to become a part of the United States as quickly and easily as possible. To the clash of these ideals was added another issue that continued to prove divisive—the situation involving Oriental labor. Many in the islands feared that Hawaii would be swallowed up by the Asian immigrants and ultimately become a part of Japan. In opposition were the sugar growers who needed the Asian workers to do the hard, gritty work in the fields that others had shown no inclination to do.

The king himself was proving to be either a problem or the best hope, depending on the point of view. In 1887 the reciprocity treaty had been renewed, which pleased the sugar planters, but this time the old question of Pearl Harbor had cropped up again and Hawaii had to allow the U.S. Navy to use the harbor. Internal affairs, particularly the question of a constitutional convention, plagued the king, and he became increasingly hardened in his positions. Cabinet officers resigned, new ones were appointed and there were differences of opinion that often cut along racial lines. In 1891 the McKinley Act went into effect giving American sugar producers a bounty of two cents a pound and eliminating the duty on all imported sugar, wiping out Hawaii's advantage gained by the reciprocity treaty. The Act was to lead to a dangerous dissatisfaction by the sugar growers.

In 1891, Kalakaua, having returned to San Francisco for a relaxing visit, fell unconscious and died on January 20, at the age of 54. His body was brought back to Honolulu aboard the USS *Charleston*. The gala welcome planned for the king's arrival had actually begun before it was noticed that the *Charleston's* flag was at half-mast and her spars draped in black. The welcome became a wake. Queen Kapiolani was hysterical with grief, and throughout the Hawaiian community Kalakaua was genuinely mourned. For all his faults and excesses, he had arced like a comet across the Hawaiian skies; his reign had been sometimes illogical, sometimes quixotic, but never dull.

LILIUOKALANI

A new queen and a new beginning—it should have inspired a new confidence as well, but the problems persisted. Liliuokalani, sister of Kalakaua, shared his complexity of character, his strong will and his tilt toward the divine right of kings. She was 52 years old, a handsome and regal woman with strong opinions and a willingness to state them.

In August 1891, Liliuokalani was saddened by the loss of her husband John O. Dominis, who died at a time, noted the queen, when she needed him the most. It was understandable that she felt embattled; her enemies already were denouncing her privately and publicly for being unreasonable and for dismissing Kalakaua's cabinet immediately after taking office, a move upheld by the islands' supreme court.

As Liliuokalani began her reign from Iolani Palace she seemed to embody contradiction. She was firm in her opinions, but she listened to a German medium, Fraulein Wolf. She was a Christian whose closest friends ignored Protestant morality. She could write some of the more sensitive and beautiful music the islands would produce, yet be blunt, even coarse, in conversation.

Looking out across the capitol grounds at her city, the queen probably noted contradictions there, too. Honolulu was still and unmistakably a seaport and a rough-and-ready haven for sailors, but it also had a few paved streets and paved sidewalks. There were still torches lighting the native *luaus*, or feasts, but there was gas lighting in some buildings. (Iolani Palace itself was wired for electricity by 1887.) The old-fashioned days of barter were gone, and the kingdom had its own coinage and paper money. Honolulu also boasted a police force, a fire department, an ice plant and a smattering of hotels. There was a library and public parks.

There were also the Chinese and Japanese who could not vote, the Hawaiians who would support the monarchy (and whose numbers had so diminished that they seemed to haunt great events like ghosts,

Ukulele (opposite, left) believed to have belonged to Queen Liliuokalani (opposite, right); the song is one of many composed by the talented monarch. Firemen mourn the 1891 death of King Kalakaua (below).

appearing strangely distant and unable to control the happenings of the day), and there was the *haole* establishment which, from headquarters downtown on Merchant Street, grew more and more disenchanted with the queen. Liliuokalani did little to appease the *haoles,* and took a series of actions that further estranged them.

She named a new cabinet and signed a controversial bill creating a national lottery. She then attempted to force through the legislature a new constitution, restoring to the throne many of the powers lost in 1887 when Kalakaua had been coerced into accepting a more democratized constitution. At the last minute, two cabinet members refused to sign the new constitution. The queen was infuriated, as were many of her Hawaiian supporters. One who refused to sign fled from the queen's wrath to the law office of William Owen Smith, a partner of the influential scion of missionaries, Lorrin A. Thurston. The cabinet member, John Colburn, relayed to a gathering crowd the queen's intent to adopt a new constitution. A Committee of Safety was formed and met that evening at Thurston's home, where the talk quickly shifted from maintaining the monarchy to a consensus that Liliuokalani must go.

In the following two days, the reformers scoured Honolulu for guns and ammunition and scheduled a mass meeting for the next afternoon. The queen's supporters countered by scheduling a meeting of their own at the same time at Iolani Palace. In the afternoon, the Committee of Safety requested of the U.S. minister, John L. Stevens,

that an American warship in the harbor, the USS *Boston,* land troops to protect Americans and their property. Later that day, 162 U.S. sailors and Marines marched ashore fully armed, including Gatling guns and artillery pieces, and accompanied by medical corpsmen. Most took up positions within a hundred yards of Iolani Palace, although most Americans and their property were located on the other side of town.

Late that night the reformers asked Sanford Ballard Dole to head the new government. Dole countered with the proposal that a regency be established until the heir to the throne, Princess Kaiulani, came of age. The reformers wanted no part of that. Dole then suggested that the firebrand Lorrin Thurston head the proposed new government, but the reformers held out for Dole, who agreed the following morning to take the post.

The next day, Tuesday, the reformers gathered for a walk to the government building near the palace to proclaim the end of the monarchy and the establishment of a provisional government until such time as the United States annexed Hawaii.

On the way to the gathering, Dole stopped off at Stevens' office and gave the U.S. official an advance copy of the proclamation. It was, Stevens reportedly told Dole, a great opportunity.

Word came back that Liliuokalani had agreed to abide by the old constitution. Whether it was because of the U.S. forces near the palace or because she had been unable or unwilling to mount a serious

H. Vierra's Beehive Saloon on Nuuanu Street at the turn of this century.

Members of Queen Liliuokalani's royal staff, including three kahili (feather standards symbolizing nobility) bearers pose on the veranda of Iolani Palace, circa 1893.

An 1893 special commission regarding annexation included, top left and counterclockwise, L.A. Thurston, W.C. Wilder, W.R. Castle, J. Marsden and C.L. Carter (left). Liliuokalani and her court pose at Waipio in 1893 (opposite, top). The royal party at Waimanalo, John A. Cummins' country house, included Liliuokalani, seated second chair from left (opposite, bottom).

counterrevolt was not known. At any rate, the reformers decided, it was too late for concessions.

A block away from the office where the reformers gathered, one of their members, Captain John Good, was driving a wagon load of guns and ammunition up Fort Street when a Hawaiian policeman grabbed the reins. Good unhesitatingly shot the policeman through the shoulder, wounding but not killing him. The shot drew off the other Hawaiian policemen who had been watching the gathering of the reformers, and Dole's group took the opportunity to walk unmolested to the government building. On the steps of the building, to an audience of a few Hawaiians and some government clerks, the proclamation was read and a messenger sent off to Stevens asking that America recognize the new government.

Meanwhile, volunteer militiamen began to arrive at the government building, and Dole felt the reformers' power growing. He declared martial law, ordered all the saloons closed and began to request recognition of the provisional government from other foreign delegations.

The messenger to Stevens had gotten his answer and relayed it to Minister of the Interior Samuel Parker—America would extend de facto recognition to the new government. Later it was claimed by some of the queen's supporters that Stevens had said U.S. forces would intervene if the queen's followers attacked the reformers. Liliuokalani, eyeing the U.S. troops and dismayed by the quick recognition of the new government, decided to surrender—not to the reformers, but to the Americans. It was January 17, 1893.

The monarchy was toppled—for the second time. Liliuokalani may have reflected on the days when Lord George Paulet had, for a while, secured the islands for Great Britain.

With the monarchy overthrown, Dole hurried a delegation off to Washington to ask for Hawaii's annexation to the Union, among them the tireless Lorrin Thurston, who ran a skillful and effective public relations campaign all across the United States. In Washing-

ton, the delegation asked for status and carefully de-emphasized the role of U.S. armed forces. President William Henry Harrison was not overly concerned with the Hawaii affair, leaving it to the incoming Grover Cleveland.

Liliuokalani wrote an impassioned letter to President Cleveland, noting the futility of armed action against the United States and putting her faith in Cleveland's sense of fairness. In time, the ex-queen was able to get her own representatives to Washington, and Cleveland now was faced with opposing delegations. The representatives of the provisional government were able and vigorous, while Liliuokalani's representatives seemed to have missed the point. They argued less about the use of U.S. troops and the threat of force than about the best financial arrangements they could get for the deposed Liliuokalani and the former princess, Kaiulani.

Back in Honolulu the city was full of rumors of a counterrevolution. Dole and his wife feared for their safety and moved out of their home, and the U.S. minister, Stevens, agreed that the United States would assume the responsibility for keeping order. On the first day of February 1893, the American flag was flown over the government buildings, and American Marines took up guard positions.

Cleveland, meanwhile, sent a representative to Honolulu to look over the state of affairs. The representative, James H. Blount, promptly ordered the U.S. flag lowered and the American sailors and Marines back aboard ship. After his investigation he informed the president that the reformers had received significant aid from the U.S. forces—which the provisional government repeatedly denied—and Cleveland reached a decision. The taking of Hawaii into the Union under such circumstances was immoral, he said, and he would not support it. Cleveland also asked the provisional government to restore the monarchy. The reformers promptly refused and events suddenly took a curious turn; it now was possible that the U.S. might use force to restore the monarchy. With the passage of time, however, the threat of conflict faded away.

THE REPUBLIC

The provisional government now formed the Republic of Hawaii with Honolulu as its capital, and wrote a new constitution. Mainland newspapers and politicians were divided on the issue of annexation. While the argument raged on, an American naval officer quietly and effectively made a convincing argument for the Union's grasping Hawaii in some capacity. Captain Alfred Mahan, destined to become the foremost proponent of seapower as a means of survival, wanted Pearl Harbor for the Navy at any cost. It would be, he reasoned, an absolutely vital coaling station for ships using the sea lanes of the Pacific. The British and Germans took Mahan to heart and modernized their navies; powerful Americans were listening as well.

Late in 1894 the rumors grew of a countercoup, and Iolani Palace was fortified against a possible raid. This time the rumors were correct, for on January 5, 1895, a group of royalists gathered past Waikiki, on the far side of Diamond Head, and distributed firearms.

Word got out that an armed force was gathering, and the following day the provisional government sent a patrol to the area. On the slopes of Diamond Head, shots were fired and a government man killed—an attorney on President Dole's own staff. The royalist forces retreated up Diamond Head and finally scattered. A few who remained on the old volcano were fired on by artillery pieces. Others escaped and fled up Manoa Valley to the north of Honolulu; the counterrevolt was broken.

The government was more than a little annoyed at the attempted revolt. In less than two weeks, Liliuokalani was arrested by government officials and held in two rooms on the second floor of Iolani Palace. She was charged with knowledge of the revolt and failing to report it to the government.

Liliuokalani's days as a prisoner in Iolani Palace, where once she ruled as queen, were fateful ones. She insisted that she knew nothing of the royalist plot, but arms and ammunition had been unearthed from the grounds of her home. She was sentenced to five years at

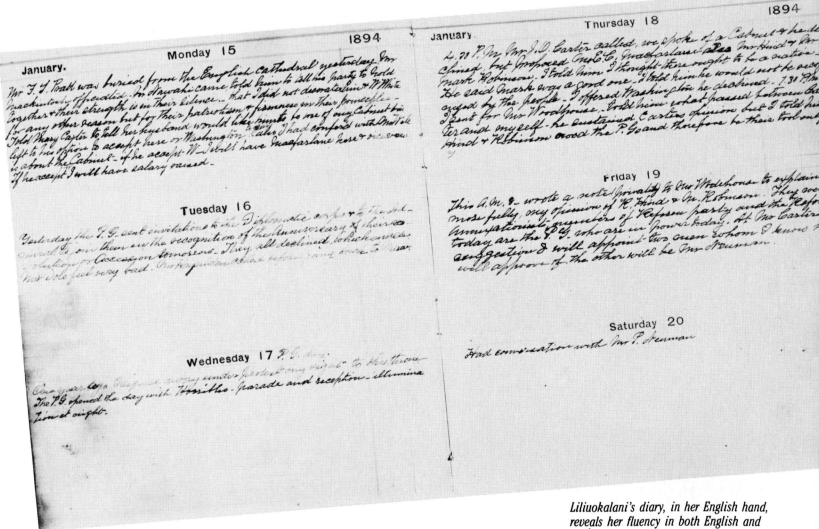

Liliuokalani's diary, in her English hand, reveals her fluency in both English and Hawaiian (above). Paul Neumann makes his address on behalf of the former queen at her trial in 1895 (opposite, top), while Liliuokalani, with R.P. Waipa, A.M. Brown and Colonel Fisher, mount the steps to Iolani Palace after her arrest (opposite, bottom).

Connie and Martha Afong express their moral support during the Spanish-American War in 1898 (above) as "The Boys of '98" stop in Honolulu on their way to the fighting (opposite).

hard labor and fined $5,000, with the hard labor commuted. Hardest for her to bear, in all likelihood, was what the government, acting in a deep and bitter enmity, forced her to do. She was made to swear allegiance to the new government, then sign her abdication as queen of Hawaii. She was released.

Liliuokalani, in some ways the most *Hawaiian* of the monarchs, lost her throne not only to the changing balance of power in the Pacific, not only to the hard geopolitical facts of Hawaii's size and location, but also to the changing times. The world was whirling into a new century. Great events were taking place that would affect Hawaii profoundly, but which the tiny kingdom was powerless to control. One such event took place far away in April 1898—the Spanish-American War.

Hawaii's President Dole had initiated discussions on Hawaii's role if the United States became embroiled in the war. Some in Hawaii, noting the presence of the Spanish fleet in the Pacific, urged neutrality. Lorrin Thurston, in Washington at the time, fired off a letter accusing Hawaii of wanting all the benefits of a U.S. connection and none of the responsibility. Meanwhile, Dole had made his decision and offered Hawaii's help to the United States in any way.

American newspapers had begun to view a closer relationship between America and Hawaii as desirable, now that war was declared. Hawaii, in fact, was going to be essential to the war effort as a Pacific naval base—proving the efficacy of Captain Mahan's argument. Hawaii was the most likely staging point for attack on the Philippines, which the Spanish currently occupied. A group of senators called on President McKinley asking him to annex Hawaii immediately.

As the war got underway, the same ship that had brought Kalakaua's remains home, the USS *Charleston,* arrived in Hawaii, followed soon by three troopships. The troops got an enthusiastic welcome. Patriotic ferver, at least among the islands' *haoles,* was rampant. More ships would follow, and in their wake the U.S. Congress began to lean strongly on annexation as a way of facilitating the war against Spain. On June 15, 1898, a joint resolution for annexation passed the U.S. House of Representatives, and was passed by the Senate on July 6. The following day it was signed by President McKinley.

On August 12, 1898, the grounds of Iolani Palace were packed with spectators—most of them Chinese and Japanese who had no influence on the events that had prompted the day's ceremonies. There were a few Hawaiians, who took no part in the ceremonies. On the steps of the palace were Sanford Ballard Dole and U.S. Minister Harold M. Sewall. After they spoke, the Hawaiian national anthem was played and colors were sounded. Guns fired a salute and everyone stared at the Hawaiian flag as it slowly fluttered to the ground. Then the American flag was hoisted, the national anthem played and again there was a 21-gun salute. Dole was sworn in as chief executive officer and sailors from two U.S. warships marched in review.

Years later, those attending the ceremonies at Iolani Palace remarked about the air of restraint, or tension, that hung over the rites. Hawaii had ceased to be a monarchy, ceased to be a republic, and now was a territory of the United States of America. Given all that had gone before, it seemed strangely anticlimactic.

Sailors from the U.S.S. Philadelphia *stand at attention while the Hawaiian flag is lowered, and the U.S. flag is raised (below). Hawaii becomes a U.S. territory as President Sanford Ballard Dole transfers sovereignty from the Republic of Hawaii to U.S. Minister Harold M. Sewall (inset).*

The Punahou School (formerly Oahu College) football team (above) takes a time out in front of Pauahi Hall—dedicated in 1896 by Charles Reed Bishop in memory of his wife. Prince Kuhio may have taken this photo of a Hawaiian in front of the prince's tent on an outing at Hanauma Bay (below).

CHAPTER SIX

CAPITAL
OF A
TERRITORY

Prince Jonah Kuhio Kalanianaole and his Princess ride in an early automobile (below). A Hawaiian family, circa 1900, embraces both the old ways of Hawaii and the new ways of the West (above).

Following annexation, the Organic Act of 1900 automatically made U.S. citizens out of Hawaiians, although there was still some trepidation in Congress. The recurring question was whether a group of islands with such a diverse population could really aspire to the ideals of Americanism. Statehood, of course, was out of the question.

In the islands, the *haole* infrastructure had no such problems. It had manipulated affairs so that sugar now was protected—and from sugar all economic benefits flowed—and the Islands were guarded against the capriciousness of the monarchy. Although Hawaiians could vote, and were in fact the majority voting bloc, they could be led; and the Asian laborers did not have the vote. The status quo was easily maintained.

Honolulu was the center of a centralized government that was predominately *haole*, Republican, conservative and business-oriented. The descendents of the missionaries still held a great deal of influence and a creeping paternalistic attitude began to flower, in which *haole* bosses could speak of "their Hawaiians" and look out upon a collection of islands that seemed in most ways an earthly paradise.

The city itself was taking on an air of permanence, becoming at last a metropolis.

A citizen of whatever ancestry could look over Honolulu and be pleased with most of the vistas. On several of the streets horse-drawn covered trams provided smooth and easy transportation from one part of town to another. There were the beginnings of stately St. Andrew's Cathedral, center of the Anglican faith in Hawaii and one of the longest building tasks in Hawaiian history; it would take almost a century to complete, although it was pressed into service as early as 1866. Nearby, the Cathedral of Our Lady of Peace, built with blocks of coral reef, was a magnet for those of the Catholic faith, now free to worship openly. Beautiful Washington Place was occupied by the deposed Liliuokalani. Not far away was another building originally planned as the residence of kings but converted to an administrative center—Aliiolani Hale, designed by Australian architects for Kamehameha V, who decided the building would serve the people better as a site for the judiciary, the legislature and other office functions.

In front of Aliiolani Hale stood a statue, eight and a half feet high, of Kamehameha I, arm outstretched. It had a curious history. During the reign of Kalakaua, a five-man committee commissioned the statue from Boston sculptor T.R. Gould. Gould created it from drawings by the French artist Louis Choris, who had drawn Kamehameha I from life in 1816 and 1817. In 1880, the statue and four plaques for the pedestal were started by ship for Honolulu, but the ship caught fire, burned and sank off the Falkland Islands in the South Atlantic.

The work had been insured, however, and Gould was able to make a second casting. Meanwhile, the original statue was recovered by a salvage crew and sent on to Honolulu, where it was repaired and put in place—not downtown, but in the tiny, remote village of Kapaau in the Kohala district of Hawaii Island, near Kamehameha's birthplace. When the copy arrived it was mounted in front of Aliiolani Hale, called the Judiciary Building. (More than 70 years later, yet another copy of the statue was made. It is one of two—the other being Father Damien—representing Hawaii in the Statuary Hall of the U.S. Capitol).

The citizen could look upon a state office building, an archives building and royal mausoleums. On the "arid plain" of old there was now a growing community.

Between the palace complex and the harbor the busy streets of Honolulu were being wired for telephones, electricity and the telegraph. The first authentic high-rise, the Stangenwald Building, threw a six-story shadow over Merchant Street by April 1901. There were public parks, the original Royal Hawaiian Hotel downtown, a few flush toilets (the first was installed in the home of Kamehameha IV in 1856 and was not an unqualified success), a roller-skating rink and several photo studios. The first automobiles, both electric, arrived in Honolulu on October 8, 1899, joined a year later by another electric and a steamer—one of them ran two bicyclists off the road at the intersection of King and Kalakaua streets, in what probably was Hawaii's first automobile-related accident.

In what had been a yam field belonging to Kamehameha I, businesses spread and thrived in an area that became the complex of King, Alakea, Beretania and Nuuanu streets. Kamehameha was at home near the harbor in today's lower Bishop Street. The street names themselves had taken on meaning: Beretania Street was named for Britannia, a tribute to the British influence in Hawaii; Queen Street was named for Queen Kalama, wife of Kamehameha III. Miller Street honored the first British consul general. Church, Chapel and Kawaiahao streets were all named to honor Kawaiahao Church. Bethel Street was named after a sailor's church. Alakea Street ("white" in the Hawaiian language) was named for its white coral paving.

Just to the left of downtown was Chinatown, with its long mountains-to-the-sea street called Maunakea. In Chinatown, the opening of the new century was catastrophic. In fewer than 50 acres were crammed almost 7,000 people, not only Chinese but other Asians and more than a few Hawaiians. When a case of bubonic plague was discovered just before the new year of 1900, armed guards were posted to keep people from going in or out, and the Board of Health ordered a number of "sanitary burnings" to clean out what was described as deplorable living conditions. The displaced persons of Chinatown were sent to live on the outskirts of town in quarantined areas.

On January 20, a sanitary fire had been burning for about an hour near Beretania Street and Nuuanu Avenue, when the wind suddenly whipped sparks across rooftops and out of reach of the firemen. The fire leaped Beretania Street, went out of control and began to race before the wind, with flames leaping ever higher and the residents

---

FIRST TO RISE, FIRST TO FALL

Among the "firsts" in Hawaiian history the name of Joseph L. Van Tassell may not rank among the better known, but his feats were all spectacular in their way.

On November 2, 1889, Van Tassell piloted a balloon from Waikiki to more than 5,000 feet in the air—becoming Hawaii's first successful flyer.

While at that exalted height, he leaped from the balloon and parachuted to earth—becoming Hawaii's first successful parachutist.

On November 18, Van Tassell attempted to duplicate those achievements, launching his balloon this time from Punchbowl, the volcanic crater near the heart of Honolulu. A change in the wind carried him off course, so that when he parachuted he was over the water of Keehi Lagoon, near Honolulu Harbor.

Unfortunately, Van Tassell landed in the water and drowned—becoming Hawaii's first aerial fatality.

Refugees watch the Chinatown fire of January 20, 1900 (below). After antiseptic baths and new clothes, Chinatown residents are evacuated to quarantine camp at Kakaako Rifle Range (opposite, left); the Honolulu Board of Health collects personal effects during the plague (opposite, right). The Kaumakapili Church burns during the fire (right).

A Japanese couple's attire reflects old world and Western influences.

of Chinatown fighting to get out of the fire's path. A great column of smoke formed over the city and lesser fires began to spread. When brought under control at last, the fire had destroyed 38 acres of Chinatown. Thousands of Chinatown residents lived in the quarantine camps for months afterward and many Oriental businessmen were ruined. The inevitable claims against the government were not settled for months, and then not to everyone's satisfaction. There was a dark suspicion among the Chinese that the fire had been allowed to spread in order to give the *haoles* more room downtown to expand their businesses.

That such a suspicion could exist and spread reflected the social dynamics of the day. The Chinese were a growing merchant class whose potential made the *haole* establishment nervous—in spite of the fact that the immigrant Chinese had turned out to be relatively docile (compared to the more militant Japanese). The Chinese intermarried, principally with the Hawaiians, and moved into town, opening shops and stores and achieving a kind of middle-class respectability. Unlike the Japanese, they did not band into strong union movements, but were linked by familial ties in a chain as strong as steel. The *haole* establishment was years in learning that the vastness of China and the diversity of its people did not make for strong nationalistic feelings among the Chinese immigrants. Hawaii's Chinese, especially the Punti and the Hakka, had no great affinity for one another unless, somehow, they were linked by family ties. As elsewhere, the goal of the Chinese was to perpetuate the family.

The goal of the Japanese was to make a better life for the next generation, and to find the proper status in the fabric of Hawaiian society. The Japanese were regarded as more troublesome than the Chinese because they were ambitious, tenacious and tended to form unions. Each generation concentrated on education for the children as the way to commercial and social success and pursued that goal with a vengeance. Although the Japanese all appeared similar to the

NOTICE THE MISSING BILLBOARDS

*S*ooner or later every visitor to Hawaii begins to realize one thing that is different from many other places—there are no billboards on the highways.

Once, there were.

Billboards dotted the highways on Oahu, extolling tobaccos, foodstuffs and soaps. That was in 1913 when Hawaii was a territory, and merchants felt they had to use accepted advertising techniques.

On May 10, 1913, The Honolulu Advertiser *devoted an entire edition to a group of energetic and determined women called "The Outdoor Circle." That intrepid group published photos of the billboards—unquestionably a blight on the landscape—and also ran letters from angry residents and visitors.*

For more than ten years, The Outdoor Circle kept up the battle, alternately losing and gaining in the struggle. By 1927 most of the billboards were gone, but The Outdoor Circle was not yet finished. That year the women helped get an anti-billboard provision through the territorial legislature. The law is still on the books and Hawaii is still billboard-free.

Billboards in Hawaii, like this one advertising the Waikiki Inn, were later outlawed due to the influence of the Outdoor Circle.

haoles of Honolulu, they nurtured their personal prejudices, too. Japanese immigrants from the provinces of southern Honshu were appalled at being regarded no better than the immigrants from Okinawa.

Other groups pursued their self-interests. The Portuguese who came to Hawaii were rebuffed by the local establishment. Despite their European background, the *haoles* were disinclined to accept them as whites and grouped them with other racial classifications. A proud and independent people, the Portuguese spent considerable energy striving for acceptance. Germans, Koreans, Scandinavians and others tried to carve out the best possible situations for themselves. The people of the Philippines—again diverse within their own race, such as Ilocanos and Visayans—differed from other groups in that they wanted to earn all the money they could and go home to the Philippines, rich and honored in their *barrios.*

The elite of society were the *haoles,* who dominated not only the business world but also education, religion and all the more important aspects of island life. They caused the rise or fall of local politicians, the success or failure of local businesses. They developed the private schools that would be bastions of conservative outlook. They formed interlocking directorates whereby business and social groups were controlled by the entwining of establishment corporations. Some said the situation was incestuous; others claimed it was simply a better way of doing business and right for its time.

The most tragic of the racial groups were the Hawaiians. Decimated by diseases, bewildered by the continuing successes of all but themselves, trapped to some extent by old traditions in a century that was passing them by, the Hawaiians saw their influence virtually disappear. Although the majority voting bloc at the turn of the century, they were unable to bring this weapon to bear to improve their lot. They became victims of a mind-set that could not countenance the aggressiveness of the *haoles* or the capacity for routine of the Asian immigrants. Kalakaua had tried to bring about a rebirth of Hawaiian culture; Liliuokalani had tried to preserve the kingdom. Nothing had seemed to work, and the Hawaiians appeared destined to disappear, as many feared they would.

Intermarriage may have saved at least the remnants of the Hawaiian race—certainly it preserved a good deal of the language, customs, gentleness and spirituality. The tolerant Hawaiians were able to accept other races as equals. Other races found far less stigma in intermarriage in Hawaii than they would have faced in their native lands, and so the marriages took place. The many splendid facets of an ancient culture were kept alive in half-Hawaiian children, perpetuated by families who found the Hawaiian lifestyle, unsurprisingly, well-suited to the Hawaiian milieu. The race would go forward, not as "pure" as before, but infused with a new vitality and new numbers. Between 1912 and 1934, nearly half the *haole* men in Hawaii married non-*haole* women, a good many of them Hawaiians. At the same time, ten percent of the *haole* women in the islands married non-*haole* men, usually part-Hawaiians. The marriages did not erase the distinctions between the racial groups, but softened them, and contributed to the acceptance that in later years would permit *haoles,* Asians and Hawaiians to sit together not only in corporate boardrooms, but in one another's living rooms as well.

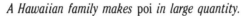

A Hawaiian family makes poi *in large quantity.*

THE GREAT WAR

The Pacific was a long way from Europe, but when word came over ships' wirelesses that World War I had broken out, each country was forced into a quick assessment of its position vis-a-vis the realities of a vast ocean. European fleets now prowled the Pacific as a matter of course. The United States continued to appreciate the foresight of Captain Mahan—Hawaii was a strategic, mid-ocean American base.

Until the United States entered the war, Hawaii was a neutral port in which ships could seek asylum; foreign vessels began to nose into Honolulu harbor to await further developments. The rule was that a ship could remain for repairs as necessary, but after a specified time must put back to sea or be interned for the duration of the war.

One that eased into Honolulu harbor was the German gunboat, the *Geier*, followed by her collier, and eventually by the Japanese battleship *Hizen* which remained outside the harbor not far from the

channel entrance. In the ensuing days, the *Hizen* captured and then sank a German sailing vessel. The captain of the *Geier*, knowing his ship to be badly outgunned, overstayed the allotted time in harbor and allowed his ship to become interned. The crew of the *Geier* may have been among the more fortunate, because they were able to enjoy liberty ashore, where they were tolerated for a time. After a while, sentiment began to turn against them when it became known that the Germans were conducting unrestricted submarine warfare.

In time, the diary of the *Geier's* skipper became public, implicating the head of one of Hawaii's largest businesses—the firm of H. Hackfeld—in pro-German plots. In the resulting uproar, manager George Rodiek lost his U.S. citizenship (although it was returned four years later), and control of the company was taken out of the hands of its owners, most of them Germans.

A controlling majority of H. Hackfeld stock was seized and sold by the U.S. government to a group of American businessmen who changed the name of the company to American Factors, Ltd. For decades after the war, the original German owners tried to regain at least

---

DUKE KAHANAMOKU
HAWAII'S GOODWILL AMBASSADOR

Probably the best-known Hawaiian of modern times was a carefree, well-built, smiling man who loved playing his ukulele and surfing, living the life of a beachboy.

He had a talent that he enjoyed but never exploited until one day in August 1911, when he went swimming in Honolulu harbor to race against a friend in a match sanctioned by the American Amateur Union.

To the astonishment of the AAU officials, Duke Kahanamoku broke the existing American record in the 100-yard sprint. To prove it wasn't a fluke, he broke the 50-yard sprint record the same day. Clearly, a new swimming sensation had arrived.

Duke Kahanamoku went on to become an outstanding competitor without taking it all too seriously. Selected for the U.S. Olympic team, he went to Stockholm for the 1912 Olympics and nearly missed them—he was taking a nap when his event was called. A friend got him up just in time to beat the world's best swimmers. On July 10, the beachboy was given his gold medal by King Gustavus of Sweden.

The Olympics of 1916 were cancelled because of World War I. In the 1924 Olympics, an older Duke Kahanamoku placed second to another swimming sensation, Johnny Weismuller.

A year later, Duke Kahanamoku used his swimming prowess to rescue eight men who almost drowned in a boating accident in Southern California. A lesser swimmer might not have saved them.

The Duke continued to swim, mostly for fun, and even did some acting. He was a great ladies' man, but at the age of 50 he married and settled down. He became Hawaii's unofficial goodwill ambassador and its official sheriff, serving thirteen terms.

For many years, the Duke continued to be Honolulu's official greeter, a role he enjoyed and handled in charismatic style. He died in 1968 at the age of 78, but the legend lives on.

Duke Kahanamoku shows off his big board.

some financial interests, with only a modest success. The company remained American.

The uproar over Rodiek's perceived guilt touched off a fever in Honolulu, inspiring schools to require a loyalty oath and triggering the organization of vigilante groups to root out any pro-German proclivities. German language courses were dropped from the school curricula, and Hawaiians with German-sounding names often came in for undeserved persecution. For many Hawaii citizens, World War I couldn't end soon enough.

The war also brought greater recognition of Hawaii as a soldier's outpost. Schofield Barracks, established in 1907 in the northwest portion of the Island of Oahu, grew to be the largest U.S. Army post in existence. Fort Shafter, to the west of the city, became an important headquarters complex as well as post. More and more naval vessels worked the sea lanes in and out of Pearl Harbor.

The influx of military people occasioned an uneasy truce between the local people and the *malahinis,* the newcomers. The tension was fueled in great part by the *haole* servicemen who tended to view the

World War I Yeomanettes salute (above) and officers-in-training practice (below) at Schofield Barracks, Oahu.

Governor Charles J. McCarthy draws the first order number at Iolani Palace in 1918 (left), Hawaiian naval militia stand at attention on the palace steps (right) and the first group of draftees from Kanai line up for medical examinations (below).

local people as "natives" no matter what their ancestry, and who looked on the local populace with the prevailing prejudices of the day. The local people, in turn, viewed the servicemen as insensitive troublemakers who gave no thought for island ways, and who would be gone one day only to be replaced by some other unfeeling young men. The civilian-military division smouldered for years, with tensions heightened and positions hardened by an occasional criminal act by one side or the other.

For a certain type of military man the islands were the culmination of a dream. He found himself far from home in a strange and beautiful place, living the adventure that the recruiting posters had promised. If he were curious and open-minded, his tour of duty in Hawaii became a pleasurable experience to be recalled fondly for the rest of his life. If he were close-minded and biased, the islands could be a tropical purgatory.

Perhaps unwittingly, some military officers fueled the racial fires by living a life that the local people could only envy. On many a pleasant evening the Japanese paper lanterns swayed in the cool winds over a lawn party at which officers in handsome dress uniforms, and their ladies in cool summer dresses, stood on a lawn manicured that day by Filipino gardeners. They were served drinks by an efficient Japanese maid, while other servants offered delicious hors d'oeuvres prepared by a Chinese chef. A group of hefty Hawaiian musicians played *ukuleles* (a Portuguese import) and sang as only Hawaiians can sing.

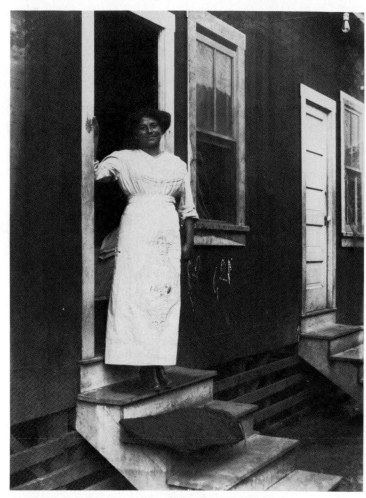

A woman stands in front of Iwilei house of prostitution in 1912 (right). Firemen knit for the war effort at the Makiki Fire Station in 1918 (below).

The Japanese War Savings Stamp Committee (above) in 1918. A racial mix composes the Boys Working Reserve Group at Pier 12 during World War 1 (below).

Harvesters place freshly picked pineapple (below) on conveyor belts (inset). By 1960, Hawaii was producing 90 percent of the world's pineapple.

It was heady stuff, and affordable only by a few islanders, most of them the *haole* elite. The military men who lived such a life usually clustered together in well-tended ghettos. Too often, they seemed remote and uncaring about the people who helped make their lives more pleasant. There were exceptions, but the rule was isolation from the local community and the outward appearance, at least, of an expensive and unattainable lifestyle. Such scenes did have one rewarding aspect. The maids, gardeners and cooks often went home and talked about the splendid evenings, firing the aspirations of whole generations of young men in Hawaii to rise above poverty and prejudice to more meaningful and pleasant lives. Happily, many of them succeeded.

The insensitive servicemen were tolerated by the establishment because of the growing importance of the military expenditures in Hawaii. Federal dollars were becoming a vital part of the islands' revenue, and if the servicemen were not loved, they were recognized as important. Their presence set off the resurgence of an old trade that many islanders deplored—prostitution. It was particularly rampant in an area just southwest of the downtown business district known as Iwilei. Honolulu's government regarded prostitution as a military problem; the military in turn regarded it as a necessary evil, arguing that its concentration in Iwilei exercised a measure of control. In any case, prostitution grew to be an enormous business in its own right. The situation continued through the years after World War I and into the opening of a new conflict that came upon the islands with appalling suddenness.

Pan American Airlines' famous Sikorsky 42, the first large flying boat to cross the Pacific in connection with the airline's exploratory flights, cruises over "the old Waikiki," with Diamond Head in the background (below). Pan American's China Clipper is assisted into its hangar at Pearl City terminal following its epochal flight as the first commercial airplane to fly from San Francisco to Honolulu (left).

*Nalani Jones and Princess Kalanianaole
enjoy the beach in turn-of-the-century summer fashions (top). H.G. Creel and an
unidentified girl are adorned with leis upon
their arrival in Honolulu (above).*

CHAPTER SEVEN

A TIGER
AT DAWN

The dawn came up like thunder that Sunday morning in December, came up to the whine of engines on aircraft straining to be launched from the decks of carriers, came up to the throbbing beat of ships' engines and the cries of men preparing for combat. It came up to a calm sea and scattered clouds over a group of islands that were the most remote inhabited landfall on earth, came up to a day, a moment, that ended a dream and began a reality for an intelligent, implacable Japanese officer of the Imperial Navy.

He was Isoroku Yamamoto, who wore the insignia of Admiral of the Imperial Navy, but was known on sight as the man who nurtured a vision of victory in the Pacific. Yamamoto was no idle dreamer, and not given to wishful thinking. He knew that a war with America would be disastrous, and that Japan's only hope in the Pacific was destruction of the American fleet. Consequently, he planned a move that would accomplish that end, if it could be accomplished at all, and save Japan from the retaliation that he was sure would follow. In his heart, Yamamoto's bold strike against the Pacific Fleet was as much a defensive move as it was an opening gambit. He called it "Operation Z."

In December 1940, Yamamoto told the rest of the Japanese navy what he had in mind. During the ensuing months at Kagoshima, the plan was put into practice. At best it would destroy the American fleet, at worst it would trap the Japanese task force far from home in hostile waters.

In January 1941, the United States ambassador to Japan, Joseph Grew, picked up a rumor that the Japanese were planning a surprise attack against Pearl Harbor in the Hawaiian Islands. For many, Grew's rumor was no more than that; it was thought that while a Japanese attack was a possibility, it would be made elsewhere.

In August 1941, the Japanese made a number of unacceptable proposals to the United States, centering around Japan's willingness to stop any advance in IndoChina if the United States would restore trade with Japan, discontinue aid to China and persuade China to recognize Japan's authority in IndoChina.

In September 1941, the Japanese Imperial Conference decided war would be necessary if the United States would not agree to Japanese demands before October. In that same month, spies in the Japanese consulate in Honolulu were ordered to report on the presence or absence of U.S. warships at Pearl Harbor.

Two months later, the Japanese presented a "final proposal" in Washington. In the same month, a task force of 31 ships sailed from the remote Kurile Islands to cross the North Pacific and carry out a surprise attack on the Pacific Fleet.

On the first day of December, the Japanese Privy Council authorized the attack, and the following morning the Japanese ambassador in Washington was ordered to destroy his code books.

December 7, 1941.

At 3:45 a.m., Hawaii time, the U.S. minesweeper *Condor* sighted a periscope off the entrance to Honolulu harbor and so notified the destroyer *Ward*. At 6:30 a.m., the *Ward* spotted a submarine trailing the target ship *Antares* toward the harbor entrance in an area where no submarine should have been. The destroyer opened fire, and its second salvo blasted away the submarine's conning tower. The *Ward* raced over and dropped depth charges, knowing the submarine was finished. The destroyer reported the action, taking care to make it known that this was no false alarm but the actual sinking of an unidentified, unauthorized submarine. The message took almost an hour to reach the Pacific Fleet commander-in-chief, Rear Admiral Husband E. Kimmel. In the uneasy atmosphere of U.S.-Japanese relations, Kimmel asked for amplification of the message.

In the meantime, an hour before the *Ward* made her run on the enemy submarine, Washington was alerted to the possibility of an attack on the Pacific Fleet and sent a message to that effect to the fleet in Hawaii. It did not arrive in time.

At 7:55 a.m., the first of 360 Japanese bombers, torpedo bombers and fighters crossed the northern coastline of Oahu. Ten thousand feet below, the island lay clear and green in the morning sun. The

---

"GOD'S GRACE HAS BEEN SET UPON ME."

The man who led the attack on Pearl Harbor later bought a Bible on a streetcorner in Japan from one of the crewmembers of the aircraft that dropped the first atomic bomb on Hiroshima.

That bizarre coincidence of World War II changed the life of Commander Mitsuo Fuchida, actual leader of the raiding aircraft on December 7, 1941. Fuchida survived the war, but during the peace that followed he was depressed and disillusioned.

Fuchida purchased a Bible from an equally disillusioned American and went on to become a Protestant minister, serving in the United States. The former Japanese officer also became a writer, and of that awesome Sunday morning in Hawaii, he wrote:

"That morning . . . I lifted the curtain of warfare . . . [later] I determined to send out into the world a book entitled, 'No More Pearl Harbors,' . . . . [after reading the Bible] My mind was strongly impressed and captivated. I think I can say today without hesitation that God's grace has been set upon me."

Mitsuo Fuchida, right, and the Reverend Abraham Akaka, pastor of Kawaiahao Church, on the 25th anniversary of Pearl Harbor.

Battleship Row, sitting ducks, at Pearl Harbor on May 26, 1940 (above).
Ford Island, in Pearl Harbor, under attack on December 7, 1941 (below).

dive bombers climbed to 15,000 feet and split into two groups, one heading for Wheeler Field northwest of Pearl Harbor, the other aiming like an arrow at the harbor itself. The torpedo bombers dropped to near the surface of the water and began their approach. The radio operator in attack commander Mitsuo Fuchida's aircraft tapped out a prearranged signal, "To .. To .. To . . ." that told the Japanese task force that the first wave had been committed. Moments later, the longed-for second signal came, repeated and repeated. It was the Japanese word for tiger, "Tora .. Tora .. Tora."

The following minutes were filled with explosions, burning oil, the screams of sailors and the terrifying noises of ships dying. The scene became one of massive destruction that seemed to go on and on and on. The great ships rocked and shuddered and buckled under the onslaught of bombs and torpedoes. As they were being torn apart, other Japanese aircraft were destroying aircraft on the ground at Wheeler and Hickam fields and across the island at the Naval Air Station at Kaneohe. It was a terrible hour in Hawaii's history—and that of America.

When the extent of destruction was tallied it was appalling. Of the 96 ships in Pearl Harbor that Sunday morning, eighteen were sunk or heavily damaged. The *Arizona* took five torpedoes and a number of aerial bombs and went down with more than 1,000 men aboard, entombed forever. The *Oklahoma* capsized. The *Pennsylvania* was blasted by bombs. The *West Virginia* sank at her moorings. The *California* went down at her berth. The *Tennessee,* moored inboard, escaped the torpedoes but was ripped apart by aerial bombs. The *Nevada* was hit but got underway, heavily damaged. She was ordered to run aground rather than risk sinking at the harbor entrance. The *Utah* went down. The *Maryland* was devastated.

These battleships had been the backbone of the Pacific Fleet, but they were not the only targets. The cruisers *Helena, Honolulu* and *Raleigh* were heavily damaged. The minelayer *Oglala* was sunk. Severely damaged were the destroyers *Cassin* and *Downes,* the repair ship *Vestal* and the seaplane tender *Curtiss.*

Ninety-two navy aircraft were destroyed and 31 damaged. The Army Air Corps lost 96 planes and had 128 damaged. Among the day's casualties, excluding the Japanese, were 68 civilians killed and 35 wounded in the total of 2,403 dead and 1,178 wounded.

The attacking Japanese force lost 29 aircraft—fifteen dive bomb-

The U.S.S. Shaw *explodes on the Day of Infamy (top), while the headline (below) cries "war." The U.S.S.* Arizona *(right), three days after the Pearl Harbor attack.*

ers, five torpedo bombers, nine fighters and the two-man crews of five midget submarines. One lone prisoner was taken from one submarine on the windward side of Oahu—the first Japanese prisoner of war for the Americans in World War II. The Japanese force also lost a larger, I-class submarine. Total Japanese casualties were 185 killed, one captured.

But the Japanese had made a number of serious mistakes. As the task force steamed back toward Japan, Commander Mitsuo Fuchida was of two minds about the attack. It had been a success, but it had not been enough. He had tried to get the task force commander Vice Admiral Chuichi Nagumo to authorize a second attack, but the cautious admiral, fearing American retaliation, had ordered the task force to turn north and run for home. Fuchida had the uneasy feeling the task was not finished. He was right.

The Japanese had failed to catch the American aircraft carriers in harbor at the time of the attack. They had failed to destroy the fuel storage tanks that would be so vital in the months to come, or to destroy the submarine base at Pearl Harbor, allowing American submarines to go into action almost at once. They had also failed to destroy the shipyard repair facilities, which went into instant operation. America was able to salvage and repair vessels and get them into action much faster than the Japanese thought possible.

Of the battleships, the *Arizona* was a total loss (but today remains in commission, graced by a memorial to the war dead). The *Oklahoma* and *Utah* were total losses. The *Nevada* was salvaged, refloated and employed throughout the war, eventually to be used as a target vessel in the Bikini Atoll bomb tests. The *California, West Virginia, Tennessee, Pennsylvania* and *Maryland* were salvaged, repaired and put into action, as were the *Helena, Honolulu, Raleigh, Cassin, Downes, Vestal* and *Curtiss.* For all of the destruction and devastation of that bloody Sunday, the Japanese attack proved to be an incomplete victory—at best a near-triumph.

Yamamoto was among the first to realize it. In a little-known inci-

dent during the early days of the war, the admiral decided to take action against the Pacific Fleet's aircraft carriers, and ordered a reconnaissance run over Pearl Harbor again, trying to pinpoint the carriers. On March 4, 1942, Japanese aircraft once again appeared over Pearl Harbor—and once again it was less a triumph than a desperate action.

Nine days after the initial attack, a Japanese I-class submarine surfaced south of Oahu and launched a type-96 limited-range scout seaplane. In the next few weeks at least six other such flights were made, all designed to get a good, visual sighting on Pearl Harbor and its damages, and to test the island's defenses for a reconnaissance flight. Yamamoto then ordered into action two Kawanishi flying boats—long-range, four-engined aircraft with a bomb load of up to two tons, a cruising speed of 160 knots and a range of up to 5,000 miles.

On February 15, 1942, the two aircraft left Yokosuka, Japan, and flew to Kwajalein Atoll, then in Japanese hands, and waited for favorable weather. On March 3, they left their sanctuary and flew to French Frigate Shoals, 600 miles northwest of Hawaii, and landed inside the reef. Through the long evening they took on fuel from two I-class submarines pre-positioned and waiting for them. The aircraft took off with a full moon shining and every expectation of good weather over Oahu.

Instead, they found a light rain falling and then a sudden mass of dense clouds that blotted out the island. It was shortly after 2 a.m. when they dropped their bombs, the reconnaissance mission a failure. The bombs from one aircraft landed harmlessly in the water at least a mile from Pearl Harbor. Bombs from the second fell in a forest on a mountainside above Honolulu, about six miles from the center of town, causing no casualties but ripping out algaroba, monkeypod and eucalyptus trees and throwing the nearby residents into shock. It was March 4, 1942, and the incident was almost forgotten in the aftermath of the Day of Infamy.

The flag at Hickam Field (left) was saved throughout the war and taken to Japan, where it was raised after the Japanese surrender. One of five Japanese two-man subs (opposite) lost during the Pearl Harbor attack.

DEATH IN PARADISE

In Honolulu on December 7, the initial reaction had been shock and disbelief, which was normal, and a certain amount of fear. The possibility of a Japanese invasion was uppermost in the minds of many residents, and amid the accounts of death and destruction were reports that Japanese paratroopers were landing in the hills above Honolulu.

The first damage reports started reaching Honolulu police shortly after 8 a.m., and built to a picture of awesome destruction on the military bases, but not as extensive as might be expected in the city.

A building supply house was hit and exploded . . . a woman hit by stray bullets, dying seconds later, in upper Nuuanu Valley above the city . . . the roof of Lunalilo School was blazing . . . and Japanese Zeros were strafing cars and pedestrians on the roads in and out of Pearl Harbor. At Hickam Field, even closer to town than Pearl Harbor, three civilian firemen were killed trying to stop a raging fire; seven others were injured. A welder standing more than 200 yards from the *Cassin* when it exploded watched pieces of metal bounce nearby without touching him. At the corner of Nuuanu and Kukui streets, a lunch stand was blown apart and several people killed. At King and McCully streets an entire block of buildings was threatened by a widening fire, sending dozens of families out into the streets. In Iwilei a large gas tank caught fire and burned, subsided, and flashed again hours later.

"This is no drill," an announcer kept telling his radio listeners. "Pearl Harbor is under attack. This is no drill." North and west of the city in the community of Wahiawa, a shell crashed through the roof of a store and four rounds tore through a nearby hospital. A Japanese fighter plane trailed smoke and slammed into a pineapple field, starting a fire which raged through the field and burned down five homes.

At Kamehameha School an exploding bomb knocked down a wall. Closer to the heart of town a shell detonated near the driveway of Washington Place. Inside the historic house the governor, 72-year-old Joseph B. Poindexter, escaped injury, but shrapnel from the shell sliced across Beretania Street, killing a Chinese man. Four men were killed by attacking aircraft as they rode in one car toward Pearl Harbor to help in rescue efforts.

The governor went on the air to proclaim the inauguration of the Hawaii Defense Act, giving his office full powers in wartime, but the Act was superseded by Lieutenant General Walter Short, who met with Poindexter in Iolani Palace and told the governor that martial law should be declared. Poindexter telephoned President Roosevelt who agreed with Short, and Hawaii came under martial law.

What followed was totally necessary in the viewpoint of the military personnel in Hawaii; it was a shameful chapter in American history in the civilian view. Martial law was underway, Short declared himself "military governor" of Hawaii and civil courts were closed.

Short—and Admiral Kimmel, at Pearl Harbor—soon were relieved of their commands. Short's successor was Lieutenant General Delos Emmons. On the civilian side, Poindexter's term expired, and he was replaced by Ingram M. Stainback.

By early June 1942, the Japanese had suffered a crucial defeat in the Battle of Midway, and there were no longer fears that Hawaii would be invaded. Still, martial law continued and took some nasty turns, one of which was the occupation of Iolani Palace by the Army. The territory's attorney general, J. Garner Anthony, opened talks with Stainback about discontinuing martial law; Stainback, agreeing, suddenly found himself in the middle of a fight with the Army. The military was not about to relinquish command of the islands, in which it now held sway over almost all facets of life. General orders flowed from military headquarters in a relentless stream, and the military position was supported strongly by the business establishment. Even after the initial burst of patriotism had steadied into a determination to help with the war effort, even after Hawaii men were in combat under the U.S. flag, and even after the dangers of invasion were but a memory, the military high command in Hawaii held onto the convenience of martial law in defiance of all logic and reasonableness.

Anthony kept up the fight. He got the Army to move out of Iolani Palace, at least, but in the end he and the governor found it necessary to call in some high-powered help. In late 1942, the two of them flew to Washington to ask Secretary of the Interior Harold Ickes for aid. It was, they told Ickes, a matter of principle. Whereas it might have been a matter of practicality in the beginning of the war, martial law had gone on too long in Hawaii and had become much more than a method of establishing control—it was now a military dictatorship that defied the rights and privileges of the U.S. citizens of Hawaii. Ickes agreed. Through his influence he was able to get nearly 200 of the Army's orders rescinded, and the civilian government was allowed to take a measure of control away from the military. But it was not until October 24, 1944, that President Roosevelt abolished martial law in the islands.

THE NISEI

Honolulu during the war years suffered some affronts to its dignity. One was the long lines of servicemen standing outside the brothels—a sight which further hardened some local positions against any mixing of residents and the military. Another was a curfew and blackout that went on until two months *after* the end of the war in Europe—much too long, in the opinion of most local people. The worst indignity, by far, was the direct challenge to the loyalty of the nearly 170,000 Americans of Japanese ancestry who lived in the islands in the opening days of the war. In the view of the military command, the Japanese-Americans were not to be trusted. (In the first days of war hysteria, there were wild claims of sabotage and spying by the local *nisei,* the second-generation Japanese; all turned out to be unfounded.)

But the *nisei* amounted to about one-third of the population of the islands; they could not be locked away in camps, as were their counterparts on the U.S. mainland, and they could not be isolated forever without damaging the delicate workings of the territory, in which they held a number of important jobs. While the military governors of the islands hesitated, the Japanese-Americans conducted themselves with great dignity and the situation eased. There was, however, one other problem—what to do with the young *nisei* who wanted to prove their loyalty to America?

Lieutenant General Emmons fired the opening shot, and it was a humiliating one for the *nisei.* As military governor of the territory, he ordered the dismissal of the Territorial Guard's *nisei* members, more than 300 young men. Half of those dismissed promptly went to work as laborers for the Army Corps of Engineers, calling themselves the Varsity Victory Volunteers. Still there were nearly 2,000 *nisei* and part-Japanese men in the National Guard. The decision was made to form them into a battalion and send them to the U.S. mainland for training. Implicit in the order was the nation's unwillingness to let *nisei* go into combat against the Japanese.

They sailed from Honolulu in June 1942, and arrived eventually at Camp McCoy, near Sparta, Wisconsin, and six months later at Camp Shelby, Mississippi. They were being formed into the 100th Battalion.

Back in the islands, the Businessmen's Military Training Corps was formed, its mission to police the loyalties of the Japanese-Americans by collecting data on suspicious persons—in effect, to spy on the local Japanese. Conversely, it was decided to allow the remaining *nisei* to volunteer for military duty in a special combat unit. The Army hoped to get as many as 1,500 men; nearly 10,000 volunteered, almost half the *nisei* of military age left in Hawaii. The nearly 3,000 who were accepted were sent to Camp Shelby for training and formed into the 442nd Regimental Combat Team.

Late in the summer of 1943, the 100th Battalion took the first step in a long and deadly odyssey. They landed in North Africa and shifted to Italy, where they saw their first combat at Salerno, and by turn, Volturno, the Papido River, Cassino and Anzio. Casualties were high. In June 1944, the 442nd arrived and was thrown into action north of Rome, with the 100th joining them as a battalion. The following September, the 442nd was in action in southern France as part of the 36th Division. Again, casualties were high. Near Biffontaine, a Texas infantry battalion was cut off and isolated for seven days, and the 442nd was one of the units asked to attempt a rescue. After three days of incredible combat, the *nisei* troops cut a path through to the Texans and helped evacuate them—an action that won nationwide acclaim for the Hawaii unit.

When the war ended in Europe there was a victory parade in Italy of all Allied forces, led by the men whose loyalty had been questioned at the outbreak of the war. Later, on July 15, 1946, President Harry S. Truman awarded the unit a Presidential Unit Citation—its seventh—and told them, "You fought not only the enemy but you fought prejudice, and you won."

It had been at a terrible cost. In addition to the seven Presidential Unit Citations, the unit had won nearly 6,000 individual awards including the Medal of Honor, and had lost 36 officers and 614 enlisted men. Another 4,500 had been wounded. The casualty rate was three

Civilian employees gather in front of the Pearl Harbor Paint Shop during World War II (below), and members of the 442nd Regimental Combat Team assemble in front of Iolani Palace before departing for training and combat duty overseas (opposite).

Within a month following the Pearl Harbor attack, the Bishop Museum staff demonstrates mandatory practice of gas masks issued to all civilians (below). A cruiser in West Loch Channel, Waipio Amphibious Base, and landing craft at the docks in May 1945 (inset).

The plotting board at the Fort Shafter, Oahu, air warning center was manned by the Women's Air Raid Defense (WARD) unit (left). A newsboy in downtown Honolulu holds up the V-J Day extra edition of the Honolulu Advertiser on August 14, 1945 (opposite).

times the average of the rest of the American Army.

Altogether some 30,000 island men joined the military during the war. In addition to the *nisei*, there were other Japanese-Americans at work in the Pacific as translators and interpreters—extremely dangerous work in areas where anyone with an epicanthic fold and dark skin was considered the enemy. Hawaii men of all racial background did their duty and came home to pick up their civilian lives again.

(The victory parade in Honolulu marking the end of the war and the recognition of Hawaii's part in the victory was not led by a member of the 442nd, but by a part-Hawaiian. Captain Alexander Kahapea was Hawaii's most-decorated soldier, earning a battlefield commission in France and, among other decorations, five Purple Hearts for the five times he had been wounded in combat.)

Hawaii's *nisei* had proved their loyalty. The men of the islands had proved their willingness to serve their country—and it *was* their country. J. Garner Anthony and others who fought the restrictive martial law principles right up to the Supreme Court, also won a victory, although it came late for Hawaii. Veterans of the war were en route home when Supreme Court Justice Hugo L. Black issued an opinion that martial law was authorized for the defense of the islands against invasion, but that it did not authorize ongoing military tribunals in place of civil courts. Black noted that responsible military and civilian officials should recognize the boundaries of military and civil power.

The war that changed so many lives and the destinies of so many nations had a profound effect on the future of Hawaii. It was, at first, an effect so subtle, so intangible, that it went almost unnoticed. With the passage of time, however, historians were able to see the phenomena for what they were. First, the men of Hawaii, particularly the *nisei,* were exposed to the relationships—both good and bad—that

THE HILL OF SACRIFICE

*I*n a volcanic "tuff" cone near downtown Honolulu is one of America's most imposing and impressive national cemeteries, The National Memorial Cemetery of the Pacific.

In ancient Hawaii the volcano was called Puu O Waiho Ana, from which is derived Puowaina, the hill of placing, or laying up (of sacrifices) . . . the hill of sacrifice. It was a place where sacrifices were made of persons who had broken a kapu, a commandment.

In more recent times the volcano has been known as Punchbowl, from its shape, and it was here, in August 1948, that construction began on the National Cemetery. It was dedicated on September 2, 1949.

The land area of the cemetery is 114.54 acres, containing some 28,000 plots. Additionally there are columbaria to accommodate cremated remains, and there is a Court of the Missing in which the names are inscribed of those missing in World War II, the Korean conflict and the Vietnam conflict. The names total 28,745.

The first public burial in the cemetery was that of Ernie Pyle, legendary correspondent of World War II, killed by gunfire on Ie Shima on April 18, 1945. Pyle and four other Americans killed in combat were buried on July 19, 1949.

Since that day millions of visitors have walked through the serenity of Punchbowl, and the cemetery has become a reminder of the sacrifices demanded by war.

existed in other parts of the world. The training time in Mississippi taught them something about the Southern outlook, but conversely many of them came home to Hawaii with French or Italian war brides. Those marriages, among the strongest in postwar Honolulu, added still more racial mixtures to the islands and helped refute racial stereotyping. Secondly, many servicemen who transited Hawaii or were stationed in the islands for a time during the war went away with tales of the beauty of the islands, a beauty that endured in spite of the civilian-military dichotomy. These mainlanders spread the word also that races could, and did, live together in mutual respect. A large number of mainlanders settled in Hawaii after the war, most of them in Honolulu, and contributed to a kind of growing internationalism. The war had, in essence, broadened the horizons not only of the Hawaii men and women who went elsewhere in connection with war service, but also spread the Hawaii ideal abroad through visitors and immigrants. A third plus for Hawaii was the good will generated by the 442nd through the widespread publicity of its exploits during the war.

Finally, there was the technological breakthrough, the beginnings of development of long-range aircraft. In time, the technology would prove as important as the social subtleties that paved the way for Hawaii's acceptance. For the fast, far jets would shrink the distances from the U.S. mainland to the islands, create a new leading industry, expose the islands to people who would never have made the longer and more arduous trip and make Hawaii a familiar word that, for better or worse, prepared the islands for statehood.

Howard Kiyama and his father are reunited at the end of World War II as the all-Nisei 442nd Regimental Combat Team returns from Europe. This world-famous photograph was nominated for a Pulitzer Prize, but prejudice against the Japanese at the time kept it from being one of the published finalists.

CHAPTER EIGHT

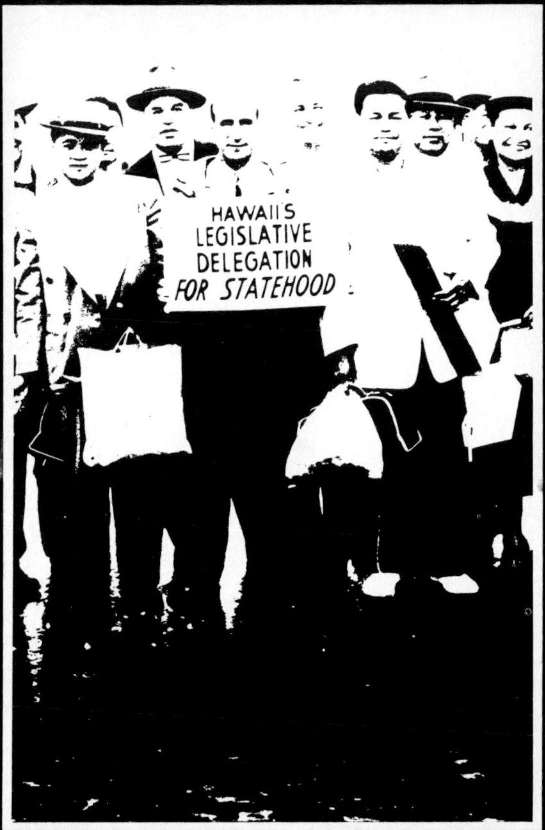
HAWAII'S
LEGISLATIVE
DELEGATION
FOR STATEHOOD

CAPITAL OF A STATE

Servicemen enjoy the nightlife at Club Hubba Hubba in Honolulu in 1958 (above). The Korean War wounded are returned to Hawaii to convalesce (below); Governor Samuel Wilder King, in civilian hat, stands at right.

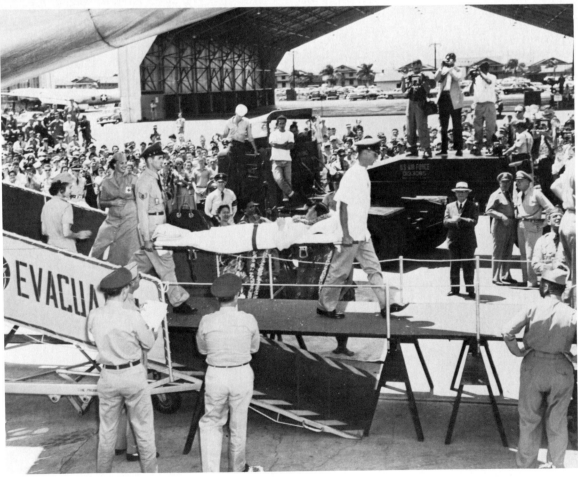

The end of the war was like sliding open a *shoji* door, revealing yet another room, a new dimension. Looking beyond the door, the Hawaii veterans of World War II could sense that their world somehow would change, and that they would be the instruments of that change. They would step into a new Hawaii, one of their own making.

The Americans of Japanese ancestry, the AJAs, had set out to prove themselves worthy Americans with their combat record in World War II; they had succeeded beyond their wildest dreams. When they arrived back in the islands as the most decorated unit in the American Army, it was not an end, but a beginning. There was an aura of freshness and gaiety throughout the city, but also a sober sense of purpose. A menace had been met and overcome; it was time to get on with the building of a new Hawaii.

In the eyes of the returning AJAs, it would necessitate two approaches, a two-front war. First, the war veterans had to become highly politicized, educated and qualified to take over key positions in the territorial government, with a view of breaking the hold the *haole* conservatives had maintained for years. Secondly—and in this they would have the cooperation of most of the territory regardless of political persuasions—Hawaii had to march on to its obvious destiny of becoming a state of the Union. Anything else would be an affront to the people of the islands, who had felt for years they were second-class citizens; anything else would negate the sacrifices the veterans had made in combat.

Territorial status was acceptable to some, but many disliked what it implied—that the people of the islands, in all their ethnic diversity and pride, were unworthy or incapable of making their own decisions. The tradition of a strong central leadership—first the monarchy, then the *haole* businessmen—supervising a core of workers who knew their place and kept it was patronizing, it was in error and it was unfair. Hawaii residents, whether native-born or immigrants, were not permitted to vote in the presidential elections. The governor of the islands was not even an elected official but a presidential appointee. The people of Hawaii could elect a delegate to Congress, but he had no vote. Only by the power of his arguments or the extent of his influence could he win concessions for the islands. Furthermore, even though Hawaii residents were more than paying their way (less than a decade after the war, they were paying more federal tax each year than nine of the 48 states) they still had no voice in the setting of taxes. Congress could establish or abolish legislative positions in the islands; it could, in fact, eliminate the territorial government if it chose.

The people who did not object to this situation were the people for whom change posed a certain amount of risk, notably the entrenched establishment. Their arguments had some cogent points, but the underlying logic was that a good thing should not be tampered with (a good thing was defined as whatever was good for the establishment). In their objections to statehood they were joined by a hard-core *kamaaina* society and by many Hawaiians; both groups deplored the passing of an older and more gracious time. But time and numbers were against them. In 1940, a plebiscite showed that two out of three voters favored statehood. Ten years later, a convention was called to draft a constitution for the moment Hawaii became a state; at that convention, 85 percent of the registered voters went to the polls to elect delegates. (The state constitution as written in 1950 would be used intact nine years later.)

The majority favored statehood, and if the establishment dragged its feet on the question, powerful others did not, including all the governors appointed to lead Hawaii after the end of World War II—

The war over, Mother Nature blasts the islands with a tsunami in April 1946.

Ingram M. Stainback, Oren E. Long, Samuel Wilder King and William F. Quinn. The territorial legislature favored statehood. The local newspapers, the *Honolulu Advertiser* and the *Honolulu Star-Bulletin,* were in favor. All operated in their various ways to bring statehood to fruition, and on the mainland, hundreds of newspapers supported the concept of statehood for the islands. Admittedly, the *Honolulu Advertiser* was cool to the idea for a time, and Honolulu's part-Hawaiian mayor, John Wilson, took advertising space in other newspapers to blast the *Advertiser's* stance—particularly the views of Lorrin P. Thurston who owned most of the paper. Thurston feared that the islands would fall into the hands of Communists, and his fear was shared by others. In time, Thurston's views would change, and by 1957 he would be chairman of the Hawaii Statehood Commission.

In the meantime, the AJAs had embarked on their campaign to revamp the islands' political structure which, in essence, meant the overthrow of control by the Republican Party. The Republicans unwisely had rebuffed the first groping overtures by the young veterans, and the AJAs had turned to the Democratic Party. In some respects it appeared to be a foolish move, for the Democrats in Honolulu were weak and divided. So divided, in fact, that even Democratic presidents of the United States appointed Republican governors to administer the islands. In desperation, the Democratic Party opened its arms to the war veterans, and, equally desperate, the veterans seized the party as a vehicle for change. With the single-mindedness of men who believed in their ultimate success, the veterans built slowly and steadily. They went to college on the GI Bill and came back from Michigan, Stanford and other mainland schools bearing degrees in law or political science. They met at one another's homes and talked endlessly about strategy, about supporting various candidates who could help them in their own upcoming campaigns.

In 1950 yet another contingent of island men went off to war—this one an undeclared "police action" in Korea. In what was now a

ILWU Local 142 head Jack Hall, right, with J.P. Blaisdell, president of the Employers Council in 1945 (left); with Dwight Steele, president of the council from 1947 to 1959 (center); and with Philip P. Maxwell, president in 1964 (right).

tradition, they served with valor, while at home the military bases at Pearl Harbor and Schofield Barracks once again were overflowing. Thousands of servicemen roamed the islands on leave or convalescent time. Honolulu clubs and restaurants were packed, and the city accepted them with a certain aplomb and a sense of *deja vu.*

The political campaigns that led up to the elections of 1954 were different from most of the previous campaigns. The Republicans exploited the danger of Communism at every turn, trying to link Communism and the Democratic Party in the minds of the voters. The anti-statehood forces talked darkly of Communist spies in control of a state of the Union, and of Communist infiltration and control of the labor unions. The AJAs, moving at last, targeted Republican weaknesses and now—supported by the proper degrees and an aura of stability—went after Republican candidates in a vigorous and unflinching grab for control of the state legislature.

And they won. For the first time in history, the Democratic Party controlled both houses of the territorial legislature. To be sure the governor, Samuel Wilder King, was a Republican, and he used his veto 71 times in the next legislative session; there was nevertheless a great sense of accomplishment among the veterans, an anticipation of more victories to come. In the 1956 elections, the Democratic Party retained its power. The political control of Honolulu and the islands had changed hands.

ous leadership. For Hall, Hawaii was "a different place" and he wanted to stay. He was eager and willing to work for unionism; he had both the intelligence and the stamina to challenge the Honolulu establishment and, when necessary, his own union. As the years rolled on, Hall was alternately loved and damned, praised and hated. It rolled over him without leaving so much as a scar. He had powerful supporters and powerful enemies and it was said that he often couldn't tell which was which. He carried on a running feud with the ILWU's Harry Bridges on the West Coast. He was a friend to governors and saw no contradiction in it from a union point of view. He was, in the end, a masterful politician.

Hall's union was a direct challenge to the establishment, particularly the firms known as the Big Five—American Factors (formerly Hackfeld & Co.), Castle & Cooke, Alexander & Baldwin, Theo. H. Davies & Co., and C. Brewer & Co.—which had interests in virtually every money-making venture in Hawaii. The ILWU and several other unions took on the Inter-Island Steamship Company in 1938 in a contest between unionism and the power of Castle & Cooke and Matson Navigation Co., which provided financial backing for Inter-Island. The unions refused to work the docks and went out on strike. Inter-Island brought in strikebreakers and, in a confrontation on the waterfront in Hilo, Hawaii Island, shots were fired by police with shotguns. No indictments came out of the shooting incidents,

STATEHOOD FEVER

As statehood fever seized the islands and residents now looked more than ever toward America for acceptance, the International Longshoremen's and Warehousemen's Union (ILWU) came in for a detailed scrutiny from both pro- and anti-statehood forces. The ILWU—the largest, most militant, best-led, controversial and often most maligned labor union in the territory—had been blamed for harboring Communism. At its very heart was its singular leader, ex-merchant seaman Jack Wayne Hall.

Hall and the ILWU thrived on controversy and had a long history of it. Hall was brilliant, hard-drinking and as pragmatic as it is possible to be. He first turned up in the islands when in his 20s—a tall, skinny kid and a member of the Sailor's Union of the Pacific. His arrival in Hawaii in 1934 and his decision to stay on coincided with the expansion of the labor movement and its drive for new and vigor-

Harry Bridges (left). Sugar plantation laborers rally at the Hawaiian Agricultural Company in the late 1940s (opposite).

although several strikers were wounded and one permanently crippled. Management had shown its teeth and in time the strikers went back to work. But unionism was on its way; by 1941 the ILWU, through persistence, hard work and by a membership campaign that cut across and through racial and class barriers, had organized the docks. It had then turned its attentions to the sugar and plantation workers. Although it suffered setbacks during the war years, the ILWU hung on. By the end of 1946, it had organized the sugar and pineapple workers and now controlled powerful segments of Hawaii's workforce. A labor-management clash was inevitable.

On September 1, 1946, more than 20,000 sugar workers walked away from the plantations. After 79 days the strike ended in a union victory. In its growing strength, the ILWU began to evolve politically and moved to take over the moribund Democratic Party.

Like the Republicans, the Democrats had no great history in the islands of being blind to race and color. The ILWU concocted a strategy of appealing to all races and colors and electing the candidates

Striking dock workers picket Castle and Cooke during the 1949 ILWU maritime strike (opposite), and the Hawaii Seven receive their guilty sentences following a seven-and-one-half month trial in 1953 (below).

they selected. It ended up with control of the Democratic Party, the legislature and the workforce. The spectre of Communism would hang over the union, however, and come up time and again to divert the ILWU focus on politics.

On May 1, 1949, a second strike rocked the islands—this one more devastating than anyone had foreseen. The ILWU walked off the docks in Honolulu and elsewhere throughout Hawaii in a wage dispute. Only 2,000 men left their jobs and for a time it appeared as though this handful of men could not do that much damage. But Honolulu, then and now, looked to the seas as a lifeline. During the strike, nothing entered Hawaii—no goods, materials, resources, assets. By the end of 60 days, there was a rash of failed businesses. By midsummer, nearly 35,000 people were unemployed, and the territorial legislature met in a special session on August 6 to pass a dock seizure act which Governor Ingram Stainback signed into law the next day. It proved futile, for ILWU members on the West Coast, the origin of most of Hawaii's shipping, refused to handle ships to and from Hawaii. In late October, the union and the companies reached agreement on a contract. Although Hall and the ILWU claimed victory, the union faced a massive public relations task—that of selling itself to the people of the islands who were badly hurt by the 177-day strike.

In the wake of the strikes, the territorial legislature created the

Samuel Wilder King, delegate to Congress, and his family are served tea as they await their sail to the mainland—a custom, alas, no longer observed.

Subversive Activities Commission and asked for a visit by the House Committee on Un-American Activities. A subcommittee turned up in 1950 and a number of witnesses went before it, invoking the Fifth Amendment. Jack Hall and 38 others, who subsequently became known as the Reluctant 39, were cited for contempt of Congress, but a federal judge ruled they were within their rights in refusing to say whether they were, or were not, members of the Communist Party.

On the morning of August 28, 1951, Hall and six others were arrested on the basis of new testimony and charged with conspiring to overthrow the government by force and violence. The case languished for almost a year because of legal battles, and the trial itself went on for months. The Hawaii Seven were found guilty, sentenced to five years in jail and fined $5,000 each. They immediately appealed and were freed on bail. Their case was not considered until January 1958, when all seven were acquitted by an appeals court on grounds that their activities had not constituted a conspiracy to overthrow the government.

The whole affair had thrown the spotlight on Communism and its influence, or lack of influence, in Hawaiian affairs. Honolulu spawned several anti-Communist entities—some private—as well as the official Subversive Activities Commission. The mood was cautious and often argumentative. Was there a Communist menace, or was it

an excuse by the establishment to break the unions and keep the working class in its place? How many Communists were too many? Did they pose a danger, or were they as justified in pursuing their beliefs under a free system as any other political group?

If nothing new surfaced in this scrutiny of Communism, nothing old was forgotten. In 1956, Senator James O. Eastland of Mississippi brought another subcommittee to the islands and reopened old wounds by bringing back to the witness stand some of the same people who had appeared earlier. Eastland got no better answers than those offered six years before.

Other social dynamics were at work in Honolulu. The veterans had found a champion in a blunt, introverted former police officer, John A. Burns. Burns was emerging as the head of the Democratic Party chiefly because he had accepted the AJAs and worked to get them equal treatment, any time and any place. At the same time, the ILWU fell short of its bid to take over the party, and while there were many politicians who owed their jobs to union support, the party and the union were growing equally, if not together. The overriding factor in Honolulu was the population growth of the Japanese—now the majority voting bloc in Hawaii—and the fact that they now had their own candidates. There was a diversion from old problems and a new concentration on realities; the *haole* establishment still controlled

Members of the statehood Congressional Investigation Commission tour Kilauea Military Camp in 1935.

business, but the ILWU and lesser unions controlled the workforce, and the AJAs controlled politics.

And now, as the fear of Communism in the islands began to fade, there was a concomitant rise in desire for statehood from all of the power groups.

The Hawaii Statehood Commission under chairman Lorrin P. Thurston published a number of pamphlets explaining the unfairness of denying statehood to Hawaii. Most were written by the *Honolulu Advertiser's* then-city editor, Buck Buchwach. Buchwach's articles, first written for mainland newspapers, then used as reprints by the commission, were widely circulated and had an impact. Among other things, Buchwach pointed out that the ILWU men from Hawaii who had served in the Korean hostilities had gone off to join in combat against Communism and had performed as well or better than other U.S. servicemen.

There were other realities. Hawaii had been under the U.S. flag since 1898, it was paying taxes, it contributed to the national economy, it was considered enough a part of America to push the U.S. into war when Pearl Harbor was bombed. Additionally, the argument that it was noncontiguous began to weaken when another noncontiguous area, Alaska, also asked for statehood.

With Alaska in the picture, the question of statehood began to take on deeper political coloration, and discouragement set in. The U.S. Senate, equally divided between Democrats and Republicans, had assumed Alaska would send two Democrats to the Senate, Hawaii two Republicans. With the Democratic takeover of 1954 and beyond, the question got more tangled—would there now be *four* new Democratic senators?

Opponents of statehood in the U.S. Congress had tied the issues together, putting Alaska and Hawaii in the same admissions bill. It doubled the bill's chances of failure. Finally, after years of delay, the Hawaii delegate to Congress, John A. Burns, the former policeman and champion of the AJAs, began to sense a shift of mood in Congress. He returned to Honolulu with the feeling that if Hawaii allowed Alaska to win statehood first, there could be no reasonable justification for denying it to Hawaii. It was a position the territorial governor, William F. Quinn, could live with, and support for that strategy began to grow in the inner circle of people who had fought so long for statehood.

There were last-minute frustrations. Yet another congressional committee came out to the islands for a first-hand look, and once again Senator Eastland and others voiced their objections. Their voices, this time, were all but lost in the rising echoes of support for Hawaii statehood.

Some 116,000 signatures were collected in a day-long rally for the Hawaii "Statehood Honor Roll" in Honolulu in 1954 (opposite). A Hawaii Statehood delegation (above) presented the names to Congress later that year to no avail. The successful Hawaii Statehood Delegation of 1958 (below) included former Governor Oren E. Long, congressional delegate Mrs. Joseph R. Farrington, last-appointed Governor William F. Quinn and chairman Lorrin P. Thurston.

STATEHOOD

In May 1958, the Alaska statehood bill passed the House, and in June it passed the Senate. Alaska, not Hawaii, was the 49th state, but in Honolulu the Alaska victory was greeted with jubilation, for it was a portent of Hawaii's own triumph. No man of conscience now could reject Hawaii's appeal.

In February 1959, the House Committee on Interior and Insular Affairs voted favorably for statehood for Hawaii. A similar bill emerged from the Senate's committee in March.

On March 11, 1959, the Senate passed the statehood bill, and the following morning the House of Representatives also passed it.

On March 12, there was an air of expectancy in Honolulu. When the news was flashed that Hawaii, at long last, was a state of the Union—the 50th state—church bells began to peal all over the city. People poured out of buildings and houses and greeted one another in the streets. Newspaper crews readied extra editions and civil defense sirens sounded. Bartenders were the busiest people in downtown Honolulu all that afternoon and into the evening, and police officers were more concerned for the safety of drivers than they were in booking them. That night there were bonfires on the beaches where Kamehameha I had assembled his war canoes, and on other beaches around the islands. For many there was great elation. For others, such as the Hawaii Statehood Commission, there was the realization that it was over—they had won and now they were out of business, at last. Impromptu parties sprang up as old friends got together and toasted the new idea that they were now genuine, bonafide U.S. citizens— they could vote, participate in the processes of government. They could bring change if they wanted to, and be listened to when they talked about how they wanted their taxes spent. Some groups gathered in churches to hear ministers invoke the blessings of God on this new state; one such group met in historic Kawaiahao Church where a prominent Hawaiian minister, the Reverend Abraham Akaka, told them that statehood was like the lifting of clouds of smoke from the islands, and that now all the people would have new opportunities.

Akaka was right, but despite statehood, new opportunities would not come immediately, nor would they be easy.

While the pealing of the church bells still echoed through the soft spring morning, there were those in Hawaii for whom statehood brought deep and intense concerns. Many of the old *kamaaina* families, for whom the status quo had meant splendid lives surrounded by lands and servants, looked apprehensively to a future in which there would be opportunities for all. Such opportunities might threaten the class structure of their lives. There were less fortunate but equally historic Honolulu families who also looked apprehensively toward the new status—they were not rich, but their position now seemed insecure. The *haole* establishment feared—rightly as it turned out—that it would be challenged by new and diversified businesses pouring into Hawaii. Now that Hawaii was a state, it was assumed to be a safer place for investments, and new capital no longer feared venturing out into the Pacific.

There were socialites who foresaw new faces and fashions that would disrupt long-standing social patterns; they, too, were correct. There were politicians who began to think of Hawaii representation in

Young Dodi Bacon's face lights up at statehood news, March 12, 1959 (left).

151

A bonfire marks the statehood celebration in 1959 (below) as the Royal Hawaiian Band leads festivities at Iolani Palace (inset, left), and a procession heads for a statehood service at Kawaiahao Church (inset, right).

The dying tradition of throw net fishing was introduced by the Japanese. A girl cleans an island delicacy, squid (inset), as part of Kamehameha Schools' Malama O Ke Ola program.

Washington; there were construction industry executives who hoped statehood would bring a resurgence of building in the islands, and whose hopes were realized on a scale they would not have believed. Once the euphoria of statehood had passed, individuals, families and businesses in all walks of life began to ponder what changes statehood would bring.

And there were a few—perhaps only a few—who looked not toward Washington and not toward the future. They looked back in time and southeast toward Tahiti, and they remembered. In their mind's eye they saw the grandeur of the Polynesian race at the height of its adventurous and epic voyages, saw the double-hulled canoes on the horizon and then the settlement along the shores of a new land.

They saw the old, powerful, complex, vibrant society that sprang up around the harbors in Honolulu and Lahaina, and it seemed to them that the land was greener, somehow, when it was planted in taro and there were no large and heavy structures. The few who looked back saw the coming of the tall ships and the subsequent spread of diseases that killed and killed and killed. They saw the decimation of a race and its ensuing loss of influence, of control over its own life and its subordination to yet other strangers as the years rolled on. Statehood, which seemed to bring so much joy, removed them in a sense even farther from their beginnings, taking them into a society that might be more intolerant. These few—and there were perhaps only a few—looked back and wept.

A SPLENDID REMINDER

*H*awaii's State Capitol, unlike some others, sits near the center of the main city of the state. From downtown Honolulu it is an easy ten-minute walk to the Capitol—and an unusual capitol it is.

A Committee of Fifteen, comprised of legislators and private citizens alike, selected John Carl Warnecke of San Francisco to be the master architect, and charged him with producing something "different," something that would be evocative of Hawaii's past, yet modern and functional.

Ground-breaking ceremonies were held on November 10, 1965, and just over three years later the building was dedicated with suitable ritual.

What had been produced was a soaring building with an open atrium, a building in which even the functional columns and supports suggested something from the past, such as trees or sails.

The building sits in the center of 80,000 square feet of reflecting pools. Cone-shaped legislative chambers recall the islands' birth in volcanic eruptions.

The building cost almost $22 million, in part because of the use of fine arts and furnishings to decorate it. Huge tapestries, giant chandeliers and at least 60,000 pieces of mosaic tile from Italy add to its grandeur. Another asset is the koa wood doors, paneling and furniture. The wood is a reminder of Hawaii's past because it is from a tree that grows naturally only in Hawaii.

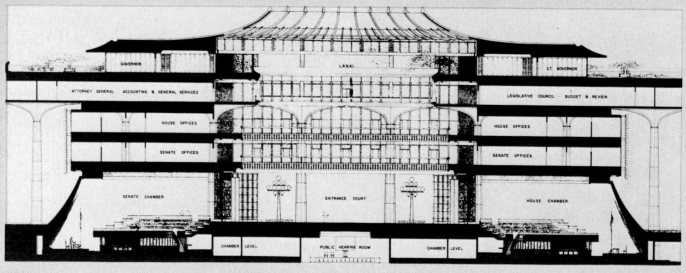

Cross-section of Hawaii State Capital.

CHAPTER NINE

THE
CROSSROADS

For many Americans, Hawaii suddenly appeared on the horizon like a tropical *Shangri-la,* newly accessible and perhaps even affordable. It was as if the mists had parted to reveal the islands, now judged to be safe and secure enough for investment purposes, convenient to visit and maybe a nice place to live. A surprising number of Americans learned that in Honolulu, at least, English was spoken and was the language of commerce. There was no need for passports or visas, yet the locale was exotic. No immunizations were required and the currency was familiar. Even better, the air was clean and the streets were safe. What also made Hawaii enticing was the jet engine—instead of lumbering across the Pacific on twelve-hour ordeals, visitors could fly from the West Coast of the United States in just over four hours. It was all too good to be true, yet it was true. Visitors began to pour into the newest state, changing its appearance by their numbers and their needs.

The first area to undergo a metamorphosis was Waikiki.

For years, Waikiki had been a somnolent, charming section—not particularly impressive as far as the local people were concerned. It had nice beaches, and the residents, who lived simply in old-fashioned frame houses, liked the out-of-the-way ambience. Doors were never locked, and people who met on the streets were apt to know one another. There were a few hotels—the Moana, the Niumalu, the Royal Hawaiian, the Halekulani, the SurfRider—but the tourists did not intrude. Then suddenly the homes began to disappear in the rush for new hotel sites, and there were more accommodations for tourists in hotels that began to reach higher and higher—the Waikiki Biltmore, the Reef, the Edgewater, the new Princess Kaiulani. Waikiki's pace became a bit faster as new clubs opened, and local entertainers found a ready market in tourists avid for good times and local color. Tourism leaped from around 500 visitors in 1939, to 500,000 in 1959, the year of statehood, and it was only the beginning. Just two decades later, the visitors would number more than four million a year and spend more than $3 billion each year in Hawaii, making tourism the state's leading industry. Most of those visitors would stay in Waikiki, which would become packed with high-rises, bars, clubs, restaurants and concessions unabashedly aimed at the tourist trade. To most local people, Waikiki, once the playground of the *alii* who loved to surf, had been transformed into a kind of tourist ghetto. For the visitors, it seemed to retain a kind of kinetic charm, and the number of repeat visitors increased as Waikiki lured them back year after year.

Outside of Waikiki proper there were other changes. In a swamp between Waikiki and downtown Honolulu, the Dillingham interests put men and machines to work to reclaim the site of one of the world's largest shopping complexes. Simultaneously, it gave visitors and residents a glossy new area packed with a variety of shops and stores, and caused consternation in downtown business circles which viewed the proliferation of regional shopping areas as a direct threat to the urban center. Finally, downtown businessmen rose to the challenge and pledged a resurgence in construction, residential units, services and attractiveness. Systematically, then faster, the face of downtown Honolulu began to change.

Adding to the change was the influx of new entrepreneurial capital—a gauntlet hurled at the local establishment (now less *haole* and more mixed, as the biological fusion of Hawaii continued). The streets of Honolulu bore new signs as businesses poured in from the U.S. mainland. Entrepreneurs discovered Honolulu, and Honolulu discovered that there were ways of doing business that were somewhat faster than the old ways. One who taught that lesson was a *haole* who had come out earlier for a vacation and stayed on to have an impact. He was an industrialist who built ships during the war, and who

seemed to do most things on a vast scale. He is credited, perhaps erroneously, with the saying, "Find a need and fill it," and his accomplishments in Honolulu prove how avidly he followed that dictum. Recognizing the coming need for hotels and housing, Henry J. Kaiser turned a slice of Waikiki into the Hawaiian Village Hotel, complete with its own lagoon; to the east of Honolulu he conceived and constructed thousands of homes which, in effect, became a second city, although spreading urban areas eventually closed the open space between them. He built golf courses, a shopping center and a hospital. He introduced a new health plan to Honolulu. He built a lavish home on the beach, and his huge catamaran, painted pink, was a common sight offshore of Honolulu. His feats undoubtedly encouraged other investors to give Hawaii a try.

The delights of Honolulu and Hawaii were now being sampled by a steady stream of visitors, some of whom neglected to go home again. Still others came to Honolulu with the intent of making a home and a living, and there were fresh waves of immigrants, mostly from the Philippines this time as immigration quotas were relaxed. The result was a visible quickening in Honolulu. As the city's population began to increase by at least two percent per year, the buildings got higher and the press for land became more acute. Every other housewife began looking into real estate sales as a way of supplementing the family income, and a visitor looking out over the skyline of Honolulu could count dozens of cranes atop tall buildings as construction gave Honolulu a "boom town" appearance. It was as if Honolulu, which had waited so long for its Americanization, was embracing it with a fervor unmatched by anything in its history.

With equal fervor the new state turned to Washington; the resi-

The beach crowd suggests the summer outrigger regatta season on Waikiki Beach (opposite). The red hibiscus is Hawaii's state flower (above).

President John F. Kennedy joins Hawaii Governor John A. Burns and U.S. Senator Daniel K. Inouye in an open-car ride through Honolulu during a June 1963 visit.

Back in Honolulu, the friend of the AJA war veterans, John A. Burns, suffered a political setback when he was defeated in the gubernatorial race by the last territorial governor, William F. Quinn. It would be four more years before Burns would become Hawaii's governor as well as the titular head of the Democratic Party in the islands.

EVOLUTION

The statehood boom changed the face of Honolulu in dramatic ways. Not only were buildings growing taller and becoming more numerous, now there were freeways that connected the urban core with outlying areas and divided the city into zones. On the outskirts of the city, cloverleafs and on- and off-ramps sprouted like orchids, and it was conceded that nothing could slow the urbanization of Honolulu.

Hawaii's constitution has made it possible for the state legislature to organize local governments, and the islands were now split into four counties. Hawaii County was the Island of Hawaii; Maui County was the islands of Maui, Lanai, Molokai and Kahoolawe; Kauai County was the islands of Kauai and Niihau; and the city and county of Honolulu was made up of Oahu and all other islands not in the other counties. The city limits of Honolulu stretched some 1,600 miles north and west to embrace the islands all the way to Kure. Despite this maritime orientation, Honolulu took on characteristics of mainland U.S. cities, right down to the air conditioned high-rises in a tropical zone swept by reliable trade winds from the northeast. More concrete covered more green space; more automobiles, particularly from Japan, began to crowd the freeways; and the population began to rocket upwards—from around 250,000 in the mid-'50s to close to a million statewide (mostly in Honolulu) by 1982. Landmarks such as the Aloha tower, near the site where Kamehameha I liked to relax, and the Waikiki Natatorium, built as a memorial to Hawaii's war dead, began to fade in the rush of developments. Many *kamaainas* decried the changes, but the consensus was that they could not be stopped.

dents of Hawaii could make their wishes known through that old American use of the vote. To carry the message back to Washington, the islands elected the first U.S. Senator of Chinese ancestry, Hiram Leong Fong, and sent him off in tandem with a former governor, Oren Long, to the Senate. Fong was a millionaire whose boyhood in Honolulu had been difficult at times; his election to the Senate capped a lifetime of upward mobility. On the House side, the Representatives got their first look at a U.S. Congressman of Japanese ancestry, Daniel K. Inouye. A veteran of the 442nd Regimental Combat Team, Inouye had lost an arm in action against the Germans in Italy, and had returned to Hawaii to become one of the bright young veterans dedicated to making changes. (In 1962, Inouye would be elected to the Senate and go on to distinguish himself.)

The Waikikian Hotel was an architectural pacesetter in post-World War II Hawaii—an example of the renaissance of Polynesian influence that is now characterized as distinctly Hawaiian.

Rice fields of Waikiki and McCully contrast with the Royal Hawaiian Hotel in a late-'20s aerial view of Waikiki (above). Waikiki today, as seen in a 1983 aerial (below), is among the most expensive real estate in the nation.

A Hawaiian monk seal in his native habitat (left), carefree flight (below) and a structured swim at Sea Life Park (inset).

WILD AND NOT-SO-WILDLIFE

*I*t's widely known that there are no snakes in Hawaii; other aspects of Hawaiian wildlife are less known but just as interesting.

Hawaii has a species of bat which reached the islands, incredibly, under its own power, a remarkable achievement for a land-based mammal. The Lasiurius bats are found now on most islands, and may still move among them; they still store up fat for long flights although it's unlikely they are making long trips nowadays.

Another remarkable migrant is the monk seal, very likely the first mammal to live in the Hawaiian Islands. Its origins are in the Caribbean and the Mediterranean, indicating another mammal with long-range capabilities.

Rats, which came to Hawaii as stowaways in Polynesian canoes, take their toll of local bird life and have caused extensive damage to sugarcane. The introduction of mongooses to kill the rats proved an unwise choice—mongooses venture out by day and sleep at night, while rats do the reverse.

Hawaii has been an unfortunate port of call for other animals. A brown bear from Kamchatka, in Russia, arrived in Honolulu aboard a ship in 1841 and was given to the townspeople, who ate it. The same thing happened to a second bear in 1846. For years it was rumored that a third bear was loose in the hills behind Honolulu, the bear having broken away from a circus held in the mid-1950s. There have been no recent reports of bear sightings.

Similarly, reports of wallabies in the hills behind the city persist, although again there have been no reports of sightings of these kangaroo-like creatures.

There are wild pigs in Hawaii. Hunters chase them regularly in the more remote areas, spotting their hangouts by the devastating holes they dig in the forest floor.

Dogs have a long and honorable history in the islands, having made the voyage with the Polynesian settlers. Dogs were used for food, as pets and in religious rituals. Some feral dogs exist today in remote areas of the islands.

I.M. Pei visibly established the lofty goals of the East-West Center Administration Building in an elegant architectural statement.

There were many positive developments that won everyone's approval. Peace Corps training camps sprang up in Hawaii's tropical setting. In Honolulu proper, ground was broken—by Governor John A. Burns and then-Vice President Lyndon Johnson—for a center of learning that would house scholars from East and West and allow them to exchange concepts and learn about one another. The East-West Center for Technical and Cultural Interchange opened its doors adjacent to the University of Hawaii campus; Asian nationalists who would not speak to one another in their own countries were discoursing at length in Honolulu's happy climate. The university itself began to emerge as a serious institute of learning despite its tropical location. Honolulu elected a part-Hawaiian mayor, Neal Blaisdell, followed by a mainland-born American of Italian ancestry, Frank Fasi, followed by a woman, Eileen Anderson—undeniable evidence of a minimum of prejudices. To underscore the cosmopolitan nature of the city, a Japanese capitalist, Kenji Osano, became the owner of more Waikiki hotel rooms than anyone else in or out of Hawaii.

Large hotel chains such as Sheraton and Hilton made huge investments in Honolulu property, and were followed by myriad fast-food

BUILDING AN ARCHIPELAGO

*T*he Hawaiian Islands are the tops of a mountain range built by volcanic action along a northwest-southeast rift in the ocean floor. The mountains extend from Kure Island in the north some 1,600 miles to the southernmost point of the Island of Hawaii, largest in the archipelago.

Hawaii is the newest of the islands, but perhaps not the last. It was built by five volcanoes which merged to form the highest volcanic mass on earth. Mauna Kea (the White Mountain in Hawaiian, named for its mantling of snow several months of the year) and Mauna Loa (the Long Mountain, actually the world's largest—nearly six miles—when measured from the ocean floor to the summit) are both near the 14,000-foot mark. Hualalai Volcano reaches 8,000 feet. The Kohala Mountains are old volcanoes which formed the northwest portion of the island, and Kilauea on the slope of Mauna Loa is one of the world's most active volcanoes.

The most famous volcanoes are not on Hawaii Island, but on Oahu, and are both very visible. Punchbowl, near the heart of Honolulu, was a hill of sacrifice in ancient Hawaii. Today it is the site of The National Memorial Cemetery of the Pacific. Diamond Head, called Leahi (the brow of the ahi fish) by the Hawaiians, is a landmark which identifies Waikiki.

It has been thousands of years since either Oahu volcano erupted, but technically they are not considered dead, and no volcanologist would predict they will never erupt again.

In the same vein, no scientist will say there will never be an addition to the island chain. As the decade of the 1980s opened, there were some indications of magma (underground molten lava) moving and shifting underneath the ocean to the south of Hawaii Island, giving rise to the possibility that nature, at some future time, will resume construction on an archipelago that was begun eons ago.

Honolulu Theatre for Youth, one of the city's most illustrious cultural assets, presents works highly suitable to the community's multi-cultural composition (above). The Bodhisttva Kuan-yin, seated in the position of "royal ease" at the Honolulu Academy of Arts, is a thirteenth- to fourteenth-century Chinese wooden art piece (left) The Honolulu Symphony performs at Neal Blaisdell Concert Hall (below).

A Zen archer demonstrates an elegant Japanese activity, executed in matches in Kapiolani Park in Waikiki (left). Downtown Honolulu comes alive during a Chinese New Year Lion Dance (above).

AND EVER THE TWAIN SHALL MEET . . .

*F*rom the time Captain Cook opened the Hawaiian Islands to the West, the population has been racially mixed and today it is becoming even more so.

In a population of about a million, Caucasians comprise the largest racial bloc although percentages are dropping, from nearly 32 percent in 1970 to 26.3 percent today. Similarly, the second-largest racial group, Americans of Japanese ancestry, have dropped from nearly 28 percent in 1970 to 23.5 percent in 1980.

The third largest group, Hawaiians and part-Hawaiians, make up almost 19 percent of the population of the islands, followed by the Filipinos at 11.2 percent. A rapidly growing group, the Filipinos are helping to make the population more diverse, as are the 10.6 percent of the populace classified as "other," which includes the latest wave of immigrants—the Vietnamese, Khmers and Laotians from embattled Southeast Asia.

Other racial blocs each make up less than two percent of the population and include blacks, Samoans, Koreans and Puerto Ricans. The Chinese, whose ancestors were among the first Asian immigrants in Hawaii, make up about five percent.

As the racial mixing continues, the two larger blocs—the Caucasians and Japanese—are expected to lose their dominance in numbers.

Hawaii has a declining birth rate—from 19.9 per 1,000 residents in 1971, it dropped to 18.6 in 1981. At the same time, the number of people moving to Hawaii from the U.S. mainland in 1971 was 63,452, while a decade later it had dropped to 37,312, bringing about an overall decline in the growth rate.

That decline, however, from 2.3 percent in 1970 to 1.4 percent in 1980, still was higher than the national growth rate of 1.2 percent.

Over the past decade the median age of residents has risen sharply, from 25 to 28.4 years, a situation attributed to the declining birth rate.

franchises. Beachfront property became impossible to buy. The city shot outward and upward at an alarming rate. For every resident who found it bewildering, there was one who termed it progress and argued, often convincingly, that it was for the best.

In the midst of the boom there was an interesting but largely unnoticed situation. In the jungles of Asia the United States had become involved in yet another war, slowly at first and then with an increasing tempo and with a mounting loss of life. It was a divisive conflict that triggered protests and led to the decision of an American president not to stand for reelection. Vietnam was the stuff of high drama and high tragedy and in the midst of it, there was hardly any mention of Hawaii men of Asian ancestry who quietly went off to serve their country in combat with absolutely no question of their loyalty to the United States. The legacy of the 100th Battalion and the 442nd Regimental Combat Team and other units was one of such unswerving loyalty, that twenty years later the willingness of Hawaii men to fight in Asia was never questioned and never discussed. No doubt the fact of statehood contributed to the assumption of loyalty.

In downtown Honolulu, the business leaders looked to the boom as healthy and invigorating. They reacted less well to the challenge of mainland capital and ideas, but in the end the Big Five and other companies began to diversify. Tourism and military spending grew to be the leaders, but as leadership changed and many of the *kamaainas* retired or were replaced, a new and adventurous spirit siezed the business community. Honolulu-based firms began to export ideas and services. Honolulu-born or trained technicians were turning up in Iran, Japan, Saudi Arabia, Egypt and Hong Kong. And the number of millionaires in Honolulu increased; more than a few were non-*haoles*. Orientals and part-Orientals had proved they could learn, they could fight, they could lead—they now proved they had a gift for making money as well.

The city boasted a symphony, an opera, an enviable art academy, a famous museum, a zoo. It had become a crossroads for businessmen dealing with Asians and the entrepreneurs of the other Pacific islands. It was still far out in the Pacific, but its location had become strategic in terms of transportation and communications. Satellites began to link Honolulu with other major cities, and all at once much of the isolation had gone. Perhaps some of the romance had gone as well.

A demonstration in Bishop Museum (below). The statue of Kamehameha I (opposite) in the Kohala district is the original of famous duplicate in Honolulu. The historic chief and his descendants are further honored with the Kamehameha Parade (inset).

CROSSROADS OF COMMERCE

Aloha Week Parade.

*H*onolulu's geographic location makes it an ideal crossroads in the Pacific, now linked by satellite and other modern devices to anywhere in the world. Honolulu has thus become home to more than two dozen multinational corporations with Asia/Pacific operations.

The firms locate in Honolulu in part because, as part of the United States, Hawaii has political stability. Firms appreciate the familiar tax laws which allow them to plan ahead with a degree of certainty. Compared with Hong Kong and Tokyo, Honolulu also is inexpensive, and busy executives can fly either east or west without losing too much valuable time.

A large plus for Honolulu—the quality of life is exceptional, a blend of American convenience with Oriental flavors and a Polynesian patina. Executives' families appreciate the schools, shopping and the ambience.

A drawback—many foreign business people are so beguiled by the image of Honolulu and the spell of the islands, they cannot believe Honolulu is a place where serious work is accomplished.

Diving off "the rock" at Waimea Beach Park, Oahu (left). An elderly Oriental woman enjoys the May Day program (inset, top); plumerias adorn a hula dancer's hair (inset, middle); and a caucasian girl, with haku lei, at the end of a race (inset, above).

A boy works with Kumu, an excellent fish (top). Hawaiian fruits, including pineapple, tangerines, starfruit, oranges and papayas, create a colorful display at market (above). The sugar cane is burned before it is cut (right).

WHAT PRICE PARADISE?

*M*any people came to Hawaii to escape the weather, traffic, drabness and hectic pace of other places—but found they cannot escape the price of paradise. Living in Hawaii is expensive.

Since 1955 the U.S. Bureau of Labor has been compiling statistics showing the cost of supporting a family of four in Hawaii compared to supporting that same family in 24 mainland cities. Comparisons were made in three general income groups—lower, intermediate and higher.

In 1980 Hawaii led in all cities except in the lower income range, where Anchorage, Alaska, ranked first and Honolulu second.

For example, goods that would cost a mainland family in the lower income bracket $100 would cost the Hawaii family $132.

The problem in Hawaii, among other things, is the higher combined tax load, which has increased from 30.1 percent of per-capita income in 1970 to 31.7 percent in 1980.

Hawaii's poor families have been hurt by other increases—housing costs for them were 43 percent higher than those for a mainland family; food costs, 28 percent higher.

NEW WAVES

The tragedy in Vietnam brought a new wave of immigrants to Honolulu as the boat people from Vietnam poured into the city. They would be joined by refugees from Laos and Cambodia. Hawaii took more than its per-capita share of the refugees in its tradition of opening its doors to strangers. Refugees in their native dress appeared before prospective employers in Honolulu, determined to contribute to their adopted home; more than half of the newcomers quickly got off the welfare rolls and into jobs, however menial, as they prepared to redirect their lives in a free land.

The refugees arrived at a time when other's ambitions had been achieved. One historian said of Hawaii in the mid-1930s that each ethnic group had its different goals—the *haoles* to control, the Hawaiians to recapture the past, the Portuguese to be considered *haole*, the Chinese to win economic independence, the Japanese to be accepted, and the Filipinos to return to their homes in the Philippines. Years after statehood the *haoles* no longer controlled, but neither did anyone else—the biological mixing of races was making racial backgrounds all but meaningless except for a sentimental clinging to old cultures in a modern context. The Portuguese had made such a contribution to Hawaiian life that it was useless to think of a time when they were not a part of leading social and business circles. The Chinese had not only won their economic independence, they had accomplished lofty goals of owning and managing lands and investments throughout the state, especially in Honolulu itself. Similarly, the Japanese won their acceptance, and now were the most prominent force in local politics. Many Filipinos fell in love with Hawaii and stayed on.

As for the Hawaiians, throughout many of the post-statehood years

Kuma hula *(hula teacher)* Iolani Luahine and Kahu *(pastor)* Abraham Akaka take part in rededication ceremonies at Iolani Palace in 1978.

IT AIN'T NECESSARILY SO

There are misconceptions and stereotypes about Hawaii and its people that most residents have to deal with from time to time—and try to clear up.

This is not a place where no serious work is done. Honolulu and Hawaii have their share of inventors, writers, musicians, engineers, academicians and technocrats. Hawaii is the home of serious marine researchers, astronomers and other space scientists and, of course, geologists whose natural habitat is the high volcanoes of the Island of Hawaii.

Poi, the staple made from the root of the taro plant, does not taste like library paste. It is quite delicious to those with open minds and adventurous tastes, and has been proved to be good for the stomach.

The destructive waves that reach Hawaii infrequently are not tidal waves—they have nothing to do with tides. The correct name is tsunamis, *and they result from earthquakes that literally displace water and set it in motion.*

Every tourist who arrives in Honolulu is not greeted with a lei. The reason is simple. Nearly four million visitors a year alight in the islands, and the logistics would make it impossible.

"Natives" do not live in grass huts. Residents live in a great variety of housing, most of it expensive. Honolulu is as modern as any other city.

Hawaii is not a foreign country, despite the quantity of mail that arrives each year that seems to designate the islands as an independent kingdom once again. Since 1959, Hawaii has been a staunch part of the United States. Even before that, the islands were a territory of the United States, reaching back to the turn of the century.

A tutu (grandmother) dances in the Kodak Hula Show, a Waikiki institution (above). Mauna Kea Observatory (opposite, top). Kamehameha Schools' leadership program instructor gathers taro leaves (opposite, bottom).

*K*ings encouraged it, missionaries damned it, practitioners raised it to a high art and dozens of Hollywood starlets failed at it in some terrible movies.

The hula's beginnings are lost in antiquity, but today it thrives as never before since the arrival of the missionaries. According to one authority, some 200,000 of Hawaii's one million residents can dance a hula, or fake it pretty well.

There are unanswered questions about the hula's origins, but in old Polynesia it could be many things. The missionaries considered it a dance of extravagant sensuality, and it could be. It also could be a form of worship for specific dieties. It could enchant kings by telling stories of events that

took place in ancient times. It could be accompanied by meles, the mythic, rhythmic chants that kept alive the old legends of Hawaii and its people.

One of the most influential teachers of the hula was the late Iolani Luahine, who dedicated her life to perpetuating the dance as an art form and more—a symbol of Hawaiian strength and spirituality.

Today the dance is no longer damned but avidly encouraged and taught, both by private teachers and in the schools. Hula contests and festivals are annual, colorful events— well attended and much appreciated.

The hula is a much appreciated part of Hawaiian culture, both in the present (below) and in the past (opposite), as exemplified by the voluminous costume, maile lei *and corn husk anklets of the dancer, circa 1900.*

A dancer, in three views (original sketches in Bishop Museum), performs an informal hula before Captain Cook at Kealakekua Bay in 1779 (left). Dancers of all ages represent hula of the old style (insets).

they continued to languish near the bottom of the social and economic ladder. They were involved in proportionately more than their share of local crimes; there were many Hawaiian names on the welfare and unemployment rolls; they seemed to care less about education and their children became drop-outs. But in the mid-1970s there was a sudden new stirring in the Hawaiian community, as if a race had shaken itself out of lethargy and begun to face some hard facts about itself and its future. Quietly but consistently, there began to appear new and dramatic Hawaiian art, literature and music. A sudden outpouring of sympathy for Hawaiian causes on the part of non-Hawaiians was married to a revitalization of Hawaiian values by the Hawaiians themselves. The Hawaiians became a potent community force. Observers called it a Hawaiian renaissance; the Hawaiians themselves, buoyed by a new-found pride, began to speak of *aloha aina,* love of the land, and other ancient cultural traits.

In 1978 a constitutional convention in Honolulu created the Office of Hawaiian Affairs (OHA) in which Hawaiians would work for the betterment of their race. Nine OHA trustees were sworn into office on January 17, 1981, and provided with an office and staff. The concept was to address the problems of Hawaiians and their relationships with others, as well as their position within modern society. Although community leaders publicly supported OHA, some were privately fearful that dealing with the Hawaiians as an isolated group would do more harm than good to a race already damaged by history. Still others feared what they thought they already had detected—an element of racism in the rising expectations of the Hawaiian people.

Once again, nothing in the history of the Hawaiians was to be easy, or simple. As they strove for their own place in the islands their ancestors discovered and settled, there would be tides that would bring them alternately closer then farther again from the realization of their dreams.

A view through the palms of Pearl Harbor in the 1880s.

EPILOGUE

Let us pretend that the demigod Maui, who has snared the sun and altered time, has worked other tricks as well. It is the 1980s, but the canoe with the odd, claw-shaped sail has just appeared over the horizon to the south, and the unknown Polynesian adventurer is but hours away from stepping ashore. Already he has seen land birds and coconut husks in the water, and for the past several nights he has observed new constellations. Now he catches the scent of flowers. On the underside of the distant cloud mass he sees the reflection of water more green than blue, an indication of shallow seas and possibly land. He turns his sturdy craft and follows his instincts and his experience toward shore.

He beaches his canoe on the white sand of Waikiki and stands, transfixed. Nothing has prepared him for this.

What does he see?

Not the taro and ti that he is accustomed to; not the men making bone fishhooks and the women pounding poi or making tapa. Later in his Hawaiian adventure he will see them in outlying places, principally on other islands, where a few souls are trying to keep alive a once-vibrant culture.

He sees a great city, modern and moving with a pace that can equal anything in the kinetic atmospheres of New York or Hong Kong, Chicago or Tokyo. He sees people of his own race and myriad others, and traces of his race in many of them. He sees familiar palm trees, not as many as there were at one time, and other foliage that he knows, as well as a great diversity of other plants that are new to him. He learns that outside the city there is a slower and more gracious way of life and, somewhat bemused, he discovers that most of the people live in or near the city instead of the countryside, mostly because they find the city a place of charm and beauty, with a downtown that rivals anything in the America to which this land now belongs.

He discovers there are problems, but they are the problems that afflict every metropolis—crime (but less than elsewhere), traffic (annoying, but manageable), a need for civic improvements (but the leadership is aware of it and taking steps), and quality of life (which all in all seems better in this Honolulu, this Fair Haven, than it is in any city he will visit later).

The Polynesian adventurer, with all the quick adaptability of a maritime race, realizes that some things are constant. The sea is still the primary lane of commerce. The sky is still of a high, blue, vaulting clearness that remains unpolluted and bright. A great yellow sun still lays a soft and warm patina on the land and seas below. The tradewinds from the northeast still push steadily across the land, making each day a delight to the senses. The Polynesian smiles. Now he is less awe-struck and is becoming appreciative. He could have fared worse, for now he will become part of a place and a city that seems always in transition but always the same—a city that grows and changes and evolves and modernizes and still keeps reaching back to the past for the lessons that only time can teach.

Maui frees the sun and time begins to move again. The Polynesian voyager in a soft tropical suit and conservative tie is carrying a briefcase and on his way to a meeting, where he will sit down with an attorney of Japanese ancestry, a haole developer, a financier whose grandparents were born in Guangdong, and others. They will talk about land projects that will, once again, change the face and many of the fortunes of Honolulu and its people.

The Polynesian turns down Merchant Street toward Bishop, and walks with a light step, moving easily with the flow of people going in and out of the warm heart of a great city.

A friendly driver from S. Hasequawa Candy Store stops along his delivery route to exchange sweet talk with some townspeople, circa 1926.

Ahupuaa. Property that usually encompassed the ecological necessities of life in the Hawaiian Islands; i.e., a wedge-shaped parcel that usually ran from the mountains to the sea.

Alii. Noblemen, a hereditary group ranking just below the royal house, possessors of great powers over lesser Hawaiian groups.

Aloha Aina. Love *(aloha)* of the land *(aina),* a concept going beyond possessiveness of property to mean a genuine reverence for the spiritual qualities of a place.

Aumakua. A guardian spirit, not as fearsome as the principal gods and more concerned with the individual's personal well-being. Popular *aumakuas* were owls, sharks and other fauna.

Haole. Originally, any stranger; in time the word came to signify Caucasians.

Heiau. A Hawaiian temple, sometimes a sacrificial place, but in all cases sacred.

Kahuna. A Hawaiian priest, sorcerer, shaman, holy man, political advisor to the powerful. A modern, and questionable, interpretation is that there were "good" *kahunas* and "bad" *kahunas.* What is known is that the *kahunas* were a powerful class and a powerful influence on both the ruling class and the commoners, and were generally held in respect by both.

Kapuna. A respected elderly person.

Kamaaina. Native-born. A modern interpretation (open to challenge) is anyone who has lived a very long time in the islands. The opposite of *kamaaina* is *malihini,* the newcomer.

Kapu. A tabu. A *kapu* placed on an area meant that the area was to be shunned. Similarly, a *kapu* on a person made that person an outcast until the *kapu* was lifted. In modern parlance, to *kapu* something means to take it and keep it for oneself.

Keiki O Ka Aina. Literally, a child of the land; on another level, one whose roots are deep in Hawaii via ancestry, family and *aloha aina.*

Kuleana. In old Hawaii, the portion of land granted to a commoner as his responsibility. A modern interpretation is, simply, responsibility.

Lanai. One of seven major populated islands of the Hawaiian archipelago. Also, a porch, veranda, terrace, generally covered and, in modern times, often screened.

Luau. A feast or banquet. In ancient Hawaii, the *luau* was limited, of course, to native foods and followed a proscribed ritual pattern. In modern Hawaii, a *luau* is a feast which may feature several non-Hawaiian dishes along with the more or less traditional entertainment of *hulas* and music.

Makaainana. A commoner, as opposed to the other classes of Hawaiian society such as the *alii,* or nobility, and the *kahunas,* or priests.

Makahiki. In old Hawaii, a time of coming together for sport and entertainment, especially games of skill and contests.

Malihini. A newcomer.

Mano. A shark; an *aumakua* (see above).

Ohana. In old Hawaii, the extended family, which included not only relatives but non-relatives who were absorbed into a family grouping. In modern times, the word reflects a common cause and those who are bound up in it.

Tapa. Also, *kapa.* Bark that has been processed into cloth-like layers, from which the old Hawaiians fashioned their garments.

Ua Mau Ke Ea O Ke Aina I Ka Pono. Literally, "the life of the land is perpetuated in rightousness," the motto of the State of Hawaii, and first articulated by Kamehameha III.

Ukulele. Hawaiian for "jumping flea," the term applied to the musical instrument brought to the islands from Portugal.

Wahine. Female, as opposed to *kane,* the male.

PARTNERS IN PROGRESS

Mid-century birth in the mid-Pacific

The schooner *Louise* sailed into Honolulu harbor in June 1848 bringing news that rocked Hawaii as it did much of the rest of the world—gold had been discovered in California.

In the ensuing months and years, that event brought changes in the business and social life of the islands which might otherwise not have occurred for decades. Indeed, formation of the Chamber of Commerce of Hawaii was among many direct results of the Gold Rush of '49.

By 1850, Kamehameha III, then ruler of the island kingdom, moved his capital city from Lahaina, its historic location on Maui, to the bustling port of Honolulu on Oahu. The city was little more than a sleepy village, but the Gold Rush had turned its harbor into a thriving, though disorganized, crossroads of trade and traders, commerce and merchants—exporters of sugar and pineapple, whalers, goldseekers in transit to and from California. Great demands were made on the islands' business and agricultural resources; hundreds of miners were "wintering" in Honolulu. The resident population of all islands was 85,000, 2,000 of whom were American and European foreigners.

The event that made San Francisco a boomtown had spawned a satellite, a "boomlet," in Honolulu.

In that hurly-burly economic environment, about twenty businessmen gathered in a small store on the dusty harborfront street—today Nimitz Highway at a point near Aloha Tower and the piers which moor giant world cruise ships. The date was October 15, 1850. They signed a constitution forming a chamber of commerce "to give energy and tone . . . to securing advantages these islands offer for commerce . . . and to establish customs and ordinances." And "to maintain unity of action for the public good."

The Chamber thus became the second oldest west of the Rockies. San Francisco's chamber had been organized just six months earlier.

Those visionary merchants—propelled by the absence of order and unity in island commerce and a rare sense of the islands' future—laid the foundation for permanent institutions and practices that were to establish and nurture Hawaii's role in Pacific commerce and as a major western outpost of the United States.

Over the years, there were name changes, charter amendments and mergers with other organizations but the central theme of the original objective remained.

The Chamber became an influential force in the development of Honolulu and the state of Hawaii.

It has served its community under six forms of government—and through plague, fire, depression and war. Physical, social, economic and environmental changes in Hawaii

Photo by David E. Starbuck

The Chamber was among the first tenants of Honolulu's distinguished Dillingham Transportation Building when it opened in 1930 on Bishop Street near the harborfront—two blocks from the site of Chamber's founding in 1850. Surrounded by sleek highrise structures, the building retains the elegance of its period in its marble and gold mosaic Art Deco lobby.

and the Pacific have been cataclysmic. The Chamber itself has evolved—in structure, practices and broadened objectives—to meet the demands of the times. Its work and achievements touch nearly every aspect of business and community life—from planning to public health, tourism, transportation, taxation.

Many of Hawaii's respected, independent institutions were founded or developed by the Chamber—Hawaii Visitors Bureau, internationally recognized for its tourism promotional achievements; the Aloha United Way, Blood Bank; Better Business Bureau; Mental Health Association and Tax Foundation of Hawaii, among others.

Under Chamber leadership today are Retail Merchants of Hawaii, the Small Business Council, Hawaii World Trade Association and Manufacturers Association of the State of Hawaii.

Nearly 3,600 members represent 2,200 firms—a deep cross-section of the business community. And the Chamber is statewide; local, neighbor island and ethnic chambers are represented on its board as associate chambers. Collectively, they represent an additional 3,600 businessmen and women.

Today the Chamber works to coalesce and communicate positions of the business community on public issues and thus to influence decision-makers on public policy. It seeks to shape the community environment to best serve the interests of both business and the public at large—a purpose ordained by its twenty merchant founders.

Entirely hand-written Charter "in perpetuity" of 1883 contains names still recognized in today's Hawaii business community. Founded by a group of merchants in 1850 during the reign of Kamehameha III, the first official Charter is dated 1871 and, though amended from time to time, remains effective today.

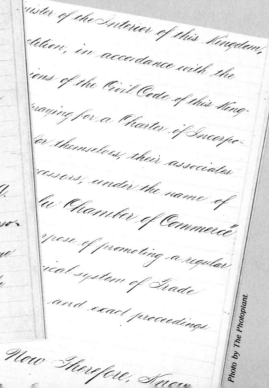

Charter
of the
Honolulu Chamber
of
Commerce.

Whereas, Samuel N. Castle, Charles R. Bishop, Alexander J. Cartwright, Theophilus H. Davies, F.A. Schaefer, and others, their associates, did on the 30th day of June A.D. 1883, file in the Office of the

Minister

...ister of the Interior of this Kingdom, ...tion, in accordance with the ...ions of the Civil Code of this King- ...praying for a Charter of Incorpo- ... for themselves, their associates ...essors, under the name of ...lu Chamber of Commerce ...pose of promoting a regular ...cal system of Trade ...and exact proceedings

Photo by The Photoplant.

Now Therefore, Know all me...

From a twelve-acre beginning to diversified Hawaii giant

In February 1869 two Hawaii-born sons of missionaries—Samuel T. Alexander and Henry P. Baldwin—bought twelve acres of land near Haiku, Maui. A year later they added another 559 acres and began growing sugarcane.

This was the start of what is now Alexander & Baldwin, Inc., a publicly held corporation with diversified operations in ocean transportation (Matson Navigation Company, Inc.), sugarcane growing and processing, property development and management, merchandising, trucking and storage, and investments. The company was incorporated in 1900 as a sugar factoring agency, one of five such companies operating in Hawaii at the time.

Land and water have been integral parts of the company's sugar operations, around which all other company businesses developed. In 1876, the founding partners owned 570 acres of land near Makawao and began work on the Hamakua Ditch, a seventeen-mile waterway designed to transport water from the rain forests of East Maui to the dry cane fields. The original ditch project grew into East Maui Irrigation Company, Ltd., an A&B subsidiary that operates and maintains a system of 74 miles of ditches and tunnels, collecting more than 400 million gallons of water daily and transporting it to the dry central valley.

By 1900, the founders had control of virtually all of the numerous plantations in central Maui and began to consolidate operations into two giant plantations—Maui Agricultural Company with headquarters at Paia, and Hawaiian Commercial & Sugar

The Alexander & Baldwin Building, a prominent downtown Honolulu landmark, was built in 1929 as a memorial to the company's founders.

Company headquartered at Puunene. These two plantations were merged in 1948, with the surviving HC&S becoming a division of A&B in 1962.

HC&S is Hawaii's largest sugar plantation with 36,000 acres of sugarcane, all of it irrigated. The company also operates McBryde Sugar Company, Limited., a 13,000-acre plantation on Kauai's south side. A&B first became agents for McBryde in 1909, and it became a wholly owned subsidiary in 1968. A third plantation operated by A&B at Kahuku on Oahu was closed in 1971.

A&B also owns Matson Navigation Company, Inc., a subsidiary and the major carrier of containerized cargo and automobiles between the U.S. West Coast and Hawaii. Matson has served Hawaii continuously since 1882. A&B became part owner in 1909, controlling owner in 1964 and sole owner in 1969.

A&B's property development and management operations grew out of the company's extensive land holdings. The company owns 71,800 acres on Maui, another 22,000 acres on Kauai and 1,900 on the U.S. mainland. Most of the Hawaii land is in sugarcane or its related uses, including watershed. Approximately 1,300 acres on Maui and Kauai are zoned for urban development.

In 1949, the company began developing the city of Kahului, Maui, one of the first planned communities in the Western United States. By 1982 more than 4,000 lots, some with houses already built, were sold to Maui residents. A 150-acre industrial park and two shopping centers were developed as the city grew in size.

In 1970, A&B began developing the 1,500-acre Wailea residential resort community on Maui's southwest coast and formed a joint venture with The Northwestern Mutual Life Insurance Company of Milwaukee in 1971 to continue development. By 1983, Wailea was recognized as one of Hawaii's premier resort destinations, with two luxury hotels, three condominium villages, three homesite villages, two eighteen-hole championship golf courses and a fourteen-court tennis club.

A&B Commercial Company, an A&B division offering building products and hardware on Maui, Kauai, and the island of Hawaii, grew out of the company's merchandising operations at its Maui plantations.

Kahului Trucking & Storage, Inc., another A&B subsidiary, also started as a plantation-related company—Kahului Railroad Company which provided passenger and freight rail services from 1881 to 1965. KT&S and its Kauai Commercial Company division provide sugar and general freight hauling and storage on Maui and Kauai.

A&B has for many decades derived a portion of its income from investments in other companies and from various short-term securities; it currently owns twenty percent of Pacific Resources, Inc., a Honolulu energy company.

A&B's headquarters are located at 822 Bishop Street in Honolulu, site of the Alexander & Baldwin Building built in 1929 as a memorial to the founders. In 1979, the A&B Building was placed on the National Register of Historic Places and the Hawaii Register of Historic Places.

Alexander & Baldwin began as a partnership producing sugarcane in central Maui in 1870; today this venture includes more than 36,000 acres of sugarcane.

Hawaii's spirit means success in the airline business

On July 26, 1946, a war-surplus DC-3 with 21 aluminum bucket seats took off from Honolulu on the first official charter of a tiny new airline that would someday become an institution in Hawaii.

The dream of the airline's founder, Ruddy Tongg, was to open air travel to all the people of Hawaii. In order to do this, he lowered fares and concentrated on hiring local employees who could understand Hawaii's unique mix of people. Originally named Trans-Pacific Airlines, Ltd., the carrier soon became known as TPA—The Aloha Airline.

Within a year, TPA had acquired three more DC-3s, and at the end of three years, it achieved a certificate to provide scheduled passenger and cargo service throughout Hawaii. TPA also added several touches of its *aloha* service to the marketplace.

Hostesses with song sheet and ukulele in hand sang and danced for TPA passengers. TPA was one of the first in the nation to offer half-fare family plans, the *puka* window (with a hole in it for picture taking) and the "One Call Does It All" program, which allowed passengers to make air, hotel and U-drive reservations with a single call.

Growth for TPA, however, was not without adversity. Cash was always a problem. Maui served its passengers from a Quonset hut— then considered the epitome of luxury. Employees on Kauai sold tickets from the back seat of an automobile. Baggage was weighed on a scale borrowed each morning from a meat market.

By 1958, TPA was in deep trouble. It was then that Tongg asked a well-known Honolulu businessman to take a look at the airline to see what could be done. The challenge and opportunity was too great to ignore for Hung Wo Ching. Within a year, he reorganized the company's finances, became president and introduced the airline's first jet-powered aircraft, the Fairchild F-27.

In the process, Ching also changed the name of the company from TPA to Aloha Airlines, Inc.

Tongg's dream had become a reality. In 1959, Hawaii achieved statehood and, with it, a boom in tourism and economic growth. Aloha soon introduced new and larger jets, including the Viscount, BAC 1-11 and the Boeing 737. In

The Boeing 737 was introduced to Hawaii's skies by Aloha Airlines in 1969 and has been flying high ever since. Aloha currently has eight Boeing 737s in its fleet—each named after a Hawaiian monarch.

When Aloha Airlines first began interisland air service in June 1946, it was named Trans-Pacific Airlines. The carrier soon became known as TPA—The Aloha Airline. Aloha flew the DC-3 until 1961.

1971, the airline carried a million passengers in a single year, up from 16,000 passengers in its fledgling year.

Aloha soon led the industry in maintenance reliability, passenger satisfaction and on-time performance. Some of the company's efforts to modernize were easy; others were not.

A computerized reservations system required linking Aloha's Honolulu offices to a computer in Los Angeles, more than 2,500 miles away. The company's short route system, conversely, allowed Aloha to bring all its

aircraft home each night for daily rounds of preventative maintenance, which helped achieve its superior reliability.

Despite changes for the entire airline industry, the basics of Ruddy Tongg's dream remain intact. High quality, reliable air transportation has become a reality not only for the people of Hawaii, but for citizens throughout the United States. The success of any airline remains dependent upon people giving service to other people.

And that is Aloha's strongest point. The company's employees have always managed to retain the spirit of *aloha*. They care about their passengers, and it shows. That's Aloha's secret to success!

Stars and Stripes fly once again aboard Hawaiian cruise ships

At a time when U.S. flag cruise operations had been dormant for nearly a decade, a group of U.S. investors met to find means of restoring all-passenger cruise service under the American flag.

In 1978, American Global Lines was formed in New York. Wishing to purchase the SS *Independence* from the C.Y. Tung Group of Hong Kong, it asked for approval from the federal government to recommission the 30,000-ton passenger liner as an American-flag vessel. A bill was unanimously approved by the U.S. Senate and House of Representatives and signed into law in November 1979 by President Carter.

It was a glorious day when American Hawaii Cruises began operations, as hundreds of American seamen and workers were once again hopeful of boosting this segment of the U.S. Merchant Marine industry. The *Independence* had been restored to her former elegance, with customized facilities and amenities for a year-round program of cruising the Hawaiian Islands.

On June 21, 1980, the SS *Independence* inaugurated her seven-day inter-island cruises and since then has become a familiar sight in Hawaii. The early success of the Hawaiian cruise program led to the purchase of the SS *Constitution*, sister ship to the *Independence*, a year later. A bill signed into law in February 1982 by President Reagan allowed the *Constitution* to be restored to her American-flag status, and on June 6, 1982, the SS *Constitution* inaugurated Hawaiian cruise service alongside her sister ship.

Both ships are considered among the finest passenger ships ever built. Constructed by the Bethlehem Shipyards in Quincy, Massachusetts, at a cost of $50 million ($345 million in today's dollars), they were originally built to carry more than 1,000 passengers on long Mediterranean cruises. The ships now accommodate 800 guests; hence, cabins are large and roomy, as are public areas, and there is much open, sunny deck space.

The SS *Constitution* has an illustrious history, playing host to such dignitaries as Glenn Ford, Anthony Quinn, Alan Ladd, Peter Ustinov and Ronald Reagan. The ship also carried Grace Kelly and her wedding party to Monaco for her marriage to Prince Rainier. After their marriage, the royal couple traveled often aboard the *Constitution*. The late

SS Constitution *and sister ship SS* Independence *are familiar sights among the Hawaiian Islands, carrying 800 passengers aboard each of the floating resorts.*

Princess Grace rechristened the ship upon its return to service in 1982 under the American flag. A public room on the ship has since been renamed in her honor. Cary Grant and Deborah Kerr are also among the celebrity passenger list; they were aboard to film *An Affair to Remember.*

Both the SS *Independence* and SS *Constitution* underwent complete restyling and redecoration for their Hawaii cruise debuts. This work was carried out under supervision of the U.S. Coast Guard; in fact, the ships not only meet, but exceed, U.S. Coast Guard safety requirements, which are said to be the highest in the world.

Dimensions of the two cruise ships are identical: 30,000-tons displacement, 682 feet in length and 89 feet in breadth. "They are large ships," says AHC president David Stollmeyer, "and there is a sense of spaciousness, without that impersonal quality that sometimes comes with great size."

With the revitalization of the American-flag passenger ship fleet, American Hawaii Cruises has uniquely benefitted from a tax reform

The late Princess Grace christened the SS Constitution *in 1982 when it was recommissioned to sail under the American flag. Prince Rainier of Monaco, Captain T.Y. Wu and other officers of the ship, and American Hawaii Cruises' chairman of the board, Alice King, joined in the ceremony.*

measure adopted in January 1983. It allows tax deductions for persons attending seminars, business meetings and conventions aboard U.S. flag cruise ships. Both the SS *Constitution* and SS *Independence* feature a convention center on board (the only cruise ships to have them) to accommodate 200 attendees. Other meeting rooms can accommodate up to 400.

In addition to reviving the American flag on Merchant Marine passenger ships, American Hawaii Cruises has revived the "Golden Age" of cruising through its special transpacific cruises between Hawaii and the Mainland. The company invites passengers to return to the days of yesteryear when half the fun of travel was simply getting there. These special cruises feature the musical entertainment of the "Big Band" era.

"The SS *Independence* and SS *Constitution* both have an all-American staff and crew," says David Stollmeyer. "Hence, there is an emphasis on service that is both friendly and enthusiastic so that passengers truly experience the Hawaiian Aloha spirit."

Since 1908, service first!

In 1908 a quarry owner, three construction men and a retired sea captain pooled their resources, a total of $15,000, to launch Honolulu Construction and Draying Company, Limited. Shortly after incorporation, the business community shortened the long name to "HC&D."

The main office was located at Queen and Fort streets. Later a red brick warehouse was acquired at the corner of Halekauwila and Bishop streets.

The tradition of dominating the aggregates industry was born in 1911 when the company gained exclusive quarrying rights in the heart of Honolulu.

Drayage operations prospered. In 1918, the company bought its major competitor, Hustace-Peck Co., and formed a moving division, housing the new operation in a wooden shed with stables for horses and a storage barn.

The company acquired a quarry site in Moiliili. During the war years, 1942-45, the Corps of Engineers operated the quarry as its major source of rock in the islands. Deposits were exhausted in 1951 and the site was sold. It later became the University of Hawaii parking facility.

By 1932, having outgrown the tin-roofed sheds, HC&D built the first all-concrete, sprinklered office/warehouse in the Territory

Then and now—whether a small mixer in 1953 (top) or the modern equipment shown below, "Service First" has always been the motto as Ameron HC&D helped to shape the face of Hawaii.

HC&D equipment repairing Honolulu's streets in July 1910. Photo courtesy of the Bishop Museum.

of Hawaii at Kawaiahao and South streets. It wasn't the best time for expansion. Employees of the era recalled that three of the building's four floors "could have been used as a roller rink—they were that empty." However, HC&D was not to be stopped by a depression.

In 1935, Concrete Products Co. was acquired, greatly expanding HC&D's manufacturing activities. Another acquisition in 1945, the Ready-Mix Concrete Co., put HC&D in a

dominant position in the ready-mix concrete industry.

The company successfully negotiated a long-term lease with Kaneohe Ranch Company in 1949 which provided quarrying rights to the state's largest rock deposits. The lease for Kapaa Quarry has since been extended to the year 2012.

Bowing to its well-known acronym, the company officially became HC&D, Ltd. in 1963.

The present corporate office building was built in 1965 on company-owned property at King and Middle streets.

HC&D expanded to Maui in 1965, purchasing Alexander & Baldwin's operations at Puunene.

In late 1967, HC&D became a wholly owned subsidiary of American Pipe and Construction Co. of Monterey Park, California (now Ameron, Inc.). This relationship evolved from years of joint venturing on contracts to supply concrete pipe for many of Hawaii's major water transmission and sewage systems. In 1977 the company was merged into Ameron, Inc. and experienced its third name change—to Ameron HC&D.

Today Ameron HC&D has annual sales of $35 million and approximately 300 employees. The vision of five men in 1908 has become the state's largest manufacturer and supplier of construction materials. Ameron HC&D has helped to shape the face of modern-day Hawaii.

Diversification keys Hawaii growth

Had German sea captain Heinrich Hackfeld kept on going, he might have landed in San Francisco during the gold rush of 1849. As it happened, Hackfeld steered his ship toward Honolulu, Hawaii, and unwittingly founded a business that would become Hawaii's largest company.

Like any true entrepreneur, Hackfeld moved to Hawaii in hopes of improving his lot and acquiring wealth and good fortune, but even the ambitious Hackfeld could not have imagined that a $2.2 billion company called Amfac would emerge from the modest mercantile operation that he opened on Honolulu's waterfront on October 1, 1849.

The astute Hackfeld recognized immediately the business opportunities inherent in an expanding whaling trade and barter generated by the gold rush. Right after opening the store he ordered picks, boots, shovels and clothing for his inventory.

By the very next year Hackfeld was doing so well he opened a second store dubbed *mauna kalika*, or "mountain of silk," in the commercial section of Honolulu. Named B.F. Ehlers & Co. after Hackfeld's nephew, this operation was the forerunner of today's highly successful Liberty House department stores.

Hackfeld quickly gained the respect and admiration of the local community for his business acumen and, by 1855, was asked to be business agent for three large sugar plantations which, like most sugar operations in Hawaii, had not yet quite gotten off the ground. Thus, business agents such as

Heinrich Hackfeld's general stores sold goods to Hawaii's coffee, pineapple and sugar plantation communities. These modest retail operations were the forebears of modern Amfac, which now has operations in 36 states.

The familiar twin-towered Amfac Center in downtown Honolulu houses the company's executive offices in Hawaii.

Hackfeld were in advantageous positions to buy floundering plantations; Pioneer Mill Co., Amfac's Maui plantation, was acquired by Hackfeld and Co. in this manner.

In 1918, H. Hackfeld & Co. was forced to liquidate its operations and vast landholdings due to a wave of anti-German sentiment generated by World War I. Under the Alien Property Custodian Act, company assets were seized and transferred to three of Hawaii's largest companies and several banks and trusts. Even the name was changed—to American Factors—to eradicate the company's German image.

During the decades following World War I, American Factors (which would be shortened to Amfac in 1966) continued in sugar, merchandising and other related activities. But the company did not grow significantly, owing to a board of directors that declared huge dividend pay outs to the company's private owners.

Then, in 1967, Henry A. Walker Jr. became president and chief executive officer. Walker, who will go down in history as the architect of modern Amfac, wasted little time in rejuvenating the company, diversifying it outside of Hawaii and into six different but complementary industries.

The Walker plan was successful. In 1969, Amfac's revenues were $304 million. In 1982, $2.2 billion in revenues were generated by six operating groups in 38 states. These operating groups are wholesale distribution, food processing, retail, hotels and resorts, horticulture and Hawaii sugar and land.

Nowhere is the strength of Amfac's diversity

more apparent than in Hawaii, where the company maintains executive offices, five sugar plantations, 49 Liberty House retail outlets, ten hotels and resorts, fourteen distribution outlets and 60,000 acres of company-owned land and more than 97,000 leased acres.

Although it has attained national prominence, Amfac was born and bred in Hawaii and remains committed to the Aloha State and its people. History shows that the stronger Amfac becomes on the continental U.S., the stronger it gets in Hawaii. Since diversifying outside of the 50th state, the company's Hawaiian revenues have more than tripled. Amfac has nearly 10,000 employees in Hawaii, many of whom have not only dedicated their working lives to the company but also to the communities in which they live. Some of these employees are involved in Amfac Community Action Teams (AMCATS), giving part of their time and talent to make Hawaii a better place to live and work. Amfac, too, is concerned about the quality of life in Hawaii and supports numerous local, cultural and charitable organizations.

Looking back, Amfac's heritage is painted with historical significance. It is a company that has survived two world wars, evolved and progressed under the socioeconomic pressures of the 1940s and struggled with its identity in the 1950s to emerge in the 1980s as a leader in Hawaii business.

Partners in Hawaii's growth for 85 years

It all started with a man of foresight.

The year was 1897. The man was Peter Cushman Jones, who had come to Hawaii from Boston 40 years earlier with only 16 cents in his pocket.

In mid-1893, Jones and his son, Edwin, organized the Hawaiian Safe Deposit & Investment Company in Honolulu. An outgrowth of the investment company was a bank that was destined to become Hawaii's largest.

Honolulu at the turn of the century was in sharp contrast to the city of today. Streets were unpaved and covered with mudholes when it rained. Four-masted schooners and other seagoing vessels filled the harbor. Horse-drawn drays hauled cargo from the docks, and residents found transportation in mule-drawn streetcars that clanged down narrow-gauge tracks. Hitching posts lined the streets while flickering gas lamps provided night-time illumination.

P.C. Jones envisioned a great future for Hawaii and the need for a special kind of bank. Along with two other friends, Joseph Ballard and Charles Montague, he established the Bank of Hawaii, Ltd. on December 17, 1897. It was the first bank chartered and incorporated to do business in the Republic of Hawaii.

When it opened for business, the bank's initial capitalization was an imposing $400,000, with its stock at a par value of $100 per share. The institution grew quickly and by 1899 had established a savings department and Hawaii's first safe deposit boxes. At year-end 1899, deposits stood at $1.2 million and capitalization was $600,000.

Bancorp Hawaii's present main branch and head office, opened in 1969.

In December 1903, Bank of Hawaii embarked on an impressive expansion program. What is still the oldest branch in the state was opened in Lihue to serve Garden Island customers, and a short time later a branch was opened in Waipahu.

In 1922, the bank celebrated its 25th anniversary by merging with the First Bank of Hilo and adding Big Island branches at Hilo, Kohala, Honokaa, Kealakekua and Kau. Eight years later, Bank of Hawaii completed its move into the major islands by obtaining Maui branches in Wailuku, Paia and Lahaina.

Expansion continued during the succeeding decades so that when Hawaii achieved

statehood in 1959, Bank of Hawaii had more than 30 offices. In that same year, it became the state's largest financial institution, a position it has never relinquished.

Hawaii's growth in the years since statehood has been dramatic. Once heavily dependent upon agriculture, the state relies now on a mixture of tourism, government spending, construction and diversified manufacturing. Hawaii's population reached the one million mark in 1983 with a gross state product topping $15 billion for the first time.

Bank of Hawaii has played a central role in that growth, supplying funds and financial advice to the state's workers, planners and entrepreneurs. Adopting new technology, products and services as consumer and business needs changed, the bank's philosophy was to be "small enough to know customers personally, large enough to serve them fully and strong enough to protect them completely."

During the 1960s and 1970s, the bank expanded into the South Pacific and Asia, establishing branches in more than a dozen locations. In 1971, to sustain growth the bank's directors authorized the establishment of the state's first bank holding company with Bank of Hawaii as its principal subsidiary. Over the next twelve years, other subsidiary companies were added, including Bancorp Leasing of Hawaii, Inc.; Bancorp Finance of Hawaii, Inc.; Bancorp Business Systems of Hawaii, Inc. and several other financial and insurance companies.

Today, Bancorp Hawaii has more than 70 offices located throughout the Pacific Basin, assets in excess of $3 billion and nearly 3,000 dedicated, capable employees. Moreover, the company is rapidly becoming more involved with mainland financial systems. In 1982, Bancorp Hawaii joined the Plus System, Inc., a national network of automated teller machines. This system permits Bank of Hawaii customers to access funds in their Hawaii accounts from almost any place in the country. That was also the year that Bancorp Hawaii helped found WESTNET, a nonprofit organization composed of several Western bank holding companies. Through WESTNET, the member banks are combining resources to market services that will mutually benefit all of their customers.

The founding fathers would certainly be amazed by the size and complexity of Bancorp Hawaii today, but surely not by its spirit. That has remained strong for 85 years and will continue to be the sustaining force as both Bancorp Hawaii and the state grow in the future.

Bank of Hawaii's second home (1899-1927) at the corner of Fort and Merchant streets.

Hawaii's shopping centers—complex and challenging

Alan C. Beall

Seattle born, raised and educated at the University of Washington, Alan C. Beall moved to the Hawaiian Islands in 1960, graduated from the University of Hawaii with a degree in economics and embarked on a career that paralleled Hawaii's real estate climb.

In 1961, 23-year-old Beall joined Dillingham Corporation's management training program as a cost engineer. With a hard hat and a pickup truck, he delivered parts to Dilco's construction sites.

Like other big local firms, Dillingham Corporation has been the training ground for many of Hawaii's successful entrepreneurs. Beall spent five years with Dillingham, but it was his assignment to Dilco's land division that eventually led to The Beall Companies' success story. At Hawaiian Land Company Beall learned the in's and out's of Ala Moana Center, one of the finest granddaddies in the shopping center industry.

In 1966 Beall left Dillingham and joined forces with real estate appraiser Don R. Cowell. A consortium of four firms was formed—Hawaii Shopping Center Corporation, Hawaii Management Corporation, Hawaii Real Property Corporation and Don R. Cowell & Associates. This merger of talents provided the rapidly booming island real estate market with a company capable of analyzing all phases of commercial development—shopping centers being the most complex and challenging. Under Beall's leadership the companies prospered and gave expertise to more than 40 commercial and shopping center projects throughout the Hawaiian Islands, the mainland United States and the Pacific. Most notable were Pearl Ridge Center, Kahala Mall, Kahuku Sugar Mill, Whaler's Village, King's Alley and Merchant Square. At that time Hawaii Shopping Center Corporation and Hawaii Management Corporation were the largest companies in their respective fields in the state.

By now Beall had become an acknowledged leader in the shopping center industry. Expanding the firm through acquisition intrigued the entrepreneurial young president and seemed a logical new direction. In 1969 Beall approached Pacific Lighting Corporation (PLC), the Los Angeles-based parent of Southern California Gas Company. PLC had just purchased another island development company, Blackfield Hawaii Corporation. After a year of negotiations, PLC acquired Beall and Cowell's interests, giving this diversification-minded utility corporation control of two of Hawaii's leading pioneers in real estate.

The two companies operated independently for a time. Blackfield's activities remained in the residential construction and financing field and those of Beall and Cowell primarily in the planning, leasing and management of commercial properties. Blackfield had begun development of the Coconut Plantation on Kauai, a 102-acre destination resort, with plans for hotels, condominiums, restaurants and shopping facilities.

The Beall companies were retained to provide the planning, leasing, management and appraisal work for the hub—The Market Place at Coconut Plantations, now one of Hawaii's most popular shopping centers.

Eventually both subsidiaries proposed a merger, and in January 1973 Beall's companies became part of Blackfield Hawaii. A year later Beall was named president.

Progress brought changes to Hawaii's real estate market. The boom of the '60s had created a surplus in the '70s, particularly in condominiums. Under Beall's leadership Blackfield eased out of the housing market and concentrated on commercial and tourist-oriented development projects. Blackfield's eleven-story 1221 Kapiolani Building is an example of the merger's combined resources.

Beall left Blackfield in January 1980 to devote full time to his private business interests. Along with investor Jay Shidler, he acquired Islander Inn Corporation, whose holdings included the Kauai Islander Inn, the Kona Islander Inn, the Waiaka Lodge and the Spindrifter Restaurant buildings on Kauai and the Big Island.

The conversion of the Kona Islander Inn to condominiums was the most successful undertaking of its kind in Hawaii's history. At a broker's auction the Shidler/Beall partnership, Inns Investment Company, sold the units on a 100-year leasehold basis, retaining fee ownership of the land.

Beall continued his involvement with Blackfield by becoming a general partner in the Market Place at Coconut Plantation.

The turn of the decade brought Beall back into the shopping center business, this time as a consultant to Shah Alam in Malaysia and to Bishop Estate's famed Royal Hawaiian Shopping Center.

Now headquartered in Waikiki, The Beall Companies provide consulting services for selective shopping centers and invest in commercial projects through partnerships managed by Beall.

Creativity and service the bywords of Hawaii's number one florist

The year was 1937. Franklin Delano Roosevelt was president, the New York Yankees were once again World Series champions and Hawaii was a territory with no dreams of statehood. Yet Shigeichi and Yukie Nakamoto had a dream of opening their own florist shop on Beretania Street in the central district of Honolulu. (Beretania is a Hawaiian derivation of Brittania, equally British in pronunciation.)

Shigeichi Nakamoto had emigrated to Hawaii from Japan in 1916 and married comely Yukie Hirano. They had four sons and one daughter. Howard, the second eldest, was born in 1937 just one week after the opening of Beretania Florist, and Shigeichi and Yukie thought that a ceremonial omen. Howard would be the one to follow in his father's footsteps as a floral artist extraordinaire.

Beretania Florist flourished and gained an island-wide reputation as the flower shop where world dignitaries ordered their favorite leis and floral decorations whenever they visited Hawaii. In those days Doris Duke and the Dillingham family were favored customers. Under Shigeichi and Yukie's direction, Beretania Florist also became central headquarters for fresh flower centerpieces and arrangements delivered daily to Honolulu's leading business firms. Shigeichi was then more commonly known as "Mr. Moto" because of his bow tie and the then-current Peter Lorre movies wherein Lorre starred as "Mr. Moto."

Through his school years, Howard Nakamoto watched and learned as his family's business grew. He voluntarily apprenticed after school helping with the creation of unusual displays and assisting in their delivery. After graduation Howard felt there was no other recourse than to join his parents—in his estimation, as the islands grew in stature and population, Beretania Florist would blossom into a large volume business. But one thing which Shigeichi and Yukie taught Howard—and to this day he has never forgotten—"Do not let the business grow so big that the personal creativity and service are neglected." This is still Beretania Florist's byword. As large as it has become since the senior Nakamotos' retirement, Howard sees to it that Beretania Florist pays just as much attention to a single flower order as it does to a request for a voluminous amount of flowers.

June and Howard Nakamoto proudly display one of their popular floral arrangements.

A unique floral arrangement reflects a distinctive island motif and the skill that has gained Beretania an island-wide reputation for creativity and service.

In 1962 Howard married June Sumida, his high school sweetheart. June became a highly creative floral administrator, supervising the Beretania Florist staff to the nth detail. Under Howard and June's direction, Beretania Florist has become Hawaii's number one florist in sales. Retaining the parent location at 1293 South Beretania Street, in 1978 Howard and June opened their Waikiki Shopping Plaza florist outlet. In October 1982, Beretania Florist Downtown opened in the heart of Honolulu's business district at Bishop Square on Alakea Street.

When queried about the most unusual floral arranging they've ever done, Howard remarks with a grin, "We've done them all. From underwater weddings with flowers that "aqua bloom" to flowers dropped from planes overhead, we do our utmost to please!"

Howard is very civic minded and promo-tionally totally aware. His affiliation with FTD (Florists TransWorld Delivery), the nation's leading florists association, led him during the '70s to inaugurate the formation of the Retail Florist Association of Hawaii. As past president, he is still active and helpful to other florists with promotional suggestions. As examples of Howard's public relations wizardry, Honolulu's business community points to National Secretaries' Week. Beretania Florist activated a Secretary of the Year with appropriate media coverage. At first only florists received any benefit, but today Secretaries' Week in Hawaii is an acknowledged business bonanza with restaurants, jewelry shops, apparel firms and even singing telegram services jubilantly participating.

Another Beretania Florist brainchild was the annual Mother-In-Law of the Year contest beginning in 1980. Howard engineered this little-known holiday (the fourth Sunday in October) into a big Hawaii state event. Howard had Governor George R. Ariyoshi proclaim an official Mother-In-Law Day, thus making Hawaii the first state to do so. Beretania Florist sponsored the contest in which only sons-in-law and daughters-in-law were allowed to enter. The winning entries were prefixed by, "I think my mother-in-law should be Hawaii's Mother-In-Law of the Year because . . ."

With three children of their own—Celeste, Coreen and Kevin—Howard and June Nakamoto look forward to carrying on the tradition that Shigeichi and Yukie Nakamoto so boldly began in 1937. "Even in this high-tech world," Howard says with a sly grin, "there'll always be a demand for the flowers of Hawaii, the most beautiful flowers beneath the heavens!"

A leading insurance company in Hawaii for 125 years

Beginning in 1878, and continuing for nearly 30 years, Bishop Insurance had offices in this building which still stands in downtown Honolulu.

When Bishop Insurance was founded, the Hawaiian Islands were best known as a place where whaling ships stopped for provisions and where sailors were given shore leave after months at sea. The year was 1859 and the company was then a department of Bishop & Co. (now First Hawaiian Bank). As the economy of the islands grew, so did the pioneer insurance department.

Charles Bishop was co-founder and the leading partner in the bank which bore his name. Bishop married the beautiful Princess Bernice Pauahi, a descendant of King Kamehameha I who had united the Hawaiian Islands. Widely respected, Bishop provided financial help and protection from the earliest days of commercial activity. These services grew as the islands expanded economically.

In 1886 a disastrous fire swept through a large part of Honolulu. Soon after, a board of underwriters was established; among the founding members was the insurance department of Bishop & Co.

Legislation was passed in the early 1900s which restricted banks to a banking business only. As a result, Bishop Insurance was incorporated in 1907 as a separate company.

From its earliest years Bishop Insurance safeguarded the shipment of sugar cargoes to the United States and foreign countries. Sugar was Hawaii's major source of income for over 100 years. Wool has been a lesser export of the islands, yet a consistent source of income since the mid-1800s when sailing ships carried it to Boston and Bremen, Germany. The company still insures these cargoes.

Arthur Berg, manager of Bishop Insurance since 1896 when it was a department of the bank, became president and manager when the agency became a separate company. During his years of leadership Bishop Insurance took important steps forward in modernization and growth. Berg retired in 1928.

In 1925 Bishop Insurance moved into the mezzanine offices of the new Bishop Bank headquarters in Honolulu. At that time the staff consisted of 22 people and the agency represented thirteen different insurance companies.

Founded in the days of the monarchy, Bishop Insurance has continued to grow through the years as Hawaii progressed from a republic to a territory—and now to the 50th state of the Union. Through this long history the people who make up the agency have given time to many different community activities—a tradition which goes back to Bishop Insurance's founding days.

In 1926 the Bishop Insurance Co., Ltd. became a wholly owned subsidiary of Bishop Trust Co., Ltd., and operated as such until 1965 when it was sold to Employees Liability Insurance Co. This company was later acquired by the Commercial Union Assurance Co. of London, with U.S. headquarters in Boston. In 1979 Bishop Insurance formed a domestic insurance company under the name of Bishop Insurance of Hawaii, Inc.

Today Bishop Insurance occupies two expansive floors in the Pioneer Plaza building in downtown Honolulu—only three blocks from the agency's place of founding. Through its whole history Bishop Insurance offices have remained in the same area, then and now the financial heart of Honolulu.

Hawaii's growth since the achievement of statehood in 1959 has been phenomenal. To keep its place of historic leadership, Bishop Insurance has offices on the neighbor islands of Maui and Kauai, two offices on Hawaii, and an office in Kailua, on the windward side of Oahu.

Bishop Insurance has shown spectacular growth during the past decade. Sales over this period have increased by 677 percent, and in 1982 the company recorded $39 million in sales. The company has 165 employees and 46 in-house agents. Clarence G. Philpotts, born and raised in Hawaii, has been president since 1965.

Honolulu Advertiser advertisement of October 7, 1876 announcing that Liverpool & London & Globe Insurance Co. was to be represented in Hawaii by Bishop Insurance.

Over 75 years of trust

The genesis of Bishop Trust began in 1858 when two prominent island businessmen, Charles Reed Bishop and William Aldrich, formed Bishop & Co., Bankers. Charles Bishop later purchased all other interests and carried on alone. Bishop & Co., Bankers in those days also provided trust services, acted as an insurance agency, drafted wills, collected rents, paid personal bills, recommended investments for customers and managed investment portfolios and real property.

The last two decades of the nineteenth century were volatile times for Hawaii, culminating in 1898 when Hawaii became a territory of the United States. Before this time, Charles Bishop had taken a partner, John H. Paty. When Paty moved to the mainland, his interest was bought by Samuel M. Damon. Damon continued to manage the bank with uncanny success. The bank continued to grow under the name of The Bank of Bishop & Co., Ltd.

Charles Bishop left a strong imprint on the islands, not only through his business enterprise, but also through the Bishop Museum, which he endowed. His wife, Princess Bernice Pauahi Bishop, endowed the Bishop Estate, which manages her real property for the benefit of Kamehameha Schools. Though the museum, estate and businesses have no connection, all retain the "Bishop" name.

By the turn of the century, banks had to follow stricter reporting systems. In 1905, the territorial legislature voted to separate the banking and trust businesses. Two days after Christmas in 1905, a group of men met and organized the Bishop Trust Company, Limited, to take over the trust services of the bank. Official incorporation papers were recognized on Monday, January 8. Samuel M. Damon, senior partner of the bank, was named president. Original directors were Henry Holmes, Alexander Garvie, R.R. Reidford and Allen Bottomley. Many of the firm's current services were begun at that time. The company bought a seat on the Honolulu Stock Exchange, ventured into real estate and made safe deposit boxes available to customers. Earnings for the year 1906 were $11,540 and net profits were $5,249.

By the end of 1922, the firm had grown

Bishop and Company Bank, where Bishop Trust Company, Ltd. was formed in January 1906.

Bishop Trust Building in the heart of Honolulu's financial district on the site of the original home of Charles and Princess Bernice Pauahi Bishop.

considerably. Net earnings for the year were $68,519. Together with the bank, Bishop Trust built a new, block-long building which is still a downtown landmark. The company was led by a series of able managers—Allen Bottomley, William Owen Smith and Walter R. Frear.

Frear, president from 1924 to 1933, expertly navigated Bishop Trust through the difficult Depression years. During that time, the firm also made another move to more spacious quarters. Gaylord Parke Wilcox followed Frear as president. During his tenure, World War II burst suddenly upon the islands in the flames

of Pearl Harbor. The new Bishop Trust building, located in the heart of Honolulu and considered to be among the island's safest structures, doubled as a bomb shelter for a time.

In 1943 Wilcox retired, and Cyril F. Damon was elected president. Upon his death in 1954, Gerald W. Fisher took over the office. In 1956, Bishop Trust celebrated its 50th anniversary. In 1959, Congress voted statehood for Hawaii and a boom time began in the islands; Hawaii became a land of opportunity. In 1963, Fisher handed the president's office over to Edwin Benner, who was at the helm of the firm during the very active transition period from territory to statehood.

Spencer A. Murphy became president and chief executive officer in 1967. To Murphy must go a great share of the credit for the revitalization of downtown Honolulu. During his tenure, the company obtained the parcel which had once been the home of Charles and Bernice Pauahi Bishop—the famous *Haleakala* or "House of the Sun." Bishop Trust's modern headquarters was erected on this site.

On January 22, 1980, the stockholders of Bishop Trust's holding company, Bishop Investment Corporation, approved a merger with Crocker National Corporation. The merger, while preserving Bishop Trust's unique presence in the islands, makes available Crocker's investment skills, strengthening the services offered its clients in Hawaii and the Pacific Basin. Clair O. Harding was named president and chief executive officer. The steady growth and stability of Bishop Trust Company, Limited, over more than 75 years of Hawaii's history, give great promise for the future.

Generations of construction integrity in Hawaii and the Pacific

Everett Earl Black, "Johnny" Black to his friends, was born in a log cabin in Vigo County, Indiana, in 1889 to a family of modest means. He graduated from Rose Polytechnic Institute in Terre Haute in 1911 with a B.S. degree in engineering. He worked for the next two years for the Portland Gold Mining Company in Colorado and the Garfield Smelter in Utah.

Black came to Hawaii in 1913, a young man of 24 with a new bride, Ruth Emens, and $250 which he had borrowed. His first job on the Waiahole Water Tunnels for Amfac's predecessor, Hackfeld & Company, lasted three months. Subsequently, until 1918, he worked for the City and County of Honolulu as a project engineer and assistant city engineer and for the Army Engineer Corps.

Black was superintendent of the E.J. Lord construction firm for twelve years before E.J. Lord retired and liquidated his firm. The "poor little Hoosier boy" bought E.J. Lord, Ltd.'s equipment and started the firm which has been identified with growth in Hawaii's construction industry. Known as the "Dean of Hawaii's Construction Industry," Black founded E.E. Black, Ltd. in 1930 and served as president until 1962, when he turned over management of the firm to his oldest son, Robert. E.E. Black continued as chairman of the board for several years and now serves as chairman emeritus.

Robert E. "Bob" Black, born in Honolulu in 1920, joined the organization in 1946 following service with the Army Air Corps in World War II. Bob received his engineering degree from the University of Cincinnati, then joined his father's organization and assisted in the expansion of its operations as a full-service general contracting company providing construction of roads, highways, highway structures, high-rise residential and commercial structures, thermal power plants, power, telephone and underground utility work, heavy industrial plants, planned-unit developments, military facilities, airfield construction and electrical installations.

In 1962, Robert E. Black was named president and remained in that position while spearheading the growth of the organization beyond Hawaii throughout the Pacific Trust Territories and in Pacific Rim countries. His insight into the firm's growth and development earned him the position of chief executive officer in 1965; in 1973 he was elected to his present position of chairman of the board.

Over the years, E.E. Black, Ltd. has constructed many of Hawaii's major structures. Among its most noteworthy projects have been the Queen Emma Gardens residential apartments, the Hawaiian Life Building (Honolulu's first high-rise structure), the historic Waikiki Theatre on Kalakaua Avenue, the Waikiki International Marketplace, the Kalihi Shopping Center, the Wilson Tunnel, the main branch First Hawaiian Bank building, the Hale Koa Hotel at Fort DeRussy, numerous Hawaiian Electric power plants and the refurbishment of the Royal Hawaiian Hotel following its military use during World War II.

A division of E.E. Black, Ltd. is the American Piping & Boiler Company which is actively engaged in the growth and development of new cost-competitive, non-fossil-fuel energy sources.

Members of the Black family and company employees have been actively involved in various community projects and educational institutions, the most notable of which are Junior Achievement of Hawaii, the Queen's Medical Center, Hawaii Pacific College and the University of Hawaii. They have also participated in the Oahu Development Conference, the Hawaiian Educational Council and, most recently, the Hawaii Business Roundtable.

E.E. Black, Ltd.'s headquarters are located in Kakaako at the same site as the original corrugated iron shed occupied by E.E. Black in 1930. The company currently employs approximately 700 people and is listed in *Engineering New Record*'s "Top 400" construction companies.

Queen Emma Gardens Apartments.

Puuloa Interchange.

197

With 40 barrels from Boston, business was begun

James Hunnewell, captain of the 49-foot *Missionary Packet,* sailed into Mamala Bay in October 1826 after a nine-month voyage from Boston. The stormy winter passage around Cape Horn had left the deck of his tired and leaky ship only a foot above water.

In the small hold were 40 barrels of merchandise with which Captain Hunnewell planned to start a trading company—the business that is now C. Brewer. In lieu of a salary, the young sea captain had agreed to accept cargo space as payment from the vessel's owners.

The *Missionary Packet* docked on October 21 in Honolulu harbor, and four days later Hunnewell unloaded his inventory of assorted goods and Yankee notions, purchased some property and opened for business.

The mainstays of the company's trade in those early years were sandalwood and livestock hides from Hawaii, merchandise from New England and tea and spices from China. By the time Captain Charles Brewer became a partner in 1836, Hunnewell had retired to his Massachusetts farm, and the business base had shifted to supplies for whaling ships.

The spring and fall visits of the Pacific whaling fleet were the islands' economic pulse in the first half of the nineteenth century, but whaling's day in the sun was beginning to set by the time Captain Brewer joined the company. Threatened by diminished catches in the 1840s and sealed by the first commercial oil well in 1859, the final doom of whaling arrived when a large part of the fleet was abandoned in an Arctic freeze in 1871.

Foreseeing the need to diversify, C. Brewer and Company turned to the sugar industry—first as a supplier of barrels, then in 1856 as the owner of a small plantation on Maui. The shift to sugar gained momentum in 1863 when the company became the agent for three Maui plantations, including Wailuku Sugar Company, which remains a C. Brewer company to this day.

When the U.S. Civil War cut off the North's supply of Louisiana sugar, Hawaiian plantations expanded optimistically and profitably, but conditions soon changed. In the 1870s, Hawaii's sugar industry was staggered by low prices, rising shipping costs, insufficient labor and high U.S. tariffs.

Committed to stabilizing Hawaii's sugar business, C. Brewer's senior partner, Henry A.P. Carter, left the firm to accept an appointment by King Kalakaua to a special commission negotiating the Treaty of Reciprocity with the United States. Under the 1876 treaty, Hawaii received preferential treatment, assuring a steady export market for its sugar.

C. Brewer, which had incorporated in 1883, consolidated its operations with William Irwin and Company in 1910, thus increasing the number of plantations it represented from five to thirteen. Within fifteen years, it was handling 25 percent of Hawaii's sugar.

During the first 50 years of the twentieth century, C. Brewer's staff devoted its energies and ingenuity to sugar, and the company became one of the famed Big Five of Hawaii—forming one of the world's most productive and efficient sugar industries.

By the end of World War II, all assets of C. Brewer were committed to Hawaiian sugar, but production costs and capital needs began to mount and competition grew sharper. Once again C. Brewer diversified and in 1959 planted its first macadamia nut orchard. Fifteen years later, the company had become the world's largest producer and marketer of macadamia nuts after expanding its own orchards and acquiring the orchards and processing facilities of Castle & Cooke, Inc. C. Brewer's Mauna Loa® macadamia nuts now are sold throughout the Western Hemisphere and also in Japan.

The addition of spice operations in Guatemala continued to widen C. Brewer's world, and today the company is one of the leading producers of cardamom.

Trucking and terminal operations, chemical and fertilizer manufacturing and distribution, and property and casualty insurance also have expanded the company's business base. Most recently C. Brewer has begun to grow and process guava fruit to produce a colorful, refreshing and healthful drink.

C. Brewer is one of the largest landowners in Hawaii, owning more than 97,000 acres and holding long-term leases on another 44,000 acres. In the mid-1970s, the company began to convert appropriate properties from sugarcane cultivation to higher uses, such as residential development.

Led since 1975 by John W.A. Buyers, chairman of the board, president and chief executive officer, C. Brewer continues its tradition of respect for Hawaii's resources and its commitment to the healthy growth of the state's economy. As the oldest company in Hawaii (the common stock is owned by IU International), C. Brewer cherishes its active role in the community as much as it honors its colorful history.

Since 1930, the C. Brewer executive office has been located at 827 Fort Street in downtown Honolulu.

A Honolulu law firm in its seventh decade

Cades Schutte Fleming & Wright, one of Hawaii's largest law firms, is proud to have played an important role in Hawaii's legal history. One of its founding partners, Arthur G. Smith, came from Boston in 1910 and served as a deputy and attorney general of the Territory of Hawaii from 1910 to 1918.

The firm (known as Smith & Wild) was formally established in 1922 by Arthur G. Smith (1882-1966) and Urban E. Wild (1891-1952) and has since grown to its present size of 60 lawyers, 20 paralegals and 95 support staff members.

Smith was skilled in the intricacies of Hawaii land and water law and Wild was a leader of the corporate and tax bar of the territory. They recruited Eugene H. Beebe, who became an acknowledged dean of trial lawyers; J. Russell Cades, a corporation finance specialist; and Charles A. Gregory, a trusts and estates expert. Each of the founding partners was a recognized technician in the law and the firm—always identified with the business community—early became and has continued as general counsel for the Chamber of Commerce of Hawaii, which since the middle of the nineteenth century has been a clearing house for information and institutionalized activity involving the business community.

With the attack on Pearl Harbor and the United States' entry into World War II, several of the lawyers went on active duty with the armed forces, and the firm represented a consortium of construction companies engaged in military construction throughout the Pacific area for the U.S. Corps of Engineers. The return of peace in 1945 saw most of these professionals resuming private practice with Smith, Wild, Beebe & Cades, as the firm was called from 1934 to 1967.

Statehood for Hawaii brought about a dramatic expansion of the islands' economy and of the law firm. From about ten lawyers, the professional staff burgeoned to today's 60-plus lawyers, as new clients engaged the firm and existing clients grew in size and activity covering local, national and some international operations.

Cades Schutte Fleming & Wright (CSF&W)

emphasizes business counseling, but for many years various partners have served in a special relationship with a number of Hawaii's leading civic, cultural and religious institutions, including the Honolulu Symphony Society, Hawaii Opera Theatre, the Contemporary Arts Center, Honolulu Academy of Arts, University of Hawaii, and have acted as advisers to many charitable trusts and institutions.

CSF&W represents one of the state's two largest banks, one of the two largest trust companies, three of the so-called "big five" Hawaii companies, the largest (in assets) and oldest domestic life insurance company, the state's largest savings and loan company, several out-of-state and overseas financial institutions and a host of other diversified businesses, large and small.

Partners have pioneered in the fields of corporate tax and financial planning, condominiums, security and exchange regulation, admiralty, freedom of speech and press, media law and sophisticated personal finance and estate planning.

CSF&W is heavily involved in complex

Arthur G. Smith (1882-1966), partner of Smith & Wild, formally established in 1922, and the successor firm Smith, Wild, Beebe & Cades, as it was called from 1934 to 1967.

securities, antitrust, water rights, constitutional rights, product liability, construction industry litigation and civil business litigation of many types.

High-technology applications of computers and sophisticated communications equipment link the Honolulu, Maui, and Washington, D.C., offices, and are employed in computerized legal research, word and data processing, document analyses, storage and retrieval. To enable its lawyers and paraprofessionals to stay abreast of the latest legal developments, the firm maintains what is probably the largest private law library in the state.

CSF&W's practice has been grouped into corporate, litigation, general practice, tax and probate departments. It carries on a continuing legal education series of in-house presentations and firm members and associates participate extensively in professional and civic affairs. Affiliations with and active participation in the American Bar Association, Bar Association of Hawaii, American Law Institute, American Bar Foundation and the American Judicature Society and other professional societies and committees have made the members and associates conversant with the problems of the legal profession. This participation has helped CSF&W personnel to discharge fairly their duties to the courts, the legal profession and the public in seeking constantly to improve the administration of justice.

Recent Hawaiian history has included a fair share of social, political, economic and even cultural controversy. But since the organization of its court system in 1840 under the kingdom of Hawaii, Hawaii has fortunately operated under a regime of law which has always been firmly rooted in the Common Law. Hawaii's legal system has been able to assist in preserving the heritage of beauty that is historically associated with the islands. The firm is grateful to have been called upon to play such a large role in Hawaii's development. It is confident that in relations among partners and associates, and with clients and the public generally, it has helped preserve this Hawaii tradition.

An impressive heritage—leadership in business training since 1917

Cannon's International Business College of Honolulu has a long and enviable history dating back to an era when graduates of business schools were often employed as "typewriters." In the late 1800s a "typewriter" could be the familiar office machine, or the person trained in operating the device. It wasn't long, though, before typewriters (the machines) became standard pieces of office equipment and typewriters (the people) became known as stenographers or secretaries.

The history of business training in Hawaii lies in the history of two major institutions which dominated the private business college environment until their merger in 1973. Honolulu Business College, founded in 1917, merged with Cannon's School of Business, founded in 1934, to create Cannon's International Business College of Honolulu—the oldest, largest and most respected private business college in Hawaii.

It was February 1917, in a private home off Alakea Street near King Street, when Mrs. A.N. Lincoln opened her doors to students interested in a business career. This one-room school was the humble beginning of Honolulu Business College (HBC) and the beginning of quality business training in Hawaii. J. Edwin Whitlow became president of the college in 1934 after the Model Secretarial School was merged with HBC. In 1935 West Commercial School consolidated with HBC, as did the Speech Institute and Sullivan's Commercial School in 1938 and 1939, respectively. The Galusha School of Business Training was merged with HBC in 1950, and The Phillip's Commercial School in 1953.

President Whitlow established the Business Educational Research Bureau in 1935. This unique group made extensive studies of training needs to qualify students for the better jobs. As a result of the bureau's studies, the basic curricula of the college

A 1937 typing class at Cannon's School of Business.

were determined. This pioneering effort is in large measure responsible for the superiority of the programs offered through the years.

HBC also pioneered in business college accreditation in Hawaii. The participation and interest of the college in accreditation resulted in HBC becoming, in 1953, the first business school in Hawaii to win national accreditation from the Accrediting Commission for Business Schools. In 1966 another milestone was achieved when HBC won accreditation as a junior college of business, conferring the associate of arts degree.

The same year that Model Secretarial School merged with HBC, Mr. and Mrs. Carl W. Cannon opened Cannon's School of Business. The date was July 1, 1934, and the location was 925 Fort Street.

Mr. and Mrs. Cannon inherited the business school expertise of Carl's father, G.C. Cannon, who founded Cannon's Commercial College in Andover, Massachusetts, in 1881. Mr. and Mrs. Cannon came to Hawaii in 1929 during the stock market crash and, after teaching several years at the West Business College, founded Cannon's School of Business with seven students.

Cannon's first graduating class had nineteen students, and the enrollment gradually grew to 100 students. At the time of the attack on Pearl Harbor, the school was closed for three weeks. Enrollment remained small until the end of World War II. Cannon's was a charter member of the United Business Schools

Association and was accredited by the Accrediting Commission for Business Schools.

When Carl Cannon retired in July 1956, Cannon's was purchased by J. Edwin Whitlow, owner of HBC. For the next eleven years both schools continued as separate and distinct institutions under the same ownership. In September 1967, the schools were purchased by Telecheck International; and in August 1968 the College of Commerce was merged with Cannon's School of Business to form Cannon's College of Commerce.

The final change in ownership occurred in 1970 when Educators of the Pacific, Inc. purchased the schools. The ultimate merging of HBC and Cannon's in 1973 united two strong institutions with a common tradition—excellence in education—to form Cannon's International Business College of Honolulu. Evelyn A. Schemmel became president of the college in 1974 and since that time has strengthened Cannon's position in the business and educational communities.

While Mrs. Lincoln's philosophy of comprehensive specialized training still prevails, the learning environment has kept pace with the demands of a changing business world. Current enrollment exceeds 800 students, and Mrs. Lincoln's one-room school has grown to a modern 25,000-square-foot facility where "typewriters" (the people) are using the latest information processing equipment to prepare for careers in the electronic office.

It's an impressive heritage for Cannon's—The Business Whose Business Is Teaching Business.

The first graduating class of Cannon's School of Business, 1935, with its founders, Mr. and Mrs. Cannon (back row, center).

Grown from an Horatio Alger story with Chinese roots

East and West are both familiar to Capital Investment of Hawaii with undertakings as far-flung as China, Guam, Hawaii and California. The reason is as obvious as the company's well-known founder. Chinn Ho is more than one of the best-known businessmen in Hawaii. Thanks to such writers as James Michener, Sylvia Porter and many others, his story has also been told to national and international audiences.

Chinn Ho grew up in Hawaii as a poor and sickly boy of Chinese ancestry at a time when Orientals were not admitted to the best clubs, were generally excluded from influential community leadership positions and were only grudgingly admitted to such things as YMCA activities.

Following such personal maxims as "Achieve Success by Contributing to the Success of Others" and "Kill Them with Kindness in Competition," Ho broke through the barriers. He not only made his mark in the YMCA and Boy Scouts but went on, without a college education, to become one of Hawaii's largest landowners and developers, a key owner of the state's largest newspaper and the operator of hotel, resort and residential facilities free of racial restrictions.

Ho personified both the democratization of Hawaii that followed World War II and the expansion of Hawaii's interests to a Pacific-wide scope.

The Ilikai Hotel, Waikiki.

The vehicle for Ho's success had its roots in Honolulu's McKinley High School from which he graduated in 1924. He made a mark of sorts by organizing a Kill Kare Carnival that got his class out of the red. This led to a post-high school association of friends, also of meager means, who entrusted their savings to him to invest.

Through the late 1920s and the 1930s Ho worked at a bank and then for two brokerage firms, with time out to visit New York and do some brokerage work in Manila and the Orient.

Thanks to relatively small but successful real estate investments in Honolulu before and during World War II, Ho was ready in 1947 to make the deal that brought his name to prominence in Hawaii. He bought a defunct sugar plantation not far from Honolulu and became the largest Oriental landholder in the history of the islands.

To swing this $1,250,000 deal—a far vaster sum in those days than it is now—Ho formally mobilized the contributed capital of others that he had been working with for years and founded today's Capital Investment of Hawaii, Inc.

From that success, Capital went on to such ventures as the construction of the landmark Ilikai Hotel-Apartment Complex in Waikiki. In the 1960s its 1,000 units ranked it as one of the world's largest condominiums.

Capital also undertook the development of the Peacock Gap planned community in California's upscale Marin County, the opening of an apartment complex and resort in the Makaha Valley outside Honolulu where the old sugar plantation had been, the management of a hotel in Hong Kong and construction of Guam's first and largest condominium complex and largest office building.

Today Capital is a joint venture partner in building the 1,000 room Great Wall Hotel in Beijing, China. On the other side of the Pacific it maintains an investment subsidiary in Los Angeles called Latipac, Ltd.

The company possesses Pan-Pacific experience in both high-rise and low-rise residential development, hotels and resorts, office and commercial properties and realty investment services.

Now retired, Chinn Ho nevertheless continues to be active with the company. The chairman today is his eldest son, Stuart T.K. Ho, a law graduate of the University of Michigan and former majority floor leader of the Hawaii House of Representatives. Capital's president is Dean T.W. Ho, also a son of Chinn, and a graduate of Cornell University Hotel School who has served as the general manager of two hotels.

Makaha Valley.

The art of service was a founding inspiration that endured

On January 29, 1954, a group of enterprising Japanese-American (AJA) businessmen, determined to meet the banking needs of Hawaii's AJA community, received the charter for Central Pacific Bank. The bank opened for business on February 15, 1954, at King and Smith streets, in downtown Honolulu. Its original officers and directors—including Koichi Iida, president and chairman of the board; Sakae Takahashi, vice president; Daniel K. Inouye, secretary; and directors Gordon Tanioka, Tokuyoshi Awamura, Ernest H. Hara, Lawrence T. Kagawa, Kazuyuki Kawano, Mitsuyuki Kido, Charles H. Kimura, Wallace Y. Matsumoto, Sadato Morifuji and Kinzo Sayegusa—perceived a unique condition of public need and business opportunity. Central Pacific Bank became the first Hawaii bank to receive an original charter since 1935.

In May 1954, the bank occupied its permanent headquarters at 50 North King Street (the corner of King and Smith streets).

Its first year-end statement of condition showed the bank had assets of nearly $6.4 million and over $5 million in deposits. This reconfirmed the great demand for financial services by Hawaii's AJA community.

In November 1955, the bank opened its first branch office in Moanalua Shopping Center. That branch was later relocated to the central Kalihi business district.

Central Pacific Bank first appeared in *The American Banker* newspaper's prestigious ranking of the largest banks in the United States with December 31, 1956 figures which ranked the bank 2,194th in the nation with assets of over $10.3 million.

Kazuo Ishii assisted in the initial organization of the bank and rejoined it in March 1957

Central Pacific Plaza.

as manager, then served as its second president from 1961 until May 1978, when Yoshiharu Satoh succeeded him. The bank grew steadily during the 1950s, 1960s and 1970s; it extended branches to the Moiliili, Kaimuki, Makiki, Waikiki, Kaneohe, Aiea, Ward and Waipahu districts on Oahu. Another branch opened in March 1980 in the Mapunapuna business district of Oahu. Its first neighbor island branch opened in Hilo, Hawaii, on September 4, 1962. A branch was located in Kahului, Maui, in 1966, and the bank provided statewide financial services when the Lihue, Kauai, branch was established on November 1, 1969.

In 1969, Central Pacific Bank surpassed $100 million in assets with over $111 million at year-end. Only ten years later, year-end 1979, the bank had attained assets of over $410 million.

Throughout the years, the bank has been privileged to have had Sadao Asato, Kazuo Ishii, Elmer F. Cravalho, Waichi Hakusui, Keiji Asano, Dr. Richard T. Kainuma and Clarence K. Karimoto serve as its directors.

A plan of reorganization, in November 1982, created CPB, Inc., the holding company of Central Pacific Bank. The original board of directors of CPB, Inc. and Central Pacific Bank included Chairman of the Board Sakae Takahashi, Vice Chairman Gordon Tanioka, Paul Devens, Alice F. Guild, Dennis I. Hirota, U.S. Senator Daniel K. Inouye, Charles H. Kimura, Sidney S. Kosasa, Eaton Magoon Jr., Wallace Y. Matsumoto, Shinsuke Nakamine, Elton H. Sakamoto, Yoshiharu Satoh, Minoru Ueda and Dr. Lester B.K. Yee. The board organized the holding company to enhance the bank's ability to meet the challenges and capitalize on business opportunities arising from deregulation of the banking industry and the accompanying intensified competitive environment. Daniel M. Nagamine was elected as a director in April 1983.

In February 1983, the bank moved into new corporate headquarters and relocated its main branch office in Central Pacific Plaza at the corner of South King and Alakea streets in the heart of the downtown financial district. The original site was retained and redesignated King-Smith Branch.

Today, under the leadership of Yoshiharu Satoh, president and chief executive officer, Central Pacific Bank has assets of over $430 million and is one of the 500 largest banks in the United States with sixteen full-service branches strategically located throughout the state. A network of "Diamond-Tel" automated teller machines augment normal banking operations and extend banking hours to meet the needs of its ever-expanding base of customers.

The growth of Central Pacific Bank has closely paralleled the development of Hawaii itself. From a bank formed primarily to meet the needs of Hawaii's AJA community, Central Pacific Bank now is proud to serve the banking needs of all the peoples of Hawaii. The bank has been responsive to the banking needs of Hawaii's residents and businesses for over 29 years, and realizes that its past and future successes are a reflection of how well it adjusts to economic and social changes while meeting the needs of the communities it serves.

Central Pacific Bank's original headquarters.

City Bank and Hawaii to celebrate 25th anniversary

When City Bank of Honolulu first opened for business on June 19, 1959, the dream of a group of dedicated businessmen and women became a reality. The group believed that another bank was needed in Hawaii—one that understood and was empathetic toward the financial needs of Hawaii's large Oriental population—as a result of the closing of three Japanese banks in Hawaii during World War II. The group's assessment was apparently correct, as total assets during the bank's first year of operation grew from $2 million to $10 million.

From the beginning, The Mitsui Bank—through its former president, chairman and counsellor, Kiichiro Satoh—was actively supportive in helping City Bank become established, and a strong bond was formed between the two banks which exists to this day. As a shareholder and advisor, The Mitsui Bank was instrumental in developing City Bank's international status. Today, City Bank also enjoys Japanese correspondent relationships with its largest shareholder, The Nippon Credit Bank (formerly known as Nippon Fudosan Bank), and with another shareholder, The Mitsui Trust and Banking Company.

The year 1959 not only marked the beginning of City Bank, but of the state of Hawaii as well. Statehood came that year, and with it the jet age. The visitor industry in Hawaii grew tremendously, bringing new residents and a boom in virtually all aspects of trade and commerce. Hawaii became the center of economic activity for the Pacific Basin.

No longer was City Bank's original concept of catering to one segment of the population a major premise for its existence. As the state's economy expanded, so did City Bank's corporate philosophy. It is now dedicated to serving the financial needs of the entire cosmopolitan population of Hawaii.

In 1961, the bank's first branch office was opened in Kailua, Oahu. Two more branches were opened in 1962, in McCully and in Kapalama. In March 1966, the bank's administrative and main offices were relocated to the new ten-story City Bank Building in downtown Honolulu. Today, City Bank has ten branches located throughout the islands of Oahu, Maui and Hawaii, in addition to its main office. There are now exterior automated teller machines (the "Green Machine") at every branch location as well as an in-lobby ATM at the main office. Total assets have exceeded the $300 million level and staffing stands at over 350 employees.

Pictured at the 1966 opening of the City Bank Building in downtown Honolulu, from left to right, Chairman Morita, former President Koichi Itoh, Mrs. Neal Blaisdell, Mitsui Bank President Satoh and the late mayor of Honolulu, Neal Blaisdell.

Much of the bank's success is attributable to James M. Morita, one of its original founders. An attorney by profession, Morita was a senior partner in the law firm of Morita, Kamo & Sakai when he was elected the bank's chairman of the board in 1961. Over the years, he has become a full-time banker. After serving a few years in the dual capacity of chairman of the board and president, Morita now holds the title of chairman of the board and chief executive officer. Active in community and industry affairs, he has held key leadership positions in American Cancer Society, Aloha United Way (AUW), East-West Center and American Bankers Association, as well as other organizations. At present, he is a trustee of Hawaii Loa College and the National Jewish Hospital and Research Center. He has also served as past president of the Hawaii Bankers Association, Western Independent Bankers, Hawaii Visitors Bureau and Downtown Improvement Association. Among the many honors bestowed upon him are the 1976 Man-of-the-Year awarded by the National Jewish Hospital and Research Center, the University of Hawaii Rainbow Award presented to its 75 most distinguished alumni on the occasion of its 75th anniversary and the 1983

Freedom Symbol award of the Honolulu Sertoma Club.

Also key in the bank's management is Richard T. Okinaka, president and chief operating officer since 1978. Under Okinaka's direction, City Bank has targeted and captured a significant share of the small- to medium-sized business market. In developing that market, he has focused particular attention on the bank's active involvement in civic affairs.

City Bank encourages management and staff participation in various community service programs. Annual sporting events sponsored by the bank have raised thousands of dollars for charitable causes. The bank has also donated manpower and dollars for worthy causes such as the United Way and Junior Achievement. The bank and its personnel have received numerous honors, awards and recognition for their contributions to the people of Hawaii.

City Bank will itself have a great occasion to celebrate, as 1984 will mark its 25th anniversary. It looks forward to that occasion and to the challenges which loom in the 21st century as the Pacific Basin becomes the hub of the world's trade and commerce.

A man's dream . . . his legacy

As a young boy growing up in the plantation town of Hakalau on the Big Island, Fred "Tosh" Kaneshiro might have become just another plantation laborer. But dirty bare feet and small-town life were not for Tosh. He had slightly bigger ideas.

For Tosh dreamed of a better life. Born in Hawaii, he was the son of immigrants who came to the islands from Okinawa in 1906. In the years to come, he was destined to leave his indelible mark on the Honolulu community for more than four decades.

Gathering up his meager belongings and his courage, Tosh made his move to Honolulu in 1930, full of that second-generation drive that has bred success for so many Niseis in Hawaii.

Teaming with his older brother Frank, Tosh took the plunge in 1941. On a bright Sunday morning, Frank and Tosh opened the Columbia Inn restaurant at the corner of Beretania Street and Kamanuwai Lane (affectionately known as "Tin Can Alley").

It turned out to be not quite what they expected, for on that opening day on December 7, 1941, other events unfolded that affected the lives of everyone in Hawaii, not to mention the world.

The doors opened for business, the bombs fell on Pearl Harbor, a few hours later a general blackout was ordered, and the doors closed.

The blackout was eventually lifted and the Kaneshiros reopened the Columbia Inn. Since that day, the Columbia Inn has been open 24 hours a day, seven days a week, 52 weeks a year.

The war brought lots of business as servicemen by the thousands poured into Hawaii. The Columbia Inn flourished during the '40s as servicemen packed the place daily looking for nourishing "home-cooked" meals and liquid refreshment. They called the Columbia Inn "The Gem in the Slums." And it was to be the favorite watering hole and dining place for Honoluluans for more than 20 years. . .until that government monster

Tosh Kaneshiro's Top of the Boulevard, a Honolulu institution for sports fans and others.

"Urban Renewal" reared its head in the '60s. The building in which the Columbia Inn was situated would be torn down soon and the Kaneshiros would have to move, the city told Frank and Tosh.

So in 1964, the Columbia Inn moved to more modern and certainly larger quarters at the top of Kapiolani Boulevard, purchased and renovated at a cost of $170,000. It was formerly the home of Times Grill, right next to the News Building where the two Honolulu daily newspapers, Hawaii's first radio station and two international wire services are housed.

Tosh plied his host magic at the new location, working harder than ever to build his clientele. Over the years, the Top of the Boulevard has taken on a homey atmosphere punctuated by a sports decor unrivaled anywhere in town. The Columbia Inn has become the unofficial Los Angeles Dodgers headquarters of Hawaii, and Tosh almost single-handedly caused Dodger games to be brought in and broadcast in Hawaii.

The combination of good food, reasonable prices, a friendly crew and a genial host have made the Top of the Boulevard a Honolulu institution. And the restaurant's success eventually lead to Tosh's being named Small Businessman of the Year by the Small Business Administration in the early '70s.

Looking toward expansion, the Kaneshiros put some money into architectural fees and preparation work, selected a site in Waimalu on the Pearl City-Aiea "border" and went out looking for financing. It wasn't easy—money was tight as the '80s rolled in—but they found the $2.5 million they needed. Ground for the new Columbia Inn Waimalu was broken in August 1980 and on July 20, 1981, the doors of the new Columbia Inn opened for business.

They were to close the next day. Fred "Tosh" Kaneshiro, who had battled to build a business during the war years, had lost a battle with cancer. Since the end of the blackout in December 1941, the Columbia Inn—first the Gem in the Slums, then the Top of the Boulevard, and now including Waimalu—has closed only once, in memory of Tosh.

Built on a reputation of good food, an extensive menu, a friendly and helpful staff and a genial host, the Columbia Inn indeed is a Honolulu institution. It's come full circle—from a fertile mind in a plantation camp to a new restaurant with a plantation decor standing where sugar cane once grew.

The Columbia Inn is a legacy—Tosh Kaneshiro's legacy.

The new Columbia Inn Waimalu has a plantation decor reminiscent of Tosh's childhood days in Hakalau.

Bringing film entertainment to Hawaii's people for nearly three-quarters of a century

A dedication to bringing the finest in film entertainment and theatre accommodations has been the ongoing concern of Consolidated Amusement Co., Ltd. since its inception in 1917. The company built its first theatre—the Hawaii, which stands today on the corner of Bethel Street and Pauahi Lane—in September 1922.

The Hawaii and the Princess Theatre, which opened three years later, became the hub of Honolulu's cultural events. In addition to movies, live shows, vaudeville and concerts were presented. Artists such as Efrem Zimbalist and Yehudi Menuhin performed, and the Honolulu Symphony played regularly in the Princess Theatre.

In September 1936, a tremendously popular event called "Pot Luck" shows were initiated. Long lines formed for the 10:00 pm Saturday night main feature film plus live entertainment by local talent. Shows changed weekly and were always a surprise. "Pot Luck" shows continued every Saturday up to the eve of Pearl Harbor.

By this time, the Consolidated theatre chain had grown measurably. There were many new neighborhood theatres on Oahu as well as new theatres on each of the major outer islands. Consolidated offices were then located on the second floor of the Hawaii Theatre building.

After the bombing of Pearl Harbor, the theatres were closed for a few days. Immediately upon reopening, and throughout the war, movie theatres did a booming business. People eager to escape the unpleasant realities of those war-torn years lined up daily to catch the latest Hollywood feature film.

During the mid-'40s, concession stands were introduced into the theatres. Previously, there had been only vending machines which offered locally made candy bars such as the "B-17" and the "Midway". With the continued installation of theatre concession stands, it became necessary for the company to open its own confectionery department to supply its theatres. This department expanded into wholesale distributing and today supplies, in addition to theatres, numerous commercial enterprises throughout the state with "luau" and party supplies, popcorn, candies and paper goods.

In September 1959, William R. Forman, president of Pacific Theatres in California, bought Consolidated. A pioneer in the industry, Forman had earlier introduced drive-in theatres on the West Coast, spurring new growth into a declining business.

He named John Traut, who had been with Consolidated since 1937, to be president. In 1971 Traut was named chairman of the board and Michael Forman was appointed president. Art Gordon, formerly of Pacific Theatres, was appointed executive vice-president and general manager.

By 1966, the corporate offices had moved to 510 South Street, remaining there until 1981 when Consolidated built and moved into a new corporate office building at 290 Sand Island Road.

Connected to the new office building is the Consolidated Warehouse Store, a retail and wholesale operation selling "luau" and party supplies and fund-raising items.

Consolidated's Film Exchange, which operated out of the old Kewalo Theatre from 1958 until 1981, was the film service company for most of the major U.S. film studios as well as certain foreign countries.

Consolidated remains one of the largest importers of Japanese and other foreign films in the United States.

Another division of the company, Consolidated Distributors, Ltd., supplies motion picture and sound equipment throughout Hawaii and the Pacific Basin. Most major equipment companies are represented, including Christie, Simplex, Altec and Dolby, as well as many others. Maintenance and repair services are also provided to most, if not all, theatres in the state.

Committed to bringing innovative ideas to Hawaii's entertainment industry, Consolidated has installed the most modern theatre equipment available in film projection, sound and patron comfort. The company currently employs nearly 500 people operating a total of 30 screens throughout the major islands.

In keeping with Consolidated's support of community activities, the company includes a Special Events Department which offers special school showings of current movies at group rates, and provides tours of its facilities to acquaint students with theatre operations and the numerous functions necessary to provide an enjoyable and memorable movie experience for its patrons.

Consolidated usherettes wore white uniforms with red leis and sashes in the early 1950s.

Patrons lined up for the popular Saturday night "Pot Luck" shows presented weekly from 1936 to December 6, 1941.

Built on two major resources—its clients and its people

At the end of World War II, two enterprising "mainland" accountants, John A. Baker Jr. and David O. Gillette, settled in the Islands. In 1951 they established the CPA firm of Baker & Gillette in Honolulu and in 1955 had offices constructed atop the historic Alexander Young Hotel Building in the space originally used as the hotel's roof-top dance floor (Honolulu's first condominium!). In the postwar years and following statehood, Hawaii developed rapidly as the hub of Pacific Basin business activity, and Baker & Gillette shared in this growth. In 1956 Manuel R. Sylvester and Howard K. Hiroki, both "local boys," were admitted as partners; and in 1963 an office was established on Maui. The Honolulu firm's concept that accountants must understand their clients' business to be of service captured the interest of Lybrand, Ross Bros. & Montgomery, which shared this same approach in advising clients. In 1965 a successful merger was effected; Baker & Gillette became LRB&M Hawaii.

Lybrand, Ross Bros. & Montgomery had its start in 1898 when the public accounting firm was established in Philadelphia. The four partners, who gave their names to the firm, opened their office with one roll-top desk, a high-standing table and a set of oak book shelves made by a client. The firm's reputation for professional service quickly established it as a leader in public accounting, and by 1902 the first branch office was opened in New York City.

At the turn of the century telephones and typewriters had won their way into every office, and the adding machine began to find a

market. However, accounting standards and agreement among practitioners were lacking. This led to the publication in 1916 by Colonel Robert Montgomery of the first American work on the subject. Eight subsequent editions of the classic *Montgomery's Auditing* followed; it is still considered the premier text on the subject.

In line with the founders' dedication to "expand its practice in a sound and conservative manner" offices opened in major cities, and by mid-century the firm was well established nationally. By the early 1970s the national firm joined with its associated firms in Europe, Canada and other parts of the world to form the international firm of Coopers & Lybrand. C&L encircled the globe.

The Honolulu office, under the direction of Jack Baker, its first managing partner, offered clients professional leadership and high-quality accounting, tax and consulting services. Baker was also a co-founder of the Hawaii Accounting Education Foundation, recipient of C&L's longstanding support. Dave Gillette was named to the International Division and established the firm's Far East Regional office in Honolulu. Gillette and partner Howard K. Hiroki (former legislative auditor for the Territory of Hawaii) were responsible for the firm's liaison and growth in the Far East.

With the advent of the 1980s, the founding partners stepped down, and Manny Sylvester was named managing partner. During his career Sylvester has witnessed and been a key part in the evolution of the firm's computer

Managing partner Manuel R. Sylvester (right) reviewing computer auditing procedures with (standing from left) partner Arthur C. Tokin, manager Edward K. Kosaki and client (seated).

auditing processes. These sophisticated techniques are in place for all computer-oriented clients. Today the Honolulu office, with eight partners and 84 staff members, is located in the Pacific Tower at Bishop Square. It is an integral part of the C&L family, with 30,000 employees in 427 offices in 98 countries.

The Honolulu team is dedicated to maintaining the delicate balance of business growth and cherished traditions in this uniquely different island state. The firm's community activities are numerous. Its annual "Toys for Tots" benefit has continued for twenty years and has become a highlight of the Christmas season. Special classes have been offered to the Honolulu Police Department to assist in investigations of white-collar crime. Courses on computer auditing, new and revised tax laws, estate planning and other significant financial and accounting matters are ongoing programs for clients, other community business leaders and government officials.

In a time-capsule letter to his successor 50 years into the future, Sylvester wrote ". . .the firm is built on a solid base. . .with its duty not only to the profession and itself, but to the community."

The Alexander Young Hotel Building with the office condominium built for Baker & Gillette atop the fifth floor (left center). Towering behind is the Pacific Tower, present location of Coopers & Lybrand's headquarters in Honolulu

"Crazy idea" develops into multimillion dollar enterprise

In the early '60s Rick Ralston, then a young college student, had a crazy idea. Looking for ways to earn money, he began hand-painting monsters and cartoons on sweatshirts. He and a friend constructed a street stand on Santa Catalina Island and surprised themselves by selling lots of shirts. They reasoned that if business was good on a small resort island, it would be even better on a larger island. So in June 1962, Ralston and his college roommate packed their easels and airbrush equipment and headed for Hawaii.

When they arrived, the 50th State Fair was underway. They set up a booth and did well; then took their business to Waikiki. They painted on the sidewalks, moving from one location to another. Business was steady throughout the summer, and they drew large crowds wherever they painted.

In September, the roommate returned to school, but Ralston stayed in Hawaii, his new home. In 1963, Ralston was working out of a thatched roof shack in the back of Waikiki's International Market Place where he continued to hand-paint shirts.

Ralston was soon pressed to find new ways to accommodate his burgeoning clientele. Production was limited to what quantity he could paint himself, so he phased into screen printing to meet the demand for more volume.

In 1966, his enterprise—Ricky's Crazy Shirts—had grown, and Ralston changed the name to Crazy Shirts, Inc. The second major retail store opened in May 1970 at Ala Moana Shopping Center. Its success was followed by stores in King's Alley, Pearlridge Shopping Center, various Waikiki locations and the

The first Crazy Shirts shop was a thatched roof shack in Waikiki's International Market Place in 1963.

Life in the '60s . . . and Crazy Shirts reflected the current style.

Neighbor Islands. Today there are fifteen Crazy Shirts locations in Hawaii, nine on the Mainland and a production operation in Tustin, California.

The company's dedication to quality has kept it apart and ahead of its many imitators. Each garment is custom-produced to strict specifications. Combed cotton plus a compacting process help Crazy Shirts hold their shape. Meticulous fabrication and careful printing processes create lasting fashion that has been popular in Hawaii for nearly twenty years.

All Crazy Shirts designs are original and unique, developed and copyrighted by Crazy Shirts. Six professional staff artists and carefully selected freelance artists are responsible for design creation and color coordination.

The Crazy Shirts retail concept combines individual design and decor for each location. Antiques, polished woods, brass fixtures, unusual art pieces and greenery make each store a unique shopping experience. In addition, high standards of customer service are maintained through intensive employee

training and awards for outstanding service.

Crazy Shirts maintains a strong commitment to supporting the community in which it has grown and flourished. Several schools and community service organizations receive donations, and a variety of sports events and health activities are sponsored and promoted by the company.

Crazy Shirts, Inc. operates from a recently constructed 46,000-square-foot facility in Halawa Valley. The natural all-cedar structure has open-air ventilation in offices as well as the production areas. There is also a 2.4 acre recreational area for employees.

The expansive complex is a big step from the original Crazy Shirts grass shack in Waikiki. Along with its rapid growth, Crazy Shirts has continued to maintain its reputation as Hawaii's favorite shirts among both the local residents and island visitors.

The common T-shirt, once always white and worn as underwear, has become a fashionable garment. Rick Ralston's Crazy Shirts has added a T-shirt to everyone's wardrobe.

Where being different made a difference

An eight-page weekly business tabloid was the foundation on which a substantial and diversified publishing company has emerged.

The first issue of *Pacific Business News,* its anchor publication, appeared March 18, 1963. With a few exceptions, it was only eight pages in size for two years. The founder and still president, George Mason, had no prior publishing experience, but he stuck to the belief that a weekly business paper that carried material from the public record—such as incorporations, civic court cases, tax liens and real estate transactions—would attract a wide and loyal readership. That proved to be the case.

Today, Crossroads Press, Inc. produces eleven business and professional publications and manages an annual office products exposition.

Its original staff of three has expanded to 35 and the space it occupies has grown from a rented 300 square feet to 6,300 square feet in its own building, with considerable room for expansion as needed.

While it took the company four years to reach the breakeven point, it has been profitable every year since. Mason attributes the firm's success to measured and controlled growth and to what might be considered unorthodox policies in the publishing field. Among these are flextime, adherence to tight credit policies, no deviation from advertising or subscription rates (and no free subscriptions to anyone).

The company's personnel are unfettered by corporate "structure" or rigid routines and rules. "If you've picked the right people," says Mason, "you'll find they work best when the only demand is to get the job done—without having to look at job descriptions, punching time clocks, or checking rule books. They know what the end result must be and that it requires teamwork. We don't allow anyone ever to say 'That's not my job.' When we have an emergency or urgent need in one department, others come to the rescue—usually without being asked."

Pacific Business News has, since 1970, had more paid circulation in the state of Hawaii than any business publication. It also has enjoyed one of the highest renewal rates among audited publications—in the 80 to 85 percent range. Most of its editions are 40 or 48 pages. The largest, its 20th anniversary edition, was 64 pages.

The company's building at 863 Halekauwila Street in the Kakaako district.

Pacific Business News' *first edition, March 18, 1963.*

In addition to *Pacific Business News,* Crossroads Press produces five monthlies called Hawaii Professional Media Group. These are *Hawaii Medical Journal, Hawaii Bar News, The Hawaiian Realtor, Hawaii Architect* and *The Balance Sheet* (for CPAs).

All About Business in Hawaii is a full-color annual produced in magazine format. Another annual is a directory of members of the Hawaii Bar Association.

A book it has published and marketed since 1967, *Taxes of Hawaii,* is the only authoritative compilation of state and county taxes and their relation to federal income taxes.

A wholly owned subsidiary acquired in 1979, Legal Publishing Hawaii, Inc. furnishes a loose-leaf service to attorneys on court decisions and also publishes a monthly eight-page newsletter, *Hawaii Real Estate Reporter,* on court and administrative decisions in that field.

Despite its name, Crossroads Press owns no presses, and it contracts out the mailing of its publications as well as some of its other needs. It does, however, have its own computerized typesetting and a large computer system for advertising, circulation and accounting.

Located at 863 Halekauwila Street, Crossroads Press is halfway between downtown Honolulu and Waikiki.

Born by need, growing by innovation, shaping tomorrow's environment

Banyan Tree Plaza.

Ala Wai Plaza and Skyrise.

Leeward Oahu Community College.

Daniel, Mann, Johnson, & Mendenhall is an international architecture and engineering firm which maintains its world headquarters in Los Angeles, California, provides planning, design and construction management services through its 40 offices worldwide.

Since its founding in 1946, DMJM has successfully executed a comprehensive spectrum of assignments exceeding $20 billion in construction costs. Much of this work has been directed toward meeting the complex requirements of commercial, industrial, institutional and governmental clients within the United States and overseas. Many of these projects have received international recognition for innovative, functional and aesthetically satisfying solutions to intricate, one-of-a-kind challenges. As a result, DMJM has built a worldwide reputation for outstanding design, technological advances, strong project management and strict cost and schedule control, providing optimal solutions to the challenges of tomorrow's environment.

In 1957, eleven years after DMJM was founded, the original four-man firm had expanded to a multidisciplined organization of over 400 with several office locations around the world. Recognizing the acute needs of the U.S. military in Hawaii, and in response to the rapid growth experienced by the islands, DMJM opened a branch office in Honolulu in association with Sam Chang.

In 1965 engineer/planner Fred Lee joined the firm, followed shortly thereafter by architect Jack Lipman, who managed the office for thirteen years. In 1966, DMJM was retained by the state of Hawaii to prepare the Oahu Transportation Study which had a profound impact upon the growth of Oahu. DMJM was charged with the responsibility of investigating, developing and recommending a modal split and transit analysis study addressing the technical, financial and operational feasibility of a rapid transit system for the Island of Oahu.

During the next decade DMJM played a major role in shaping the environment of Oahu, designing such representative and noteworthy landmarks as the Leeward Oahu Community College, whose large number of students, relatively small site and incremental land acquisition required unique solutions in developing the long-range development plan. The approach to these challenges resulted in an open-shelter concept in which the majority of activity spaces are compactly brought together between two continuous concrete decks with openings penetrating the "shelter" to create court areas capturing the special nature of Hawaii's climate. LOCC represented

the first educational facility in the islands to feature centralized multistory classrooms.

The **Banyan Tree Plaza's** entry drive was designed to encircle and create a focal point of a magnificent 100-year-old Banyan tree which distinguishes the 35-story Plaza development. It contains 238 condominium units set on a lovely site between the grounds of the historic Central Union Church and the Shriners' Hospital.

Ala Wai Skyrise offers its residents spectacular views of Diamond Head. The 36-story condominium project contains 243 spacious and airy units designed to provide maximum privacy.

Winner of four special awards for housing design, **Kukui Gardens Apartments** is the nation's largest FHA-sponsored, Section 221-D, low- to moderate-income housing project. It

offers 822 living units ranging in size from one to four bedrooms. Based on the townhouse concept, buildings are grouped in neighborhoods, each with a distinctive character.

Other representative major projects include Iolani Court Plaza, Ala Wai Plaza, and Kukui Plaza.

Today DMJM employs over 1,600 people providing architectural and engineering services from 24 domestic and 14 international locations. Albert A. Dorman, president and chairman of the board, says DMJM is proud of the role it has played in shaping Oahu and looks forward with great enthusiasm and optimism to a continued professional relationship with public, private and military sectors to serve the architectural and engineering needs of Hawaii.

Dedicated to the ideal of progressive excellence

Today's international accounting firm of Deloitte Haskins & Sells basically originated from two firms—the U.K. firm of Deloitte & Co. and the U.S. firm of Haskins & Sells.

William Welch Deloitte began his public accounting practice in London in 1845 at age 27, after he already had spent twelve years on the staff of the Official Assignee in Bankruptcy. Deloitte's firm became securely established in England during the 52 years he presided over it. In 1890, Deloitte & Co. opened its first overseas office in New York City. Offices in other major U.S. cities soon followed.

In 1893, Charles Waldo Haskins and Elijah Watt Sells first met while working to help reorganize the accounting system of the U.S. government. The close association of the two men in this work led to a continuing professional relationship. In 1895, in a small office in downtown New York City, the two founding partners opened for business as the firm of Haskins & Sells. Through the years, the partnership they formed grew into one of the world's ranking firms of independent accountants and became known as a leader in the development of innovative auditing tools and accounting methods.

The close relationship between Deloitte & Co. and Haskins & Sells began in 1925, when the practices of the two firms in Canada, Cuba and Mexico were combined. In 1952, the two firms essentially merged into one organization, and in 1978, the Deloitte Haskins & Sells name was adopted by both the U.S. and the U.K. firms.

Today, Deloitte Haskins & Sells has more than 26,000 people in over 400 offices in 70 countries, and serves an almost endless variety of clients, both private and public. Throughout its practice, the firm is dedicated to the ideal of progressive excellence. Embodied in this ideal are innovative spirit, dedication to responsive client service, leadership in professional matters and scrupulous attention to quality control.

The long history of Deloitte Haskins & Sells in Hawaii (through its predecessor firms) dates back to 1907, when five Honolulu businessmen incorporated under the laws of New York State (optimistically for a period of

The Hawaii partners, April 1983. Seated, left to right: Gary Nishikawa, George Lumsden (partner-in-charge) and Keynes Von Elsner. Standing: Alan Richardson, Gerald Ushijima, George Baumgartner, John Marrack and John Skipper.

1,000 years) the Audit Company of Hawaii. During the Audit Company of Hawaii's early years, senior staff members were recruited from Scotland. Coming to Hawaii in 1912 on a visit, chartered accountant H. Douglas Young remained in Honolulu and became executive head of the firm in 1916 when the Audit Company of Hawaii, Limited was incorporated as a Hawaiian company to succeed the original Audit Company of Hawaii. In 1926, Mr. Young, John K. Lamberton and Frederick G. Pearson organized the partnership of Young, Lamberton & Pearson as successor to the Audit Company of Hawaii, Limited.

After World War II, as investment capital from the mainland started flowing into the islands and island businesses started looking across the ocean, too, it became apparent that the firm, which by that time was auditor for all of the "Big Five" corporations as well as other prominent businesses, would need to affiliate with a national accounting firm to continue giving clients the service they needed. In 1956, Young, Lamberton & Pearson, Hawaii's largest independent audit firm, merged with Haskins & Sells. In 1958, the Hilo-based accounting firm of Henderson, Henderson & Dobbins also merged with Haskins & Sells.

During the early years, audit teams went from Oahu to the neighbor islands on month-long audit trips, staying in plantation boarding houses and, if lucky, having a last-day holiday at such places as the Volcano House while waiting for the twice-weekly boat to take them back. Today, Deloitte Haskins & Sells in Hawaii offers a complete range of audit, accounting, tax and consulting services from offices on the islands of Oahu, Maui and Hawaii.

George H. Lumsden, partner-in-charge, and his partners in the Hawaii practice believe that serving a client well requires much more than technical competence. Also required are a keen interest in clients' business affairs, sound business judgment and innovative application of professional skills. This concept of quality professional service is expressed by the firm's trademark, "Beyond the Bottom Line."

Commitment to excellence

These three words, a pledge for more than nine decades to perform to the highest standards of quality and integrity, have propelled Dillingham from one man's dream of an island railroad to a diversified multinational corporation with operations spanning the globe.

Today, Dillingham's energy, maritime and construction operations serve customers in Hawaii, Alaska, on the continental United States, Canada, New Zealand, Southeast Asia and various Pacific Basin and worldwide locations—but corporate roots run deep in Hawaii.

On a July evening in 1865, a young Massachusetts sailor was returning from a horseback ride in Nuuanu Valley. His horse reared, throwing him to the ground and breaking his leg. While recuperating, his ship left port.

The young sailor never returned to the sea, but began a new career as a clerk in a small hardware store. His name was Benjamin Franklin Dillingham.

Hawaii was still a monarchy in 1885 under

Dillingham & Co. hardware store on Fort Street in 1870. Benjamin Dillingham took a job as a clerk at $40 a month in Dimond's hardware store and later purchased the business in partnership with Alfred Castle.

King Kalakaua when Dillingham and others began organizing a project to consolidate west Oahu lands for resale and lease. The objective was to ease island reliance on the whaling trade and stimulate agriculture and shipping.

The Oahu Railway and Land Company was formed by Dillingham to provide fast, cheap transportation for the venture. Five years later, on September 4, 1889, Benjamin's railroad—dubbed "Dillingham's Folly" by doubters—made its initial mile-and-one-half

run. The railroad expanded rapidly, carrying goods and passengers between rural farmlands and the busy port of Honolulu.

This growth created an opportunity for harbor development and land reclamation in Honolulu and on the neighbor islands, and in 1902, Benjamin's son Walter Francis Dillingham formed Hawaiian Dredging Co., Ltd. Company dredges made possible the development of the Pearl Harbor Naval Base and created over 5,000 acres of usable land from tidal swamps and reefs, including most of today's Waikiki and Ala Moana business areas.

These companies were merged in 1961 to form Dillingham Corporation with Lowell Smith Dillingham, grandson of the founder, as president. Under Lowell's direction, Dillingham embarked on a planned growth program, establishing the company's major energy, maritime and construction activities.

Today, Dillingham's principal energy subsidiary, Cal Gas, is a leading LP-gas marketer on the U.S. mainland. The company operates over 270 retail outlets in 28 states and supports its distribution activities with an extensive production, transportation and storage network. Dillingham is also involved in oil and gas exploration and production on the U.S. mainland and geothermal exploration in Hawaii.

Dillingham's U.S. flag fleet of approximately 100 tugs and barges is active in ship assists, ship escort, bunker refueling and the movement of bulk cargoes in Hawaii, along the U.S. West Coast, Alaska and the Pacific Basin, the Gulf of Mexico and Central and South America. The company operates ship repair facilities at four Pacific locations and transports goods along the northeastern coast of Australia and to Papua New Guinea.

Dillingham's construction operations are divided into three principal areas—heavy, industrial, and commercial construction—serving clients in Hawaii, throughout the Pacific Basin, the continental United States, Canada, Alaska, Southeast Asia and around the world.

With more than 94 years of operation, and with annual revenues well in excess of $1 billion, Dillingham has far surpassed the dreams of its founder, the eager young sailor-merchant who took a chance on "Dillingham's Folly."

OR&L Station, Iwilei, early 1890s. By 1915, the railroad was annually hauling 700,000 tons of freight and nearly a million passengers over more than 100 miles of track.

Two decades of service to Hawaii's international travelers

The first commercial jet had landed only a couple of years before, but two resourceful American businessmen could already see Hawaii's potential as a travel destination. In 1962 Charles F. Feeney and Robert W. Miller successfully bid on the five-year concession to sell goods duty free to travelers as they depart Honolulu for foreign destinations. Feeney and Miller had just secured their first such concession a year before in Hong Kong.

The duty-free concept is simple—goods sold in duty-free shops at international airports are free of the country's tax and must be exported with the buyer. When purchased, merchandise is delivered to the point of departure at the airport and is not available for consumption in the country where the purchase was made.

Monetary benefits to the government of the duty-free port, in this case to Hawaii, are substantial. Duty Free Shoppers' obligation as a concessionaire guarantees a minimum cash payment or gives a percentage of the gross—whichever is higher—to the government. The more successful a Duty Free Shoppers concession, the more money is returned to the government—frequently to be used to keep landing fees at a competitive rate and help finance airport systems development.

Charles F. Feeney, founding director of Duty Free Shoppers.

In many ways, Feeney and Miller did for travel retailing what Hawaii's early plantation factors did for sugar—they were willing to bet on Hawaii's future and to make a daring financial commitment to the state.

From the start, Duty Free Shoppers has been committed to making Hawaii a popular destination for international travelers. In the twenty years that Duty Free Shoppers has been the official duty-free concessionaire, it has created what is now the world's most successful duty-free store system.

In 1972, Duty Free Shoppers opened, in the heart of Waikiki, the first, and to this day the only, in-bond duty-free shop off airport premises in the United States. Sales jumped substantially, increasing revenues—and, automatically, the amount of money Duty Free Shoppers remits to the state for financing of the airport system.

The majority of Duty Free Shoppers' duty-free sales in Hawaii are made at the Waikiki shop. Because goods purchased at this location are delivered at the airport, the State of Hawaii automatically receives 20 percent of these sales. Duty Free Shoppers has paid the State of Hawaii more than $130 million in concession fees in just the last five years. In 1981 alone, Duty Free Shoppers' fees exceeded similar concession fees paid *at all other U.S. airports combined.* Duty Free Shoppers is the largest single source of Hawaii's airport revenue, providing nearly half of all monies, including landing fees and other concession payments, generated at all of Hawaii's airports.

Waikiki Duty Free shopper.

Duty Free Shoppers manages non-duty-free shops at the airport, too, offering gifts, apparel and high-demand packaged foods.

Ja Ja Fashions and Kalia Gift Shop, operated by Duty Free Shoppers, provide non-duty-free retail shopping experiences for Hawaii visitors on the way to Waikiki and in Waikiki, respectively.

Today, Duty Free Shoppers has concessions or shops in Singapore, Guam, Saipan, San Francisco, Anchorage, Los Angeles and New York in addition to the original Hong Kong and Honolulu locations. The company also has sales and customer service offices in Tokyo and Osaka, Japan.

Duty Free Shoppers continues to play an active role in community service in Hawaii. Duty Free Shoppers' gifts help support the arts, education, health care and civic development. Nine Hawaii civic leaders meet regularly with company representatives to determine contribution policies to assure that the community is well served by the company.

Hawaii is also the international administrative headquarters of Duty Free Shoppers Group Limited, the parent company and the world's largest retailer specializing in merchandising to the traveling public. The company is privately owned and has more than 1,300 employees in Hawaii and 4,400 worldwide.

Robert W. Miller, founding director of Duty Free Shoppers.

Quality, service and pride

In the spring of 1971, several executives from Anheuser-Busch paid a visit to the office of Edward J. Doty, near the airport industrial park in Honolulu. While Doty knew many of these men well through industry involvement, he had no idea of the subject to be discussed during the visit. The result of the meeting was the creation of Eagle Distributors, Inc., the Anheuser-Busch distributorship of Budweiser, and Michelob, for the entire state of Hawaii.

When Ed Doty first came to Honolulu from the mainland in 1950, he went to work as a merchandiser for Johnston & Buscher, then distributors for Lucky Lager beer, Budweiser and Michelob beers from Anheuser-Busch and a large assortment of wines and spirits. At the time, the local market was dominated by the mainland beer, Acme, and by Primo and Royal, both brewed locally. However, before long Lucky Lager sales took off, and within a decade had over half the beer business in the state.

Doty left Johnston & Buscher sixteen years later, in 1966. With the help of his wife, Norma, and one other employee, he opened Doty Distributors, handling a variety of liquor products. Although the new company prospered, it lacked capital. That was obtained by selling the company to the Schenley Corporation in 1969. Through Doty's strong management ability the company had reached a dominant position in the business by 1971, having acquired the Olympia beer franchise and building the brand into more than a 60 percent market share in Hawaii.

That same year, Anheuser-Busch offered the franchise to Doty. The opportunity to be associated with the leading brewer in the world was one Doty could not resist. He parted with Schenley and started Eagle Distributors on September 1, 1972.

Starting with nine employees and a few rented trucks, Eagle Distributors applied the basics of hard work, service, honesty and a product of the highest quality. An 18,000-square-foot warehouse in the Mapunapuna area of Honolulu was leased by the new company, and three small branches were opened on Kauai, Maui and Hawaii.

Doty's and Anheuser-Busch financial executives' early projections for Eagle predicted about an $18,000 before-tax profit in the first year of operation—an optimistic projection at best, as Eagle would be the first exclusive beer distributorship in Hawaii. All other beverage companies sold multiple brands of beer, wine and spirits. The risk paid off; in a short time it became evident that Anheuser-Busch would command a major portion of the beer business in Hawaii. By 1982, the

Eagle Distributors' 60,000-square-foot Honolulu warehouse.

Anheuser-Busch brands—Budweiser, Budweiser Light, Michelob, Michelob Light and Natural Light—held a 60 percent share of market. The original list of nine employees had grown to 119, and the company boasted 35 large, gleaming beverage trucks.

Today, all branches have refrigerated, controlled-environment warehouses to guarantee the high quality and freshness of Anheuser-Busch products. The 60,000-square-foot Honolulu warehouse in Halawa Valley's Central Park development is a showplace which can store over one-half million cases of beer in refrigerated space. Six cargo bays can unload over 40 Matson containers per day.

The use of computers has simplified the logistics of a vastly spread-out operation.

Eagle Distributors' gleaming fleet of delivery trucks.

Hawaii, being an island state, is the only location in the nation with a single Anheuser-Busch distributorship covering an entire state—a situation which, additionally, is complicated by miles of ocean separating each branch.

Through the guidance and teamwork of Anheuser-Busch, Eagle Distributors has become the leading beer distributorship in Hawaii, now doing well over six million cases annually, with a gross sales volume well over $50 million dollars.

Still handling Anheuser-Busch brands exclusively, Eagle's market dominance was achieved through a quality product, foresight, service and, perhaps equally important, community involvement. Believing that a company should strongly support its community and its state, Eagle Distributors, Inc., its management and staff have always been active and visible in supporting civic and charitable projects and causes. Ed Doty is president of the Recycling Group, credited with initiating recycling in Hawaii. The company is involved as well with the fight against cancer through the Pacific Foundation for Cancer Research. Among a number of sporting events, the company and Anheuser-Busch sponsor the Ironman Triathlon in Kona and a variety of charitable fund-raising events on behalf of such organizations as the Muscular Dystrophy Association, the American Heart Association and a long list of local charities. Doty is also a member of the Governor's Task Force on Litter.

Over three decades of helping Hawaiians travel the world

After spending the first twenty years of his life trying to adjust to the cold of the Midwest, Carl Erdman was convinced that he wanted a change of climate. He decided to strike out on his own and travel to Hawaii to be with his well-respected uncle, the Reverend John P. Erdman. Little did Carl know at the time that he would spend most of his adult life helping people with their travel plans.

After bidding his family farewell, Carl boarded a train in St. Paul, Minnesota, to begin the first leg of his 6,000-mile trip to Hawaii. After several days riding the train, Carl arrived in Los Angeles, excited and ready for the second and final leg of his voyage. He purchased a cabin-class ticket for $90 and boarded the great passenger ship, the *Lurline*, which was owned and operated by Matson Navigation Company.

Carl arrived in Honolulu in January 1935 and was met by his Uncle John, who helped him get started with his new life in the islands. For the first fifteen years, he held various jobs to keep food on the table and a roof over his head.

By 1947, Carl had landed himself a job as manager of Grayline, and for several years he helped other people travel around the islands. It didn't take long for him to recognize the need for a travel agency. With Hawaii's Pacific location, people could travel to all points of the globe, whether for vacation or for business.

There weren't many travel agencies in Honolulu at that time and Carl was advised by friends to buy an existing agency to avoid the many problems of starting a new business.

It was January 1950 when the doors first opened to the Carl Erdman Travel Agency, located in the historic Stangenwald Building on Merchant Street right in the heart of downtown Honolulu, just where Carl wanted to be.

In the years that followed, Carl and his wife did extensive traveling themselves to experience firsthand the places he would be sending others to; over the years, he has always encouraged his staff to do likewise.

With conscientious attention to detail, and putting the travel client's welfare first, Carl Erdman Travel continued to grow and expand rapidly.

By 1964, Carl recognized that he needed more working capital and sold his business to the B.F. Dillingham Co., Ltd., at which time he relocated to the new Ala Moana Building while still operating under the name of Carl Erdman Travel.

Carl continued to expand his business to meet the travel needs of the islanders. In 1968, Castle & Cooke Ltd. sold its travel department to Carl Erdman Travel, making it one of the largest travel agencies in Honolulu.

Bayard H. Dillingham (left), president, and Carl M. Erdman, vice president.

In 1976, the Carl Erdman Travel Agency took the opportunity to purchase the travel department of the Theo. H. Davies & Co., at which time Carl returned to the downtown area with the opening of the Davies Pacific Center branch.

Carl Erdman Travel Agency has always been a leader in its field, and was the first travel agency in Hawaii to install "Tele-Ticketing," a system which greatly improved the speed and accuracy of airline ticketing through the use of computers.

Today, Carl Erdman Travel is still one of the largest and best-equipped travel agencies in Honolulu, with two offices and over twenty highly trained travel counselors to assist Hawaii's travelers.

Carl has been an active member of ASTA (American Society of Travel Agents) since 1951. He served as president of the Hawaii chapter from 1969 to 1973, and from 1973 to 1977 he served three terms as national director.

Since 1950, Carl Erdman Travel has advised and consulted governors, mayors and thousands of business people, including the general public. As a full-service travel organization, its business is equally divided between commercial and pleasure travel.

Carl Erdman Travel is now a corporation owned by the B.F.D. Limited Partnership, composed of members of the prominent Dillingham family.

From no-tech to high-tech: an evolution in banking

The story of First Interstate Bank of Hawaii (formerly American Security Bank) is as colorful and exciting an evolution as is banking in Hawaii itself—from banking by longhand entries in ledgers to the use of the most sophisticated satellite and land-based telecommunications networks found anywhere in the world.

Before banks came to Hawaii, money transactions bordered on the chaotic. Coins and currency from nations around the world converged in Hawaii—and exchange rates in that mixed collage of cultures were inconsistent and subject to frequent change.

The first bank in the islands opened in 1858; others soon followed. In 1916 alone, three banks opened their doors. One of those was the Chinese American Bank, organized by a group of prominent businessmen.

With the Great Depression and President Franklin D. Roosevelt's declaration of a national bank holiday, the Chinese American Bank closed its doors along with other banks in Hawaii and on the mainland. A "Central Committee for the Reorganization of the Chinese American Bank" was immediately formed to protect the assets of the depositors. After a thorough review, the committee decided to form the American Security Bank which, in turn, purchased most of the assets of the Chinese American Bank.

The committee also arranged with the Federal Deposit Insurance Corporation to cover every depositor with up to $5,000 insurance. Thus, when American Security Bank officially opened for business on April 20, 1935 at the corner of King and Nuuanu streets in downtown Honolulu, it had the distinction of being Hawaii's first insured bank.

Three years after the bank was founded, it hired 17-year-old Dennis Y.M. Ching as a messenger. Ching was to have a profound influence on the bank's future during the next 45 years. He rose through the ranks to become chairman of the board in 1975 and, until his death in 1983, guided the bank

American Security Bank, circa 1949, corner of King and Nuuanu streets in downtown Honolulu.

through an era of unprecedented growth and expansion.

In 1952, a branch in Makiki was opened, closely followed by two additional branches. The bank was gathering momentum. From 1962 to 1972, eight new branches were opened, and the bank had spread to the islands of Maui, Kauai and the Big Island. Its headquarters moved from King and Nuuanu streets to Waikiki in recognition of the importance of the tourist industry, and a plan to play a significant role in it.

The following year, the bank's main offices moved from Waikiki into its own prestigious offices at 1314 South King Street. In the short period of three years—May 1978 through June 1981—five new branches were opened, bring-

The original offices as restored in 1981, now First Interstate Bank of Hawaii.

ing the total to seventeen. Also in 1981, the original office at King and Nuuanu streets was completely restored, in the mode of the 1930s. With its roots nostalgically perpetuated in the charm of the restored office, the bank moved toward the biggest step yet in the entire history of its accelerating evolution.

By 1983, the face of banking itself was changing in Hawaii as well as throughout the rest of the United States. High-tech, non-bank competition and a deregulated environment had created new demands for advanced electronic services never before available. To compete in this dynamic environment, on April 11, 1983, American Security Bank officially became a franchised member of the nation's largest multistate banking system—the $42-billion First Interstate Bancorp of Los Angeles, California.

Although the bank's ownership, management and autonomy did not change with the franchising, its name did change to First Interstate Bank of Hawaii. And it became linked online via satellite to nearly 1,000 other First Interstate offices and a central computer base, as well as over 750 24-hour automated teller machines in the Western states. As First Interstate Bank of Hawaii, the bank could now offer what no other bank of any size in Hawaii could offer—personal check-cashing privileges for its customers at nearly 1,000 other U.S. mainland First Interstate offices. More new services, such as discount brokerage and participation in a nationwide network of shared automated teller machines, would quickly follow. But most important of all, the bank gained access to the advanced high-tech research and marketing resources of America's eighth largest banking system.

The evolution goes on. The bank that was founded when clerks made entries into ledgers by longhand has become Hawaii's leader in computerized customer services.

Serving the needs of Hawaii's industry for 75 years

Iwilei oxygen plant, 1928.

An automobile clanked up to the Acetylene Light & Agency Company on April 22, 1909. The driver bought a cylinder of acetylene for his car's headlights and thus became the first customer of a business that today is Hawaii's leading manufacturer of industrial gas products and distributor of medical, safety, and welding equipment and supplies.

Although the use of acetylene for car headlights was shortlived, the future of oxygen-acetylene for welding was bright. In 1919, a group headed by Allan Renton purchased and reorganized the company into Hawaiian Gas Products Co. "Gaspro" was long used as the trade name and, in 1954, became the official name of the company.

The welding business continued to find an increasingly important place in industry. In 1926, the company installed, in the Iwilei area, its first plant to manufacture oxygen. By 1929, the use of oxygen expanded to medical applications; ever since, Gaspro has been Hawaii's leading supplier of oxygen to hospitals and other medical institutions.

Carbon dioxide was added to the list of compressed gases in 1926 in order to service the need of the beverage industry for carbonating their products. Although initially a byproduct of an alcohol plant, by 1932 the company had installed its own plant to generate carbon dioxide from burning coke from Germany. In the early 1930s, Gaspro manufactured its first dry ice by blowing CO_2 into the drawer of a letter file. When the drawer was full of CO_2 snow, it was removed with a small grocer's sugar scoop and compressed into dry ice using a small cylindrical container and hand pump. Today the company's dry ice production, primarily

for the airline industry, is measured in tons per day.

In 1932, the company installed an acetylene plant in the Kalihi district of Honolulu on a site midway between the airport and downtown Honolulu that was to become the company's headquarters 27 years later.

In 1938, the company built a lime plant to provide a source of CO_2 and to serve the sugar industry's need for lime to clarify sugar juices in the milling process. Gaspro continued as the primary supplier of lime to the sugar and construction industries for the next four decades. This year also brought the establishment of Gaspro's first neighbor island branch, in Hilo. Subsequently, branches have been established on Kauai, Maui and in Kona. Agricultural chemicals, primarily for the sugar and pineapple industries, became an important part of the products distributed by these branches.

The year 1941 began with the purchase of the former Honolulu Brick Company. An

unforeseen demand for brick products for bomb shelters, barricades and other protective devices was brought about by the infamous attack on Pearl Harbor in December. One of the company's unusual war efforts was the construction of a secret oxygen plant for the government. It was secluded in a distant area, should the main plant be destroyed by bombing, and was in full production for over three years. Another contribution was the conversion of the company's Waianae lime plant into a cement plant for the last two years of the war.

Following the war, the company expanded into the distribution of steel pipe and, in 1957, began manufacturing plastic pipe. This business then grew into the manufacture of such other plastic products as bottles, buckets, flower pots and fiberglass-reinforced bathtubs and related bathroom fixtures.

Gaspro continued to flourish in the '60s and '70s as statehood and the increase in tourism brought about unprecedented growth. This time period coincided with increasing national and local emphasis on employee safety, with Gaspro emerging as Hawaii's leading distributor of safety equipment and supplies.

The year 1980 brought the culmination of 61 years of continuous ownership and direction by the Renton family. Since 1931, Gaspro had been a distributor for Airco, Inc., one of the country's largest manufacturers of welding equipment, industrial gases and medical equipment and supplies. In March 1980, Gaspro merged into Airco, Inc. to become part of a worldwide chain of similar companies under the direction of The BOC Group in London. This new page in Gaspro's history promises to bring a strong source of capital, engineering expertise and new products to continue to serve the needs of Hawaii's industry.

Kalihi acetylene plant, 1932.

An established tradition of service to business in Hawaii

Goodsill Anderson Quinn & Stifel is one of the oldest and largest law firms in Honolulu and the state of Hawaii. The origin of the firm dates from 1878. The firm's name has changed from time to time, pursuant to Hawaii Supreme Court rules requiring that a law firm's name reflect only active partners and also to recognize long-time achievement by active partners. From 1925 to 1931 the firm was known as Prosser, Anderson & Marx. From 1941 to 1969, the firm was known as Anderson, Wrenn & Jenks and is recognized by that name by many in Honolulu. In 1973, the firm became known as Goodsill Anderson & Quinn. More recently, in January 1983, the firm took on its present name, Goodsill Anderson Quinn & Stifel.

At its origin and for many years thereafter, the firm was engaged in the practice of business and commercial law almost exclusively. As business in Hawaii and clients of the firm grew and prospered, the firm grew commensurately. Over the years, the firm has maintained its strength in corporate and commercial law and has broadened its practice in other areas to meet business and community needs.

The firm has been involved in an array of significant transactions in Hawaii, including the first major corporate reorganization and many significant subsequent corporate reorganizations and mergers, the organization and restructuring of many of the state's principal businesses, among the first securities law registrations and filings, major corporate acquisitions, corporate liquidations and dispositions, numerous real property acquisitions and financings (among the largest in the history of the state), documentation of the first commercial condominium office complex in Honolulu (and perhaps the first in the United States), development of the largest shopping center in Honolulu and the securing of what have grown to be significant precedents in numerous areas of law. The firm is regularly engaged in securities law offerings, registrations and compliance matters, corporate financings, reorganizations, restructurings and organizations, banking law matters, public utilities law proceedings and advice, purchases and sales of businesses, federal and state tax litigation and planning, the structuring of real estate acquisitions, financing, development and leasing transactions, Hawaii Residential Leasehold Law matters, commercial and residential condominium development, real estate financing and development activity, environmental law questions, equipment leasing and financing, trust and estate matters, labor law practice and significant litigation of

(Photo courtesy Ray Jerome Baker, Bishop Museum)

In 1898, the firm's offices were located on the second floor of the Bishop Bank building at the corner of Merchant and Kaahumanu streets.

nearly every kind and character (including complex litigation supported by the firm's in house computer capability).

The firm also has been involved in advice and drafting with respect to many state and local statutes and ordinances, including many of Hawaii's principal laws governing business transactions.

From a one-man firm in 1878, Goodsill Anderson Quinn & Stifel has grown to over 55 attorneys in 1983 with offices in downtown Honolulu and Kailua-Kona on the Island of Hawaii. In addition to providing advice to its principal business and litigation clients including major corporations, the major utilities, major insurance companies, the leading Hawaii bank, the oldest and largest trust company, a leading newspaper, a principal airline and significant real estate owners, developers and lenders, the firm provides consultation and advice to newly emerging businesses and to its small business and individual clients.

The firm has been served over the years by a continuous succession of distinguished members, including the only man in Hawaii's

history to head both the judicial and executive branches of government, trustees and directors of the largest business enterprises and financial institutions in the state, associate justices and a chief justice of the Hawaii Supreme Court, officers of the state and city and county of Honolulu, the last governor of the territory and the first governor of the state of Hawaii, and a number of past officers, directors and presidents of the Hawaii State Bar Association. Firm attorneys are outstanding graduates of major law schools throughout the United States, including Hawaii, who reflect the ethnic diversity of the community and are active in professional and community affairs.

The firm will continue to expand its areas of practice to meet the needs of its clients and the community which it serves. Goodsill Anderson Quinn & Stifel is proud to have grown with the city and county of Honolulu and to have played a role in its remarkable development.

Economical, modern fleet is key to growth and success

Having only begun at the start of the 1980s, Greyhound Rent-A-Car has already made its mark on the automobile rental business in the islands. The only Greyhound franchise throughout the state of Hawaii, Greyhound Rent-A-Car is backed by the nationally known mainland Greyhound Corporation, better known for it's intercity buses since the 1930s.

Starting a car rental business in Hawaii's already overdeveloped, competitive market was a big move for Greyhound Rent-A-Car, but a move that has given Greyhound a foothold for continued growth.

Much of Greyhound's history stems from that of the bus line on the mainland, but the tour bus business didn't do so well in the islands at the end of the 1970s; Greyhound quit the tour bus business and sold its 35 buses to Gray Line Hawaii.

To fully understand Greyhound's successful return to the islands, it's important to know something about the man behind this innovative franchise—Robert C. Allen, veteran tourism executive with over 30 years in tourism, hotels and transportation. Allen's innovativeness stems from working with such greats as Henry J. Kaiser in helping to introduce the "Pink Jeep" which is used in many resort areas throughout the world. Bob Allen also purchased the famous 100-foot catamaran *Ale Ale Kai V* from Kaiser and added it to the Pearl Harbor run, which he operated under the name of Shoreline Cruises.

Allen's first ten years in the tourism and transportation industry were spent as president and general manager of Gray Line Hawaii, Interisland Travel Company, Avis U-Drive Company and Trade Wind Transportation Company. Those first ten years armed him with the experience and knowledge to succeed in bringing a new car rental agency to Hawaii. In the late '50s, Allen became president of the Roy C. Kelley hotels which had over 2,000 rooms available.

Allen was not a person to stand still; he was then, as he is today, a mover and a shaker, a person who produces results, taking the challenge and risks to explore new avenues of business.

During the '60s, Allen served as an executive with several corporate entities. Also during that time, he spent five years with the Hawaii Visitors Bureau as executive vice-president and spearheaded the Bureau's effort to make Hawaii more attractive to visitors.

In the '70s, Allen, who had already gained over twenty years of experience with the visitor industry in an executive capacity, went to the Middle East to run the Merlin Hotel chain for the Del Webb Corporation. Upon his return to Hawaii, he joined National Car Rental as marketing director and enlarged their 650-car fleet to 1,800 cars in less than eighteen months.

Allen's decision to take on the Greyhound Rent-A-Car franchise came without hesitation. He had served many years in the industry and

didn't see why another car rental agency couldn't survive, especially with the national reputation of the entire Greyhound organization.

To acquire the Greyhound license, Allen established Transportation Systems Management Corporation; he is president and majority owner along with several partners.

Greyhound Rent-A-Car offers the economy of a modern fleet of compact cars and the versatility of booking throughout the islands with other rental operators. In addition, Greyhound Rent-A-Car offers larger agency commissions to stimulate bookings.

The Greyhound Rent-A-Car sales counter is centrally located in Waikiki directly in front of the Coral Seas Hotel. Its administrative offices are just across the street in the Outrigger West Hotel, where Robert C. Allen runs his operation with skill, leadership and experience in providing economical transportation in an efficient and friendly manner.

Robert C. Allen

Reporting Hawaii's business news for over a quarter of a century

Regional business publishing is one of the fastest growing sectors of the communications industry, with over 70 publications now serving the country's major metropolitan areas. So it may come as a surprise to learn that *Hawaii Business* magazine is one of the oldest regional business magazines in the nation.

Hawaii Business began back in 1955 as an engineering journal, the *Hawaii Engineer.* Founder Joseph A. Murphy's Volume I, Number One ran 32 pages and carried eight pages of advertising. Today the company, which also publishes the national travel trade publication *Discover Hawaii* and an annual directory titled *Hawaii Buyer's Guide,* has been growing at the rate of twenty percent annually.

Hawaii Engineer gradually broadened its base of coverage, and in 1957 the magazine changed its name to reflect its coverage of industry in general. As *Hawaii Industry* it continued to grow and attract readers, and in 1962 began a conversion to paid circulation. Within a few years, with a fully paid circulation, the magazine again took on a wider responsibility and adapted its name accordingly—to *Hawaii Business and Industry.*

The last step in the magazine's evolution to a general business publication came when it changed its name to *Hawaii Business;* by now its format was well established as a general interest business publication, with a fully paid, ABC-audited circulation and the best penetration of its market of any regional business magazine in the country. Aimed at owners, managers and presidents, *Hawaii Business* boasts a total readership of 40,000 people monthly and is read by the most influential and affluent segments of the community.

As *Hawaii Business* magazine was developing, the company explored another publishing opportunity and in 1961 created the first edition of its annual *Hawaii Buyer's Guide,* now one of Hawaii's most widely used business publications.

Circulated to a list of key purchasing agents and specifiers, the *Buyer's Guide* carries some 10,000 listings of manufacturers and their Hawaii representatives and is widely used in purchasing circles. A fully computerized publication, all listings are updated annually and the book is completely revised using a specifically designed computer program.

In 1975 Hawaii Business Publishing Corp. found itself with another opportunity—one that was ideally suited to the business-oriented nature of the company's publications. In January of that year it launched the first edition of the monthly *Discover Hawaii* magazine. Aimed at the 15,000 or so Hawaii-

Hawaii Engineer, *Hawaii Business Publishing Corp.'s original publication, and the forerunner of* Hawaii Business, *was launched in 1955.*

Hawaii Industry *was an outgrowth of Hawaii Engineer, and reflected a wider coverage and readership in 1957.*

Further evolution, to Hawaii Business and Industry, *which by 1962 had a fully paid circulation.*

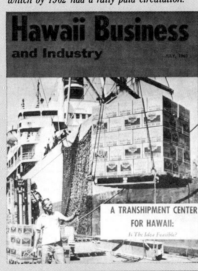

By 1983, Hawaii Business *had the best market penetration of any regional business magazine in the country.*

producing travel agencies in North America, the magazine provides a full-color report each month on all that is happening in the state's $4 billion travel industry.

Because North American travel agents sell so many different resort destinations, and because personnel turnover in the industry is so prevalent, there is a constant need for education and information if a travel agent is to sell a destination properly. That is the function of *Discover Hawaii* magazine—to show and tell travel agents what is happening in the islands. Besides the regular monthly editions, which feature a reader service card allowing travel agents to order information about Hawaii, the company publishes a twice-yearly *Discover Hawaii Sales Planner,* a directory to every product and service in the islands commissionable to a travel agent.

Highly regarded by the industry, *Discover Hawaii* provides travel agents with the most comprehensive information system offered by any resort destination in the world. The publication has won four Maggie Awards in Western Publications Association competition—the only Hawaii magazine ever to win one of the coveted Maggies.

In the years ahead, regional publishing appears likely to continue the rapid growth it has experienced in the past decade. As communications needs become more varied and more specific, regional publishing companies are destined to find more and diverse needs for their services. Hawaii Business Publishing Corp. considers itself positioned to fill Hawaii's publishing needs, whatever they may be.

Meeting the health care needs of Hawaii's people

During the 1930s, the devastating effects of the Great Depression reached across the Pacific Ocean to Hawaii. Its people suffered many hardships, including the inability to obtain needed medical care. It was in this environment of personal financial struggle together with the traditional Hawaiian feeling of caring for one another, that the roots of the Hawaii Medical Service Association were formed.

In 1935, at a now-historic Territorial Conference of Social Workers, a committee was appointed to find a way to help people, hard hit by the Depression, get needed medical care. The committee worked tirelessly for two years and in 1937 put forth a proposal for a "community association of participating members who through regular monthly dues would share their medical costs among themselves." The idea met with overwhelming support in Hawaii since the proposal provided that the association be governed by a board truly representative of the community.

On June 1, 1938, with a loan of $6,500 from many of Hawaii's most prominent businesses and a roster of 671 members, the Hawaii Medical Service Association was born. Harold W. Loper became the first official HMSA president, with William Bowman as his business manager. Dues were set at $3 per month and the plan offered up to $300 in medical benefits per year. This was the start of Hawaii's first member-owned, nonprofit organization committed to helping the people of the islands meet the burden of the cost of medical care.

The new Association moved into its first offices in the Hawaiian Trust Building in

A familiar figure in Hawaii during the 1950s was HMSA's "Billy Benefit," seen here waving from a Honolulu city bus.

Honolulu with a handful of employees. Later it was to move to Bishop Street, its home for the next 20 years.

In 1946, HMSA became part of the national Blue Shield Association and firmly established itself in the growing movement towards better health care for all Americans.

The '50s witnessed unimagined growth in HMSA membership. By 1950, the Association had expanded to Kauai, Hawaii and Maui and boasted a membership of 48,000. In 1955, HMSA celebrated the enrollment of its 100,000th member, and by 1960 its membership had reached almost 300,000.

The '50s and '60s were decades of innovation as HMSA pioneered coverage for initial office visits, home health care and

From its Bishop Street site in Honolulu, HMSA moved its headquarters to Kapiolani Boulevard in 1966 where it remained until 1983 when it consolidated its various operations into its new energy-efficient building on Keeaumoku Street.

psychiatric care. The Association also developed its highly successful dental, drug and vision plans during this period. But probably its most important contribution to the health of Hawaii's people was HMSA's introduction of expanded protection to cover the cost of catastrophic illness and injury. HMSA's first Major Medical Plan provided up to $5,000 per illness, a far cry from today's $250,000 coverage.

As government became more involved in health care, HMSA found itself performing another needed public service for Hawaii—the administration of new government health programs. In 1956, HMSA became the administrator of health benefits for military dependents through the CHAMPUS Program. In 1966 HMSA was awarded the contract to administer benefits under the newly developed Medicare Program. And in 1971, HMSA received a request to act as fiscal agent for Hawaii's Medicaid program.

Along with these new responsibilities came new challenges. Fueled by high inflation, technological advances and government health spending, the entire nation, including Hawaii, began to feel the troubling impact of rising health care costs. Fortunately, the Association was able to foresee many of the changes that were to come. HMSA began to significantly expand its efforts to contain the cost of health care through its emphasis on outpatient care and other efforts to reduce the use of hospital services, the main contributor to rising costs.

In 1972, HMSA offered its first HMO (health maintenance organization), the Community Health Program, to Hawaii with its prophetic emphasis on managed health care and wellness. The Association continued to move in this direction in 1980 when it established its second HMO, Health Plan Hawaii, as a federally qualified plan.

Through these and other trend-setting efforts, HMSA members have used far less hospital care than any state in the country. For Hawaii this has meant broader coverage and less expensive health plans.

As it entered the '80s under the experienced leadership of President Albert H. Yuen, HMSA had the highest level of operating efficiency and one of the lowest levels of administrative expenses compared to similar health plans across the country. With well over a half-million members and a community-based board of directors, HMSA still continues to meet the community need for which it was first established—to ensure for the people the best possible health care at the lowest possible cost.

The bank that Luke built

In this multi-island state with a widely diversified population, the story of Kan Jung Luke, founder and Chairman of the Board of Directors of Hawaii National Bank, is the bank's story. It reflects the fruition of the American dream in its most classic sense.

Born in 1914, the youngest of thirteen children, the barefoot country boy from a Kohala plantation on the Big Island of Hawaii learned early that only self-determination would bring his goals within reach. Primary for him was education. His educational pursuit began in Kohala, took him to St. Louis High School in Honolulu and the University of Hawaii and culminated in an MBA degree at Harvard University Graduate School of Business Administration in Boston, Massachusetts. For twenty-one years prior to the founding of the bank in Honolulu, Luke lectured on finance, investments and banking at the University of Hawaii Business School as an avocation, donating his salary to the University. He has since helped make education an attainable reality for many others with his yearly contributions to several schools and universities.

When World War II began, Luke was called from the Army Reserve to manage the Officers' Mess at Ft. Shafter, where he efficiently met the responsibility of feeding thousands of officers daily. He held the rank of Major.

Luke's perseverance to attain an education and to succeed in the military remained his guiding principle in managing the bank. This perseverance, combined with a series of creative innovations, has made Hawaii National Bank, and Luke himself, leaders in Hawaii's banking community.

The September 19, 1960 opening day deposits of $6,256,618 remain unequalled in Hawaii's banking history. In fact, according to the *American Banker* magazine, it was the largest of 134 banks opening in the United States that year. Then, only a month after the bank opened its doors, Luke initiated education loans. Hawaii National, with ten of its eleven branches presently servicing the Honolulu district, later pioneered daily

Hawaii National Bank's first office downtown, at the corner of King and Smith streets.

compounding of interest and free checking accounts in Hawaii. It was also among the first to provide bank-by-mail service and to continue offering free checking accounts for those "Age 55 or Better." The bank was once ranked in the top three in Hawaii for real estate activity, motivated by Luke's strong personal interest in real estate. Just four months after its opening, Hawaii National Bank was made prime mortgagee for the $350-million Hawaii Kai development on Oahu. Luke remains part owner of an industrial park adjacent to Honolulu International Airport and

Chairman K.J. Luke (right) celebrating the grand opening of a branch office with former Governor John A. Burns.

a partner in Moanalua Terrace Associates, the largest FHA housing project of its kind in the United States when it was completed in 1968. He is also a principal in other real estate and investment entities.

Other firsts in the Hawaii banking community have been Hawaii National's All-American Auto Loans and Prime Plus Home Equity Creditline—pioneering services for all Hawaii's people.

An appreciation for the cosmopolitan nature of Hawaii, so evident in the capital city of Honolulu itself, helped make Hawaii National Bank unique in the state. Since 1960, when K.J. Luke founded the bank on the corner of King and Smith streets in downtown Honolulu, the Board members and officers of the bank, as well as its wide range of customers, have represented Hawaii's diversified ethnic groups.

Throughout Honolulu and the state's several islands, Hawaii National Bank is known as the "Home of Warm-Hearted Bankers." No slogan could more accurately capture the philosophy of the bank or its founder, K.J. Luke.

221

Hawaii's first airline pioneers aviation advancements in the Pacific

The first Hawaiian Airlines hostesses were hired in 1943 to work aboard the carrier's DC-3 passenger flights. Prior to that, ticket agents at the airport tended to passengers' needs before the plane's departure.

Back in 1929, a great deal of energy, vision and perserverance were required to turn the daring concept of an interisland transportation system into a safe, practical reality. In the fall of that year, Hawaii's first commercial air service was initiated, under the name of Inter-Island Airways, Ltd. Actual flight operations started with a Bellanca monoplane powered by a Wright J-6 300-horsepower motor, carrying passengers on short ten-minute flights over Honolulu.

The first scheduled service of Inter-Island Airways began on November 11, 1929, with the operation of two Sikorsky amphibian planes (S-38s), each with a capacity of eight passengers. The first schedule called for three round trips to Hilo per week, with stops on Molokai, Lanai and Maui on request, and two round trips to Kauai.

With continued attention to advancing aviation technology, sixteen passenger Sikorsky S-43s augmented the carrier's fleet, accommodating not only increased traffic, but newly authorized interisland air mail service as well. During 1930, 13,043 passengers were carried—2,676 were passengers in sightseeing flights over Honolulu and 10,267 were interisland passengers.

Inter-Island Airways Ltd. changed its name to Hawaiian Airlines in 1941. That year also marked the introduction of the Douglas DC-3 to Hawaiian skies. To emphasize the reliability of the aircraft, Stanley C. Kennedy, founder of the company and long-time president, directed that delivery of the first DC-3s occur in formation for 2,500 miles from the mainland to Honolulu.

These 24-passenger workhorses of the piston era were the mainstay of the airline's fleet for many years. They were vital during wartime operations when all interisland traffic was placed under military control. Granted the first air cargo certificate issued by the Civil Aeronautics Board, Hawaiian Airlines provided an aerial lifeline to the neighbor islands during World War II.

In 1943, Hawaiian Airlines inaugurated stewardess service, with Momi Grace Jacobs hired as the first stewardess for the airline. Interisland airfares were reduced in 1945, and the fare to Hilo dropped to $15, as opposed to the 1939 fare of $30.

Hawaiian's first aircraft, the Sikorsky S-30 amphibian, pioneered interisland commercial air travel in 1929. Early flights to Kailua-Kona landed in the bay where an outrigger canoe took passengers ashore.

Hawaiian Airlines was the first airline in history to win the 20 Year Award for its accident-free safety record from the National Safety Council in January 1950. To this date, the carrier has maintained an outstanding safety record and a continuous commitment to excellence and customer satisfaction.

When interisland steamship service was discontinued in 1948, the Hawaiian Islands became dependent solely on air transportation for passenger movement. Hawaiian Airlines was ready to meet the challenge.

Two separate operations conducted in 1950 were evidence of the versatility of Hawaii's pioneering airline. Hawaiian Pineapple Company instituted a program through which employees in Honolulu and Lanai were given the opportunity to observe operations on the other island. This resulted in 60 special flights to and from Lanai during this period, carrying some 1,400 Hawaiian Pineapple Company employees. In another pineapple-related activity, over one million pounds of pineapple tops were flown from Maui to Kohala during "Operation Pinetop." One hundred forty-three flights were made from Maui to Upolu Point on the Big Island without interference of regular scheduled passenger operations.

In 1952, Hawaiian continued its lead in interisland air transport with the introduction of the Convair 340, providing Hawaii with its first pressurized, air-conditioned cabin service. The airline later purchased long-range, four-engine DC-6 aircraft for transpacific military air charters in 1958.

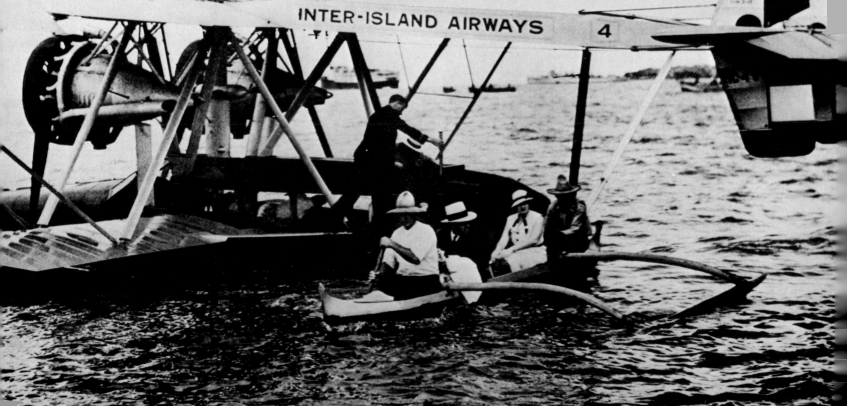

Shortly after Hawaiian's 25th anniversary, the airline introduced a fleet of five "Viewmaster" ships to its service. These DC-3 aircraft boasted four giant five-foot panoramic windows, eight enlarged convair type windows and provided seating for 31 passengers.

By Hawaii's Statehood year, 1959, Hawaiian had become the first island airline to open its own sales offices on the mainland. With offices in Los Angeles, San Francisco and New York City, sales contacts were made in 41 North American cities during that year.

In 1963, Hawaiian opened a Far East sales office in Tokyo and became the first airline serving Hawaii to release a promotional film on the islands with Japanese narration. Hawaiian was also the first island airline to issue promotional material printed in Japanese.

During the 1960s Hawaiian's interisland traffic took a sharp upward climb. Joining the company in 1964 to lead it to record profits was John H. Magoon Jr., who left a thriving laundry business to assume his new position as president and major stockholder. Under Magoon's direction, Hawaiian Airlines again maintained its pioneering stance in Hawaii aviation by introducing the first pure jet aircraft, the McDonnell Douglas DC-9. Travel time between island destinations was reduced to a brief 20 to 40 minutes.

Hawaiian accepted delivery of the first DC-9-50 in scheduled American service in September 1975. Subsequently, DC-9-80s were added to maintain a livery with the industry's most modern and advanced aircraft.

In 1973, Hawaiian's corporate identity underwent a complete change. A new corpo-

In 1966 Hawaiian Airlines introduced jet-age travel to the islands with Douglas DC-9-10 fanjets carrying 90 passengers. Larger DC-9-30 fanjets accommodating 115 passengers followed a few years later, and by 1976 the 139-passenger DC-9-50s replaced the 30s. The Super DC-9-80 now complements the airline's fleet with a capacity of 170 passengers.

rate symbol, designed by Walter Landor Associates of San Francisco, incorporated the state flower, the hibiscus, with the profile of a Polynesian woman. Resulting in "Pualani," the symbol accompanied a bold new wordmark, "Hawaiian Air," and was expressed in

On the occasion of the carrier's 35th anniversary, founder Stanley C. Kennedy, left, reviews congratulatory messages along with the airline's first pilot, Captain Charles I. Elliott, center, and president John H. Magoon Jr., right.

the new paint scheme for Hawaiian's sleek DC-9 jets.

In November 1976, Hawaiian celebrated 47 years of flying with a spotless safety record and the enviable position of being first in the airline industry in safety—holder of the world's safety record.

A milestone marked in 1978 by the airline was of particular historical note. That year, Hawaiian Air carried 3,095,191 passengers in the first ten months of the year. Previously, it took 24 years to carry three million passengers!

In another first, Hawaiian's all-female crew flew the SD3-30 to Molokai. Captain Sharyn Emminger, First Officer Karen Squyres and Flight Attendant Trude Asada flew straight into the history books as the first all-female crew on an American scheduled carrier.

Presently, Hawaiian is the state's largest airline. It operates between seven communities on the six principal islands. The entire network totals approximately 2,000 miles of interlaced routes, along which the average passenger travels only 130 miles. Employees, who reside on all the islands served by the carrier, number close to 1,000. Hawaiian Air maintains full-time sales personnel and offices in major cities across North America, Canada, London, England, Tokyo, Japan and Sydney, Australia. A success story that began with ten-minute flights over Honolulu.

223

From monarchy to statehood

On New Year's Eve 1879, Thomas Alva Edison dazzled the world with his "red hot hairpin in a bottle," the first practical incandescent light. At that time, the streets of Honolulu were lit by gas, but within just seven years, C.O. Berger and D.P. Smith were extolling the virtues of electric street lighting. Smith tried to sell King Kalakaua on Edison's new bulbs, while Berger was promoting arc lamps.

It was Berger who set up the first demonstration of electric lighting in Hawaii when he strung five arc lamps around Iolani Palace on July 21, 1886, but it was Smith who was ultimately authorized to order a 50-light electric plant, which was installed on the palace grounds. The constitutional monarchy was in the electric lighting business.

By March 1888, that system included a hydroelectric plant in Nuuanu Valley, possibly the first of its kind west of the Rockies. By the dawn of the Gay Nineties, people were demanding electricity not only for street lighting, but for their businesses and homes. But Oahu's climate did not cooperate; there just wasn't enough rain, and without it, the government's hydro plant couldn't deliver the power.

In the meantime, E.O. Hall & Sons had installed a few generators in Honolulu homes, but it soon became apparent that something more was needed. Jonathan Austin, William Hall, Edwin White and William Lockwood moved to fill that need, forming a co-partnership on May 7, 1891. Five months later, on October 13, the partnership became a corporation and Hawaiian Electric Company was born.

The company's original office and coal-powered dynamo were located in a one-story building on King Street where the 30-story Pacific Trade Center now stands, but by 1894 a larger power plant was built at the foot of Alakea Street.

A milestone for the young company was passed that same year with the construction of a line to Waikiki across the duck ponds and rice fields that separated the beach community from the city.

Ice and cold storage, added to the company's services in 1901, were offered to customers until after World War II, when electric refrigeration made that area of operations obsolete. As the use of electricity grew, so did Heco's system. Farmers and a sprinkling of residents in Kaneohe were the first rural customers to benefit after lines were strung over the Koolaus in 1914. A Hawaiian *mele* (song) was composed to commemorate the event. *"Olapa Kauila i Kaneohe"* is still popular today.

Ten years later, the first underground circuits were installed in downtown Honolulu. At that time, Hawaiian Electric offices were located on King Street. The present administration building, a Mediterranean-style landmark, was built next door and was dedicated in 1927. As new electric appliances were introduced in the 1930's, residential customers demanded more electricity, and so did the Army, Navy, the plantations and the

Heco's second King Street building in 1923. Erected in 1900, it provided needed space for offices and appliance showrooms. Four years later, a new building stood where cars are parked at left; it still serves as Heco's administrative center.

canneries. Heco expanded its generating facilities to serve them and built the first unit of the Waiau power plant on the shores of Pearl Harbor in 1938.

The year 1940 brought additional requirements for service to expanding national defense activities as the winds of war blew closer to the islands. In August of that year, a second unit at Waiau was placed in operation.

And then came December 7, 1941. The attack on Pearl Harbor that morning took place in Waiau's front yard, and the Heco men on duty ducked under trucks for protection as bullets streaked through the air. Despite the carnage and destruction just a few hundred yards across open water, the Waiau plant survived the attack without major damage.

Heco was affected during the war years by acute shortages in skilled labor and essential materials, yet the need for electric power never slackened. The critical power situation was greatly relieved in 1944 by the completion of a 35,000-kilowatt unit at the plant located at Honolulu Harbor, but even so Heco was forced to meet peak demand with power supplied by the Navy, the Army and the sugar plantations.

At war's end, plans were renewed for a new engineering complex at the company's Ward Avenue property, and that facility was completed in 1947. The postwar years brought continuing expansion. The Hicks plant, named after the company's seventh president, became the second facility on the Honolulu waterfront when it went into operation in mid-December 1954. By 1958, the first of two 138-kv transmission lines was strung from Waiau across the mountains to the Koolau substation.

Statehood came in 1959, bringing with it a period of unprecedented growth. In 1963, the first unit of the new power plant at Kahe Point went on line, and a year later, Heco stock was offered for the first time on the New York Stock Exchange. From its original $20,000 capitalization in 1891, Heco grew to become a multi-island utility. Maui Electric Company, serving the islands of Maui and Lanai, was acquired in 1968, and Hawaii Electric Light Company, serving the island of Hawaii, was purchased in 1970. Both are wholly owned subsidiaries.

The 1970's brought environmental consciousness to the community. Heco switched to the use of low-sulfur oil at its downtown plant in 1969 and at the Waiau plant in 1971; that same year, the company established its own Environmental Department.

Heco recorded unprecedented capital expenditures in the 1970s and into the 1980s. In 1976, a $10 million water discharge project

Horse-drawn wagons delivered ice in the early 1900s.

was completed at the Kahe plant. The $63 million allocated for capital expenditures in 1980 was the largest construction budget in Heco history. Part of it went to complete a sixth generating unit and tall stacks at Kahe and to build an oil storage facility at Campbell Industrial Park. Then in 1980, under Environmental Protection Agency regulations, Heco switched to low-sulfur oil at Kahe. Low-sulfur fuel oil costs increased to as high as $43 a barrel, capping a 10-year rise from $2.50 a barrel.

Beginning in the mid-1970s, Heco stepped up its interest in alternate energy sources as a solution to its dependence on oil for generating electricity. On Oahu, Hawaiian Electric participated in a highly successful test of a 200-kilowatt wind turbine erected at Kahuku in 1981. That R&D project, funded and developed by the U.S. Department of Energy and the National Aeronautics and Space Administration, was the precursor of other wind energy projects destined for Oahu.

In 1982, a 3,000-kilowatt geothermal generator on the Big Island began feeding power into Hawaii Electric Light Company's system. The electricity thus generated was purchased by Helco from the Research Corporation of the University of Hawaii and was sold to Helco customers. Additional development of the Big Island's geothermal resources became a strong likelihood for the future.

Meanwhile, on the Valley Isle, Heco's other subsidiary, Maui Electric Company, began to look at the geothermal potential of that island.

Another alternate energy program in which Heco participated was Ocean Thermal Energy

Conversion (OTEC). The company also contributed to the investigation of a deep water cable that could some day connect Hawaii's individual island power systems.

In mid-1983, the company moved closer to its goal of diversifying its operations by creating a holding company, Hawaiian Electric Industries. Under the plan, Heco became a subsidiary of Hawaiian Electric Industries while retaining Meco and Helco as Heco subsidiaries. The new holding company held the prospect for more extensive participation in the development of alternate energy and other related ventures.

The formation of the holding company could be one of the most significant developments in the unique history of Hawaiian Electric Company, the nation's only electric utility to have operated under five forms of government—a monarchy, a provisional government, a republic, a territory, and finally, a state. Throughout those years, Hawaiian Electric has provided the basic ingredient of progress—electrical energy—by adapting to the needs of Hawaii, growing from a small enterprise to become one of Hawaii's largest companies, with $866 million in assets and $687 million in revenues in 1982.

Hawaiian Electric and Hawaiian Electric Industries—satisfying the energy requirements of Hawaii's people now and in the decades to come.

Dedicated to serving Hawaii sensitively and professionally

Hawaiian Memorial Services is the new name for Hawaii's most professional memorial service organization. Hawaiian Memorial Services has grown into a company which offers a wide range of services and pays great attention to detail. All facilities are designed to accommodate all faiths, and all staff members are well-versed in the desires and requirements of the various families and faiths. The business has established itself by providing professional, sensitive, personal service and taking special care that every detail of each family's wishes are carried out.

The story of Hawaiian Memorial Services began on Memorial Day, 1958, with the dedication of Hawaiian Memorial Park Ltd. to the people of Hawaii. Located on Windward Oahu, the Park is a beautiful non-sectarian garden sanctuary of over 72 acres, overlooking Kaneohe Bay and commanding a panoramic view of the awe-inspiring Koolau Mountains that sweep aloft in a protective backdrop.

The Park won immediate acceptance from Hawaii's families, and continues over the years to be the overwhelming choice of Island families.

In July 1961, the stockholders of Hawaiian Memorial Park Ltd. sold their interest to a newly formed company to be known as Hawaiian Memorial Park Cemetery Association. Today's Hawaiian Memorial Park Cemetery Association's leadership consists of outstanding trustees who are involved members of Oahu's community—A. William Barlow, chairman; John Henry Felix, Ph.D., president; and trustees Jerry Coron, John Farias Jr., Fritz Herman, Kinji Kanazawa and Warren K.K. Luke.

Eternal lights burn at the two entrance boulevards of Hawaiian Memorial Park as a tribute to the families served; one sees the beauty of velvety green lawns, splashing fountains and graceful trees and gardens. The arches of the administration building portray a harmony of architectural design with natural scenic surroundings. It is Hawaii's largest and most beautiful memorial park and has been acclaimed on national television as the most beautiful in the United States. Many of Hawaii's visitors enjoy Hawaiian Memorial Park as one of the Island's scenic locales.

Hawaiian Memorial Park commands a panoramic view of the awe-inspiring Koolau Mountains.

Some of Hawaii's most beloved and favorite entertainers have chosen Hawaiian Memorial Park cemetery for their family memorial estates, including Gabby Pahinui, Jesse Kalima, Van Andre Kalima, Willard Kalima, Joseph "Little Joe" Kekauoha Jr., Leland "Atta" Isaacs, famous hula dancer Iolani Luahine and Bella K. Richards, a famed hula teacher and dancer.

Maui Mortuary—Bulgo's

In October 1980, a wholly owned subsidiary of Hawaiian Memorial Life Plan, Ltd.—Hawaii Mortuaries, Ltd.—was formed to purchase Bulgo's Mortuary in Wailuku, Maui. Bulgo's has a long and interesting history dating from 1924 when Senator Charles Peters opened it as Peters Mortuary. Senator Peters sold the mortuary in 1950 to John Planesi Bulgo.

John Bulgo had no previous experience in the funeral field, but he saw an opportunity to sincerely assist people when they were in need. He went on to the San Francisco College of Embalming, where he received his degree, and returned to Maui.

John Bulgo operated Bulgo's until his untimely death in a car accident in 1957,

leaving his wife, Dorothy, and his three children, Joe, Anna Mae and Mary. Joe Bulgo, his only son, took over the management of the mortuary. Joe was a great innovator in the mortuary industry.

In 1964, Joe got very involved in Maui politics and the family decided that Mary and her husband Wilfred "Sonny" Estrella would manage the day-to-day operations of Bulgo's, with Joe returning to the mortuary in 1975.

Maui Mortuary—Norman's

In June 1981, Hawaii Mortuaries, Ltd. purchased Norman's Mortuary, originally owned by Norman and Connie Garcia.

Norman Garcia received his training from the U.S. Army Mortuary in Honolulu. After receiving his certification in 1948, Norman and his wife, Connie, moved to Maui and purchased property at the corner of Waiale Drive and Wells Street in Wailuku. There they built their mortuary, which opened on April 16, 1949.

Norman and Connie and their professionalism were well-accepted on Maui; their business increased rapidly, necessitating an enlargement of the facilities.

On May 1, 1979, Norman's Mortuary Inc. was sold to a group of investors who owned and operated Valley Isle Memorial Park on Maui.

Valley Isle Memorial Park

The Valley Isle Memorial Park property was developed in 1961 by two investors who sold it

Hawaiian Memorial Park, nationally acclaimed as the most beautiful memorial park in the United States.

a short time later to Union Investments, Inc., a Honolulu-based firm. In September 1971, another group of investors purchased Valley Isle, and in June 1981, it was acquired by Hawaiian Memorial Park Cemetery Association.

Borthwick Mortuary

In January 1982, Borthwick Mortuary, the finest and most professional in Hawaii, became the third mortuary to be purchased by Hawaii Mortuaries, Ltd.

William Borthwick, an established mortician, came to Honolulu in 1914 from Seattle. In 1916 he established Borthwick Mortuary on Chaplain Lane and Fort Street in downtown Honolulu. By 1925, there was great need for a larger facility and Borthwick Mortuary moved to Nuuanu and School streets. In 1932, the need for a newer and larger complex dictated another move, this time across the street.

That same year, William Borthwick turned the mortuary over to his oldest son, James Harold, who operated it until his death in 1943; then younger son, William Mendel Borthwick Sr. took over leadership. In 1958, William Mendel Jr. succeeded his father as manager of Borthwick Mortuary, always maintaining the family's values of the finest services possible.

In 1960, the Hawaii state government began the development of Hawaii's first freeway, the Lunalilo Freeway, and purchased the Borthwick Mortuary property. So once again, Borthwick Mortuary was on the move and finally settled at its present location at Maunakea and Kukui streets.

Additional divisions of Hawaii Mortuaries, Ltd. include Pacific Casket & Memorial

Services, providing the finest memorial products available in Hawaii; Vineyard Floral Services, offering beautiful and unique floral arrangements; and Vineyard Food Services, providing complete and varied menus. The casket, floral and food services offers Borthwick Mortuary clientele a rare convenience, with all needs arranged for in one convenient location. In April 1983, Borthwick Mortuary installed Hawaii's newest and most efficient crematory facility.

Hawaiian Memorial Life Plan, Ltd.

Hawaiian Memorial Services has a subsidiary that offers a very important program for Hawaii's families statewide—the Hawaiian Memorial Life Plan, Ltd., which offers the sale of pre-need memorial services.

Hawaiian Memorial Services is a very progressive firm and has seen the need to provide the state of Hawaii with a new technical and trade school. Plans are underway to develop the Pacific College of Life Sciences at Borthwick Mortuary. The college will fill a void in the higher education field by providing education in mortuary science and thanantology. The school will be fully accredited and will offer the widest range of mortuary-related science curricula.

Looking ahead, the trustees are in the process of expanding Hawaiian Memorial park Cemetery with the purchase of an additional 200 acres. With this acquisition, the Park will be able to offer more specially designated gardens that have been requested for many years. Also, a new floral facility and information center will be constructed.

In addition, plans are currently being developed for the expansion of Borthwick Mortuary with the addition of two new chapels at the corner of Maunakea Street and Vineyard Boulevard.

Hawaiian Memorial Services is increasingly striving for excellence in service, sensitivity and professionalism, and with its current leadership, is sure to provide Hawaii's families with the best possible memorial services.

Quality and innovation—formula for successful macadamia nut chocolate manufacturer

Macadamia nuts were first grown in Hawaii in 1882, but it wasn't until 1960 that the full potential of these delicate dessert nuts was realized. That's the year a young couple from Maui moved to Honolulu and started making Hawaiian Host chocolates by hand. Although sales at first were slow, Mr. and Mrs. Mamoru Takitani were certain that their secret combination of macadamia nuts and a special blend of chocolate would be a success.

For years the Takitanis had been fascinated with the unique flavor of the smooth shell macadamia nut. Orchards on Maui were small, but the annual fall harvest was large enough to give Mamoru and his wife Aiko a start. Experimenting with five kinds of chocolate, the Takitanis created a family formula that is still used today.

Like many *kama'ainas*, Mamoru Takitani was destined to assume control of the family business, Star Ice and Soda works. But in 1959 Mamoru negotiated a "deal" with his father. If he couldn't create a successful candy business in Honolulu within five years, he would return to Wailuku, Maui.

Creativity is the key to the success of Hawaiian Host Chocolates. Takitani learned early of the need for educating the public; sales to the locally based Fourth Division Marines in Makawao, Maui, revealed that few people had ever heard of a macadamia nut. The distinctive taste and high quality of his hand-made chocolates assured repeat business, but how could he entice people to buy their first box? Success depended on quality and innovation.

On January 1, 1960, Takitani purchased a small candy company in Kaimuki. As chief executive of a little-known company, Mamoru worked sixteen hours a day as candy maker, salesman, owner and janitor. Working twice as many hours as his six employees, Takitani set his goals high—sell 100 cases a day so he could afford to bring Aiko from Maui. Sales the first month were $800, with operating expenses of $1,600. It required many months of hard work before Aiko could join Mamoru, but courage and creativity eventually paid off.

Takitani was the first candy maker to use full-color photographs on his packaging; first to create a convenient carry-on box for visitors to take aboard departing airplanes; first to produce popular Hostess Mints; and

Aiko and Mamoru Takitani (left) stand proudly next to the tiki symbol of Hawaiian Host Chocolates during the grand opening dedication of new semi-automated headquarters in Honolulu in 1973.

the first person to use the internationally known Hawaiian tiki as a trademark. Business began to flourish, and soon Aiko joined Mamoru in his nonstop seven-days-a-week enterprise.

During the early years macadamia nuts were cooked in oil, but the flavor did not meet with Takitani's standards for quality. In 1975 he perfected a method of dry roasting which captures more of the delicate taste. The result is a macadamia nut chocolate that is in demand throughout the mainland United States, Hawaii and the Orient.

Takitani's energy and enthusiasm are responsible for the growth of Hawaiian Host. Beginning as a six-person neighborhood candy company, Hawaiian Host today employs 75 people at its modern semi-automated headquarters in Honolulu which opened in 1973. The original family formula remains the same, but the variety of products and purchasers has expanded dramatically. Hawaiian Host began with an attractive offering of ten types of chocolates; today this major manufacturer markets approximately 50 different types of macadamia nut chocolates and other candies throughout the world. Although macadamia nuts are currently produced in many countries, Takitani insists on using only the finest island nuts from Hilo and Kona on the Big Island of Hawaii.

Takitani's most recent innovation met with

instant success. Combining dry-roasted macadamia nuts with smooth caramel and his special blend of chocolate, he create Maui Caramacs. As with all Hawaiian Host products, Takitani selected the packaging colors and design, then named Caramacs after his home island of Maui.

Still active twelve to fourteen hours each day, Takitani is constantly experimenting with new ideas. Over twenty years of aggressive advertising, quality control and innovation have made Hawaiian Host Chocolates the leader in a highly competitive field. While often imitated, Takitani's personal touch can never be duplicated.

Hawaii's sophisticated telephone network is built on century-old foundation

Today, computer-directed electronic switching systems process large volumes of customer calls swiftly and accurately.

When Maui storekeeper Charles Dickey installed Hawaii's first telephone lines more than a century ago between his home and his store three miles distant, he prompted the start of a statewide telephone network that today encompasses nearly eight million miles of phone lines and cable.

"Mr. Dickey rightfully earned the title 'Father of the Telephone in Hawaii' by bringing the innovation to the islands in 1878, only two years after Bell had patented his invention," said Donald M. Kuyper, president of Hawaiian Telephone Company. "Back then, there were no such things as the horseless carriage or electric lights in Hawaii households, and it took 13 days to travel by ship to Hawaii from the West Coast. The idea of talking to someone miles away was exciting to some, who, like Mr. Dickey, could foresee a day when the telephone would play an integral role in Hawaii's growth."

During 1983, Hawaiian Telephone and its more than 4,700 employees statewide celebrated its 100th anniversary, reflecting on the accomplishments of the past while concentrating on the revolutionary changes—both in technology and regulation—now occurring in the telecommunications industry.

Hawaiian Telephone, originally known as Mutual Telephone, was incorporated in August 1883 under a charter granted by King David Kalakaua and his Privy Council. The new company was organized to compete with Hawaiian Bell, Oahu's first telephone company which had been formed three years earlier.

Until Mutual absorbed Hawaiian Bell in 1894, Oahu customers had to subscribe to two phone lines in order to call customers of both networks.

By 1928, the Oahu-based company had acquired the six major neighbor island phone companies. With the addition of Molokai's and Lanai's small, privately owned systems to the company network in 1931 and 1946, respectively, the present-day, six-island network of Hawaiian Telephone was completed. Mutual Telephone was re-named Hawaiian Telephone in 1954 and remains today as one of only three phone companies in America providing service to an entire state.

"During the early years, Mutual Telephone grew tremendously, not only in the number of telephones served, but in technology as well," said Kuyper. "In 1910, Honolulu became one of the first cities of its size to have an all-dial telephone system. In 1931, radiotelephone service was inaugurated, opening up communication between each of the islands and the mainland. In 1938, radiotelephone service was extended between Hawaii and Japan, beginning Hawaiian Telephone's role as the communications hub of the Pacific."

In the war years following Japan's attack on Pearl Harbor, the company and its employees were lauded by the military for the aid rendered in maintaining a communications network critical to the war effort.

Postwar population and economic growth brought widespread demand for telephone service, and the next several years saw many changes to the phone company's operations: microwave radio systems replaced the earlier VHF-AM and FM radiotelephone systems used for inter-island transmission; toll-free dialing was established on each of the islands (the island of Hawaii is the largest toll-free dialing area in the world); the first transpacific submarine cable was laid in 1957 in a $37 million joint venture between Hawaiian Telephone and AT&T. Subsequently, two additional cables expanded calling capacity to the U.S. mainland. And the two submarine cables laid from Hawaii to Japan and the Philippines in 1964 and 1975 tremendously improved the quality of communication to the Orient.

Hawaiian Telephone entered the space age in 1966 when the first "live" television program—a football game—was beamed to Hawaii from the mainland via satellite, opening the doors to the use of satellite circuits for phone, television and data transmission throughout the Pacific.

"Satellites, together with undersea cables, provide a diversity of transmission facilities, protecting our islands from being cut off from the rest of the world should one or the other system fail," said Kuyper.

In May 1967, Hawaiian Telephone merged with GTE Corporation, the nation's largest independent telephone company. The merger provided the company with advanced technological support and financial strength.

"Although we're proud of our century of accomplishments, we must continue to concentrate on developing telecommunication services to meet the needs of today's computer-based world," said Kuyper. "Hawaiian Telephone continues to be in the forefront of utilizing such advanced technological developments as optical fibers, digital technology, microprocessors and minicomputers in bringing the people of Hawaii closer to each other and their neighbors around the world."

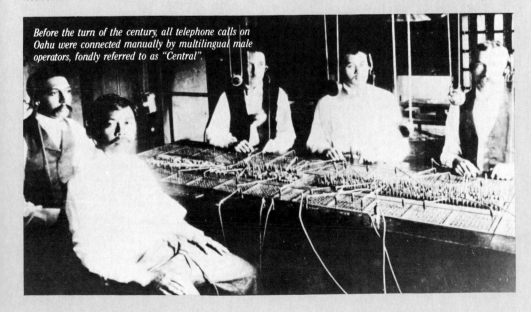

Before the turn of the century, all telephone calls on Oahu were connected manually by multilingual male operators, fondly referred to as "Central".

Serving Hawaii's people since 1898

"The building was plain and dark. The desks were wooden and very high. We all sat on stools and wore alpaca office coats. The main street was a dirt road. Every once in a while a sprinkler came through town to keep the dust down."

Although the scene portrayed is Dickensian, the location was downtown Honolulu in 1898.

The description was by Frederick W. Jamieson, whose career began in the original offices of Hawaii's first trust company where he was an office boy, and came to a close when he retired as a vice president in 1946.

Hawaiian Trust and Investment Company, Limited, opened for business on August 10, 1898, providing Honolulu's 30,000 residents with professional trusteeship and investment management of personal trusts. It was capitalized at $30,000. Its five founders were in their 20s and 30s: George R. Carter, Peter C. Jones, Clarence H. Cooke, F.C. Atherton and Robert W. Atkinson.

The fledgling caused hardly a stir in Honolulu's small business community, for the talk of the town was of annexation of Hawaii by the United States and the Spanish-American War. The former was accomplished and the latter ended just two days later, on August 12.

The company showed a profit from the beginning. The stockholder's report of January 31, 1899 showed a net profit of $5,600 and client assets under management valued at $250,000.

When the company acquired its present name in 1901, the pineapple industry had just begun. The posh new Moana Hotel opened Hawaii to tourism, offering adventurous visitors an elegant place to lay their heads.

Hawaiian Trust took the lead in pressing for legislation governing acts of fiduciaries, and by 1903 had drafted Hawaii's first trust bill. In November of that year, less than six weeks before the Wright brothers' first successful flight at Kitty Hawk, North Carolina, George R. Carter, a company founder and its manager and treasurer, became second governor of the Territory of Hawaii.

Carter was not the only company executive to become a part of Hawaii's history. Four of the founders—Jones, Cooke, Atherton and Atkinson, as well as the company's first vice president, E.A. Mott-Smith—were honored for their civic activities by a growing Honolulu when city streets were named after them.

Even during the Depression, Hawaiian Trust prospered. Elsewhere, fortunes were lost, reputations were ruined and breadlines pro-

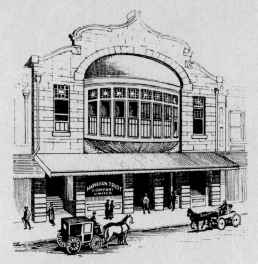

Hawaiian Trust's first home, 1898.

liferated. In 1930, the company declared a twelve percent dividend, and employees received a share of company profits equal to eleven percent of salaries paid—a profit-sharing program well ahead of its time.

Hawaiian Trust celebrated its golden anniversary in 1948. The 50 years of uninterrupted growth prompted then-president Peter McLean to remark, with considerable understatement, "the superiority of corporate management of trusts and estates over that of individual fiduciaries has been amply proved."

In 1957, Hawaiian Trust moved to a new nine-story building at King and Richards streets, opposite Iolani Palace. Two years later, Hawaii became the 50th state. When the firm moved to its present location in 1968, it was also a return to its original location. Among the buildings formerly on the block now occupied by the Financial Plaza of the Pacific was 923 Fort Street, Hawaiian Trust's first address.

Hawaiian Trust has never missed a dividend payment, a characteristic of a healthy and growing company. In recent years, its rate of growth has accelerated. A dramatic example is the value of client assets under management. The first stockholder's report showed this to be $250,000; when the firm celebrated its 80th anniversary in 1978, client assets had grown to $1.3 billion. Just five years later, that figure was $2.3 billion.

In the lifetime of the company, mankind has progressed from the horse-and-buggy age to the Space Age. Financial markets have changed enormously and the company has changed as well. In addition to managing the assets of individuals, it manages charitable trusts, pension and profit-sharing plans and corporate funds. Many of the services offered today did not exist several years ago. While Hawaiian Trust continues to develop new ways to serve tomorrow's needs, its basic role remains unchanged. It is, as it has been since 1898, a corporate fiduciary and money manager serving a unique role in a superior fashion.

Hawaiian Trust's present home, 1983.

The voice of Hawaii

"The station that best serves the public will be best served by the public," sums up the philosophy of K59 and Heftel Broadcasting Corporation. It is a philosophy that has proven both idealistic and pragmatic since the station was acquired on June 7, 1965, by Cec Heftel.

Heftel, who now represents Hawaii in the U.S. Congress, brought a new dynamism to Island broadcasting. When he purchased K59, then KGMB-AM, he also purchased KGMB-TV; the stations were seventh and third, respectively, in the Island market. Within six months both stations were number one in Hawaii and impacting heavily and positively on Island life.

Heftel Broadcasting Corporation made other swift and decisive moves, purchasing KPUA television on the Island of Hawaii; acquiring KGMB-FM and selling it as KGMQ-FM in 1976; selling KGMB-TV in April 1977; purchasing KULA-FM in January 1980.

On February 14, 1980, KGMB-AM became KSSK-AM, but continued to be popularly known as K59.

The popularity was no accident. A combination of provocative personalities, swift and accurate news coverage and a wide variety of entertainment packages meant that for many Islanders there was only one spot on their radio dial.

If listeners were accustomed to day-by-day pleasures from K59, they also knew that in times of stress it was the station to be listening to.

With K59 (then KGMB) the official news source for the Islands, Webley Edwards stood on top of the KGMB building at 1534 Kapiolani Boulevard and broadcast the news of the Japanese attack on Pearl Harbor, December 7, 1941.

In that tradition, K59 coverage of devastating Hurricane Iwa which ravaged the islands of Kauai and Oahu in late 1982 provided the most timely and comprehensive accounts of the situation and helped Islanders determine what actions to take during and after the hurricane.

Almost from the very beginning—and radio in Hawaii dates back to the turn of the century—it was K59, not only covering the news but sometimes making it, and all the while continuing to bring entertainment to its audience.

In 1932, when there were about 20,000 radio sets in the Islands, the station was supplying documentary reports on crime in Hawaii that were carried by the CBS network; that same year the station achieved 202 live remote broadcasts.

Eight years later the station would give complete coverage to the arrival of the first

Palm trees and towers of KGMB, circa 1954.

Clipper plane; would assist the Coast Guard in the search for famed aviatrix Amelia Earhart; and would describe the eruption of volcanic Mauna Loa on the Island of Hawaii so vividly it would be re-broadcast on the U.S. mainland.

In building an enviable reputation for news, entertainment and on-site coverage of special events, K59 also established a tradition of sports coverage and a special attention to ethnic affairs that included the first Japanese language program in Honolulu, on March 26, 1930.

Throughout its history the station became a fixture in the Islands, but also made its programming felt beyond the reefs. As KGMB the station was heard "loud and clear" on the Pacific Coast by spring, 1930. The following year the station was picked up in Kotzebue, Alaska, 30 miles from the Arctic Circle. In 1932, when the station joined the CBS network, it helped enhance Hawaii's growing popularity.

Adding to that image was "Night in Hawaii," a 35-minute program heard on 97 CBS stations in Canada and across the U.S. mainland. In October 1935, KGMB broadcast the first of the immensely popular "Hawaii Calls" programs to the mainland.

Ownership changes were inevitable in the station's relatively long history, and in January 1960, the *Honolulu Star-Bulletin,* a daily newspaper, purchased ownership of the station, selling it two years later to a group of local businessmen.

Acquisition of the station by Heftel in 1965 injected new life into the station, gave it more impetus toward community service, and saw a quick and decisive resurgence to the station's dominant position in Island radio.

Harnessing high technology to benefit the environment and community

What do you do when you have two kids in college, one in high school, a mortgage and all the usual expenses, and suddenly find yourself out of a job?

If you have over 25 years of engineering experience under your belt with the Territory and State of Hawaii and City and County of Honolulu, and you're ahead of your time, you make a "mid-life career change." That's what Sam O. Hirota did when he formed the company known today as one of Hawaii's leading engineering firms, and certainly the most advanced when it comes to high technology.

Back in 1962, Hirota went overnight from the position of deputy director of the State Department of Transportation—tunneler through mountains, diverter of streams, builder of airports, dredger of harbors, surveyor of virtually all he beheld—to just plain unemployed. The fateful night was election night, when John A. Burns ousted William F. Quinn as governor. Out went the old people; in came the new.

Hirota gave the new administration a hand in effecting a smooth transition before going into business for himself on May 1, 1963. He offered Civil Engineering & Surveying Services, a one-man show in a one-room office at 547 Halekauwila Street, Honolulu.

Hirota's first job was designing an interior

Computer graphics display.

road for Punahou School, a decided contrast to the superhighways and bridges of yore. By 1964, he was invited to form a joint venture with Parsons, Brinckerhoff, Quade & Douglas of New York to work on a Navy project in Guam. Later, they formed another joint venture to handle a design-management commission from the State of Hawaii regarding Interstate Route H-3.

Meanwhile, Dennis Hirota had earned his Ph.D. in civil engineering and served three years in the U.S. Air Force. He returned to Hawaii and joined the company in 1971.

By the time the company was ten years old,

it had grown to 33 employees, become incorporated and moved to the Amfac Building in downtown Honolulu. In 1977, Sam O. Hirota, Inc. moved once again to the present headquarters at 345 Queen Street where it occupies the entire fifth floor.

The firm engages in a wide range of surveying and engineering projects throughout Hawaii, the Trust Territories and the South Pacific. These include *property boundary surveys and maps* for residential lots, hotel and business parcels in Waikiki and downtown, hundreds of acres of sugar cane land in Kilauea, Kauai, and macadamia nut orchards in Kau, Hawaii; *hydrographic surveying and mapping* of Pearl Harbor, Nawiliwili Harbor, Samoa Beach Erosion Control, Honolulu and Hilo Harbors; *photogrammetric mapping* of Honolulu International Airport area (Hickam to Sand Island), Piilani Highway (Kihei to Ulupalakua) and Hilo-mauka; *subdivisions* of Princeville, Pukalani and Makena View Estates; *public works,* such as Piilani and Honoapiilani Highways, Arizona Memorial Shoreside Facilities; *flood control* of Anolani, Honokowai and Iao streams; site civil engineering for *shopping centers, condominiums, hotels and office buildings,* namely Pearl City, Windward City, Windward Mall, Waikiki Shopping Plaza, Craigside, Honolulu Tower, Pacific Trade Center, new Honolulu District Court, Central Pacific Bank, Queen Street Building, Hilton Hawaiian Village Tapa Towers, Marriott Kaanapali Hotel, Hale Kaheka, Hanalei Plantation, Makena Prince Hotel, Admiral Thomas, Canterbury Place and Sheraton Princeville Hotel.

Projects may include anything from telescope placement on Mauna Kea to hazardous waste disposal. Versatility is a company strong point.

Sam O. Hirota, Inc. has always used the latest digital and electronic equipment, often being the first to introduce it to Hawaii. A Wang 2200 computer was acquired in 1975. As Dennis Hirota became more interested in computerizing operations, a DEC 11/780 VAX super mini-computer was added in 1979.

As this medium-sized, twenty-year-old engineering firm enters its third decade, the industrial society has been pronounced "dead," and the age of information and high technology is acknowledged. Nobody at Sam O. Hirota, Inc. is feeling much future shock, however. The company's principals have already seen the future, looked it square in the eye and long ago embraced it.

Sam O. Hirota, Inc. site civil engineering project, Windward Mall Shopping Center.

Serving Hawaii with a better way to bank

It was 1929. Lawrence M. Judd was governor of the territory of Hawaii, and John H. Wilson, mayor of Honolulu. Of the territory's 357,000 residents, 56,000 toiled on plantations.

Liberty Theater in Honolulu had just been reconfigured to accommodate "moving pictures." The brand-new Pawaa and Palama Theaters had been designed from the beginning to show the current rage in entertainment.

New homes were sprouting in Manoa and Waialae, and on Bingham and Dowsett tract land.

But all was not idyllic in paradise. The erratic New York stock market was worrying local business. Production on plantations was slowing, and uncertainty prevailed. The market was soon to topple destructively into the throes of a long and agonizing depression.

One group of local businessmen, however, saw a bright future ahead and expressed confidence in the country's ability to pull out of its economic problems. They staked $8,000 in capital, set up headquarters in the Union Trust Building on Alakea Street and opened the doors of Honolulu Mutual Building and Loan Company, Ltd. on August 5. On the first day of business, W.G. Matthias of South King Street subscribed to a $500 share account with an agreement to deposit $35 per month and became owner of savings account number one. Two weeks later, the company made mortgage loan number one, to A.H. Hanna of Hibiscus Drive. Thus from the very first weeks, Honolulu Mutual already began fulfilling its stated aim and purpose :

"To encourage the formation and practice of thrift and systematic savings, and

To stimulate among members the desire for homeownership and to supply the necessary funds to aid every family to procure a home."

At the end of five months, the fledgling company had built up its assets to $15,766 and ranked last among the 21 savings and loans in the territory.

President William Borthwick believed in his company and was committed to helping people achieve financial independence. "The security back of this savings organization is the safest security on earth," he would say. "It is the earth itself."

Savings agents went from door to door and through island plantation camps to solicit and collect deposits. People saved systemat-

The company depicted asset growth from year to year through unique pyramid ads, such as this 1942 mid-year report, six months after Pearl Harbor.

Photo courtesy of Bernice P. Bishop Museum

In 1949, Honolulu Federal Savings purchased the Alexander Bros. Building (at right) at the corner of Merchant and Alakea streets and established its headquarters there. Its present main office building was erected on the site in 1966. At left in this 1941 photo is the old Theo. H. Davies Building.

ically—even when life was most difficult— undoubtedly influenced by savings promotion manager George C. Knapp and his agents, who exuded confidence. By 1939, Honolulu Building and Loan had more savings members than any other savings and loan in the territory. Assets had grown to $775,029 and the company moved into new quarters at 928 Bethel Street, "across from the Commercial Club."

The company grew quickly, passing its older, established competitors along the way. In 1949, with assets over $8 million, Honolulu Savings and Loan moved to the familiar Merchant Street location.

The company has always been a leader in service to its customers. It was one of the first savings and loans in Hawaii to open branch offices. In the 1960s it was the first to

make condominium loans and made more home loans than the state's two largest banks. Honfed was also the first financial institution locally to establish an on-line computer center to provide instantly updated savings account information for its customers.

One far-reaching innovation was the introduction of the Honolulu Federal Passcard in 1974. This magnetically encoded plastic card became the key to the convenience of Lulu automatic tellers, Instant Transfer terminals at shopping centers and supermarkets, discounts from a catalog of local merchants, periodic statements, Telephone Bill Payment Service and Lulu Bell, for pushbutton banking from home.

In 1978 Honolulu Federal surpassed $1 billion in total assets. The dreams of its original founders had come to fruition— Honfed had proved that strength and growth were the direct result of helping the people of Hawaii.

Today, over 800 people work in the various specialties at Honolulu Federal and its service corporations, including Home Properties, Inc. (real estate development), Advanced Computer Systems (financial data processing and related services such as automatic teller network switching and plastic card production), Tel-Tec Hawaii (tele-processing and electronic maintenance) and Home Security Insurance, Inc. (mortgage life and disability insurance, personal life and health insurance).

Promoting thrift and homeownership to help Hawaii's people achieve financial independence remains the company's aim and purpose. Honolulu Federal stands ready to meet the challenges of the years ahead and to serve the community which has made it Hawaii's largest savings and loan.

HONOLULU BUILDING & LOAN CO., LTD.

A Mutual Savings and Loan Institution

MEMBER.
FEDERAL HOME LOAN BANK SYSTEM
U. S. SAVINGS & LOAN LEAGUE

318 BETHEL STREET
(Across the street from Bethel St. Postoffice)
TELEPHONE 4788-4371 • HONOLULU, T. H.

Safety! plus Service! plus Progress! plus Victory!

June 30th, 1942	$1,512,547.68
December 31, 1941	$1,398,244.00
December 31, 1940	$996,028.90
December 31, 1939	$775,029.28
December 31, 1938	$668,278.47
December 31, 1937	$495,768.63
December 31, 1936	$309,414.78
December 31, 1935	$209,242.77
December 31, 1934	$142,454.42
December 31, 1933	$100,468.29
December 31, 1932	$89,960.40
December 31, 1931	$66,052.18
Dec. 31, 1930	$22,574.38
Dec. 31, 1929	$15,765.82

Built on
a Safe
and Sound
Foundation

Organized
August 5, 1929

With Confidence in the Future, and the Community We Serve, we announce:
Another Period of—Outstanding Progress!

The HONOLULU BUILDING AND LOAN COMPANY, LIMITED, is a member of the FEDERAL HOME LOAN BANK SYSTEM and operates on a Mutual Profit-Sharing basis.

There are no preferred shareholders. Dividends have been credited semi-annually without a miss.

The security back of this institution is the safest on earth—it is the earth itself!

WM. BORTHWICK, President
GEO. C. KNAPP, Vice President-Manager
MAX W. MOODY, Secy.-Treas.

EMMA ROSE TAVARES, Office Secretary
ROBT. S. TANGA, Office Accountant
JAMES N. NAKAMURA, Asst. Accountant

CAMERON & JOHNSTONE, Auditors

233

Perpetuating the spirit of its founding fathers

It was mid-1918 in downtown Honolulu when seven men—Stanley Taylor, Stanley McKenzie, Charles Marquez, Robert McLean, Percy Deverill, Ernest Clarke and Charles Crane—organized Honolulu Paper Company, Limited. All except Taylor were large users of paper and allied products, and their combined business represented a considerable volume in those days.

The founders' original philosophy was to operate a diversified business in the fields of paper, stationery and general office supplies and equipment and to cover those fields "intelligently, adequately and thoroughly." They felt that as long as businesses existed, whether times were good or bad, offices would consume supplies.

Operating out of the old Smoot and Steinhauser offices at the corner of Merchant and Alakea, with Charles Marquez as president, five employees achieved a $132,000 sales volume in 1919. With paper distribution as a solid foundation, the company barely lived through the short depression during the early 1920s. The owners therefore set out on the road to diversification and expansion.

In 1925, among the company's first acquisitions was Thrums, whose business was similar but also carried office machines, furniture and supplies. With the development of these new lines and rapid business growth, the offices were moved to the Young Hotel on Bishop Street, and large warehouses were purchased on Queen and Cooke streets. The company continued to thrive throughout the late 1920s and weathered the Great Depression successfully and, amazingly, without any losses.

The rugged 1930s brought more acquisitions and the election of Stanley Taylor as the company's third president. Under his leadership, in 1934 the company grossed $615,000. In 1939, all of the company's operations were consolidated via relocation to space on Ala Moana Boulevard and South Street, the site upon which the Stanley Taylor building was later erected in 1957.

World War II proved to be a catalyst for further expansion as the controlling interest in a major Honolulu paper business and its Hilo stationery operation was purchased. With their eyes on the outer island market, the owners formed Maui Paper Company in Kahului in 1948.

The 1950s brought the registration of Honolulu Paper's capital stock with the Securities and Exchange Commission, listing of the stock on the Honolulu Stock Exchange and last, but not least, in 1959—statehood.

(Photo courtesy of Hawaii State Archives)

Then.

Statehood led to expanded services and the opening of the Ala Moana Center retail store dba Hopaco Stationers, Inc.

The turbulent 1960s turned out to be quite inspiring. With Maui Paper doing well, a branch was opened in Lihue, Kauai, in 1963. By 1964, Honolulu Paper had streamlined its framework to include Hopaco Stationers and Maui Paper and, most importantly, had firmly established its business, having sold well in excess of $8 million for several years. These accomplishments exhibited an impressive track record for a company that had started with five employees. Boise Cascade Corporation recognized this, and in 1964 negotiated a merger with Honolulu and Maui Paper com-

Now.

panies, whose names were collectively changed to HOPACO. In connection with the merger, Maui operations relocated to a new facility. The following year, the third and final outer island distribution center was opened in Hilo.

The 1970s were heralded by the opening of a new retail outlet in Hilo's Kaiko'o Mall. The retail aspect of the business proved to be profitable, and more retail stores were opened in Pearlridge Center, on Paa Street and downtown on King Street and, in 1981, in Kahului's Kaahumanu Shopping Center.

In 1978, a move to more modern and spacious quarters in the Mapunapuna light industrial area allowed centralization of the administrative and sales staff and expansion of the company's office products warehouse.

Today, with over 200 employees, distribution centers for fine paper, industrial and office products, retail outlets on all major Hawaiian islands and a sustained record of positive and successful growth, HOPACO has earned recognition as the leader in its field. In 1983, the company expects to more than triple its 1964 sales. HOPACO has certainly perpetuated the spirit of its founding fathers in establishing a diversified distribution business to intelligently, adequately and thoroughly fulfill business needs in Hawaii; in fact, HOPACO represents an important segment of Boise Cascade Corporation, one of the largest forest products companies in the country.

A heritage of 100 years of living and working in the Islands

The year was 1883. While most islanders were preparing for the coronation of Hawaii's king, David Kalakaua, a small group of men formed a company incorporated by the Territory of Hawaii as InterIsland Steam Navigation Company.

A century later, the company—now known as InterIsland Resorts, Ltd.—is considered a pioneer in the industry.

In the beginning, the company's nine ships hauled more freight than passengers between the islands. However, the few passengers who braved the choppy voyage suggested bigger and better things to come.

The volcano, Hawaii's premier attraction, drew more and more people to the Big Island. By 1920 People's Garage, later purchased by the company and renamed Hawaii Transportation Company, was operating four-day, three-night horse and buggy tours around the Island of Hawaii. The following year the company gained control of Volcano House to provide lodging for their passengers touring the volcano area.

By 1922 tourism was considered a viable industry. The Hawaii Tourist Bureau visitor count that year totaled almost 10,000. By 1926 the number reached close to 16,000.

In 1928 the company built the Kona Inn on the beach adjoining Hulihee Palace in Kailua Kona—contrary to advice by local residents who considered the area uncomfortably warm. Kona Inn proved an immediate success and the company operated this hotel until 1978.

In 1929 the company took to the skies with Inter-Island Airways. Service began with two S-38 twin-engine seven-passenger Sikorskys, plus a six-passenger Bellanca cabin monoplane used for sightseeing and to educate people to the ease and safety of air travel. The new service cut travel time from Honolulu to Hilo from fifteen hours to a speedy three hours and fifteen minutes.

The company now offered travelers complete service: passage to the Big Island via steamship or air, ground transportation and tours as well as hotel accommodations.

World War II brought changes. Tourism came to a halt. The steamships were leased to the government and Hawaii Transportation Company hauled freight instead of passengers. The airline, now called Hawaiian Airlines, went under military control.

However, the Blaisdell Hotel in Honolulu, the Naniloa in Hilo and the Kona Inn profited well from military business.

Two weeks prior to December 7, 1941 the Blaisdell Hotel took delivery of 350 cases of liquor, more than a year's supply. There was no bar in town more popular than the Palm

Floating like a magnificent starfish at the edge of Keauhou Bay, Kona Surf is unquestionably one of Hawaii's finest luxury resorts.

Garden. The hotel fared as well. Servicemen rented rooms at all hours to rest between flights to battle areas.

Soldiers training on the Big Island turned the Naniloa from a white elephant into a real moneymaker. Kona Inn also profited.

With the end of the war the steamships were returned to the company, Hawaiian Airlines became a civilian operation again and Hawaii Transportation Company returned to carrying tourists instead of freight.

The Kona Inn, Kailua.

In 1950 the company underwent a government directed corporate dismantling resulting in three separate companies: Hawaiian Airlines; Overseas Terminals, a freight hauling and barge operation; and InterIsland Resorts, operating resort hotels and ground transportation services.

Under the direction of W. Dudley Child Jr., president, a period of accelerated growth began in 1960 and continued into the 1980s. Today, InterIsland Resorts operates more than 2,000 luxury hotel rooms on the neighbor islands with extensive meeting and convention capacity, and Gray Line Hawaii, Ltd., the largest statewide ground transportation system serving the travel industry.

A tradition of service to Hawaii's international people

International Savings was founded as the International Building and Loan Association, Ltd., on January 6, 1925. Back then, when opportunities for the people of Hawaii were not as abundant as they are today, a group of local businessmen shared a mutual concern for the local residents, many of whom were immigrants shut out from the "American dream".

Despite their varied ethnic and cultural backgrounds, these people shared a common plight—the lack of financial resources necessary to meet the demands of modern society. In response to these needs, Masayuki Tokioka, Wade Warren Thayer and a farsighted group of enterprising Honolulu businessmen created International Savings.

These men established a financial institution whose policy was to serve the people of Hawaii by giving them security and a reasonable rate of return for their savings deposits. And, recognizing that the home is the foundation of family security in America, International Savings' founders also helped to make the privilege of home ownership available to Hawaii residents of all incomes.

When International Savings first opened its doors for business, Hawaii had been a territory for only 25 years. Wallace Rider Farrington was governor, and Calvin Coolidge was the president of the United States. In the years that followed, International Savings continued to serve the people of Hawaii through the stock market crash of 1929, the following Great Depression and World War II.

In December 1935, International became a member of the Federal Home Loan Bank. Since October 27, 1936, all accounts with the company have been insured by the Federal Savings and Loan Insurance Corporation, an agency of the U.S. government. In 1956, the name of the company was changed to International Savings and Loan Association, Ltd.

All during these years the financial requirements of Hawaii's people continued to change, and International Savings continued to grow to meet the more sophisticated needs of its clients.

After 57 years of service to the people of Hawaii, International Savings embarked on a historic new era in 1982, when, as the result of a proxy vote by its customers, it became

the first savings and loan in the state of Hawaii to convert to a stock company. Conversion to a stock savings and loan expanded International's powers and access to sources of revenue that will allow it to continue to provide comprehensive financial services to its customers in the future. Besides improving International Savings' equity position, stock sales raised the capital necessary for increased mortgage lending activity, and for providing better and more efficient savings services.

Today, under the direction of Lionel Y. Tokioka, chairman of the board and chief executive officer, International Savings is a strong and widely respected financial institution. It has prospered from a one-office association to a stock corporation with assets of $400 million. And despite the many changes that have occurred over the years, International Savings has not lost touch with its beginnings, its original purpose—its dedication to serving the financial needs of all of the residents of Hawaii.

Total transportation services company connecting Hawaii to the rest of the world

In the 1950s, statehood was in the wind for Hawaii.

Its promise meant bigger government, bigger business and an upsurge in population. In shipping, containerization was about to supersede palletization as the cargo innovation of the era, calling for new types of equipment and a new marketing approach.

During the summer of 1958, Richard T. Asato, current chairman, and two other small truck operators joined together to incorporate Island Movers, Inc. The original fleet consisted of about twelve used trucks, some of them World War II vintage.

In 1960, two of the original stockholders sold their interest in Island Movers to start their own hauling companies. The company, however, continued to expand, and in the mid-'60s, current president, Donald M. Takaki, began his career in transportation by joining Island Movers. The expansion of Island Movers was dramatic. With an experienced truck operator and a young aggressive executive at the helm, Island Movers entered strongly into the household goods moving field. The expansion did not stop there. With the ownership combination of Richard Asato and Donald Takaki, Island Movers—using a blend of aggressive sales and marketing and a large measure of good personal service—is today Honolulu's largest motor carrier, providing the community with local trucking, moving and public warehousing, as well as freight forwarding and door-to-door moving services on a national and international basis.

Island Movers today operates more than 150 pieces of equipment, employs approximately 200 personnel and utilizes about ten acres of real estate to house its operations on Oahu and Maui. The Maui branch, located in the modern Kahului Industrial Park, is the first neighbor island operation for the company. Branches on the rest of the major islands are contemplated in the near future.

The modern-day Island Movers deals in freight and property transportation services in every dimension. Unlike its beginning role as a truck transporter limited to hauling cargo within the confines of Honolulu, the company today deals with the transport and forwarding of cargo throughout the world. With its own forwarding systems and those of which the company is a part, Island Movers has truly evolved its service capabilities into a modern, sophisticated transportation network.

The potential of Island Movers is just beginning to be realized. With young experienced management personnel in all areas of its operation, Island Movers will continue to expand its role as a total transportation services company, servicing the entire state and connecting Hawaii to the rest of the world.

From a fleet of twelve used trucks, Island Movers is today Honolulu's largest motor carrier, utilizing about ten acres of real estate to house its operation.

Island Movers today operates more than 150 pieces of equipment.

Island Movers, delivering cargo dockside, plays its role in a worldwide system of freight forwarding.

A royal Hawaiian heritage inspired this modern-day medical center

Kapiolani/Children's Medical Center in Honolulu had its beginnings almost 100 years ago in a simple Hawaiian cottage surrounded by palm and kiawe trees where no more than seven women at a time could give birth.

In 1983 that 100-year-old maternity hospital became officially and legally merged with Kauikeolani Children's Hospital to make Kapiolani/Children's Medical Center one of the most comprehensive health care facilities in the Pacific Basin to specialize in maternal, gynecological, newborn, child psychiatric and pediatric care.

Today's modern, eleven-story facility with its seven adjacent buildings is a far cry from the simple cottage site of the first Kapiolani Maternity Home in 1890. The medical center's story begins in 1874 when King Kalakaua and Queen Kapiolani ascended the Hawaiian throne. Dedicated to a royal motto, *Hooulu a Hoola Lahui,* "to propagate and perpetuate the race," the king established a society to carry out his royal mandate and appointed his wife to serve as its first president.

It was the queen's personal dream during the next ten years to establish a maternity home for poor and neglected Hawaiian women, who were long accustomed to giving birth to their young in very primitive conditions. With the help of nine *kamaaina* or native-born women from the Hooulu a Hoola

Kapiolani Maternity Home was a simple, rambling, Hawaiian-style cottage surrounded by a lush, tropical garden when it first opened in Honolulu in 1890.

Kauikeolani Children's Hospital, which opened in 1909, was the only hospital in Hawaii devoted exclusively to the care of children of all races from birth to age 21.

Lahui Society, the queen concentrated all her efforts on fulfilling this dream.

In 1890 the Kapiolani Maternity Home opened in a low, rambling cottage belonging to the queen's sister, Princess Kekaulike, on the corner of Beretania and Makiki Streets in Honolulu. At first the Hawaiian women were suspicious of the new hospital and reluctant to make use of its facilities, even though they were provided free of charge. Only six babies were born in the home during its first year of operation. However, with careful coaxing and persistent education, the new mothers soon began to change their opinions of the queen's maternity home.

The demand for the hospital's services grew steadily over the next few years. In 1917 the home was moved into a larger residence belonging to the August Dreier family of Honolulu. However, with nearly 500 babies being born each year in the facility, the need

for an expanded, up-to-date hospital became critical.

In 1929 a new, 50-bed Kapiolani Maternity and Gynecological Hospital opened on the medical center's present site—just 30 years after Queen Kapiolani's death. Meanwhile, another local hospital was experiencing growing pains of its own.

Kauikeolani Children's Hospital was founded by Governor Sanford B. Dole and Dr. James R. Judd in 1907 as a voluntary, nonprofit institution. When the stately, two-story building was opened in 1909, the board of directors christened it after Emma Kauikeolani Wilcox, the wife of the hospital's primary benefactor, Albert Wilcox. The name was well-chosen. In Hawaiian Kauikeolani means "healing light for the young." The hospital was the only facility in Hawaii devoted exclusively to the care of children of all races from birth to age 21.

The events of December 7, 1941 at nearby Pearl Harbor greatly affected both hospitals. The annual birth rate at Kapiolani Hospital doubled when wartime blackouts made home deliveries impossible, and plans to expand the children's hospital were promptly shelved so that the medical community could focus on the war effort. It wasn't until 1950 that the new 80-bed Kauikeolani Children's Hospital could be built, incorporating a wide range of new services, including those of psychologists, speech and hearing therapists, educators and sociologists.

With the increase in services came the need for more space in which to accommodate the growing number of patients. The medical community spent the next several years assessing the health care needs of Hawaii's population, and came up with a plan in 1972 to merge the two facilities with the University of Hawaii's School of Medicine departments of pediatrics, obstetrics/gynecology and child psychiatry.

Founded upon the traditions of these two fine institutions, Kapiolani/Children's Medical Center was inaugurated on September 1, 1976. Its administrators and medical staff take pride in providing a multitude of family-centered programs and services that address the total needs of the individual patient within the family unit.

Indeed, Kapiolani/Children's Medical Center has come a long way from that little cottage nestled in Princess Kekaulike's garden. From six births a year to more than 6,000—wouldn't the queen be proud?

Pioneer craftsman for over 46 years

Robert M. Kaya, founder and chairman of the board.

Robert M. Kaya Builders, Inc. is embarking on its 46th year of providing quality building construction services for the city of Honolulu and the state of Hawaii. The firm traces its humble beginnings through its founder and present chairman of the board, Robert M. Kaya, who in August 1937 started a small, one-man carpenter shop on McCully Street.

The 1930s were difficult economic times and for four months no business could be generated. But with fortitude and determination, Robert Kaya persevered, where others would have given up. Slowly but surely, business began to come in—primarily small repair and renovation jobs, but Kaya completed them with exceptional service and high quality. As a result, word-of-mouth referrals began a gradual and steady growth of home improvement work for Robert M. Kaya Builder until World War II.

By 1941, Bob Kaya had a staff of four people. His first major project was the building of his own new home. He was so proud of his accomplishment that he decided to have a housewarming party on December 7, 1941. Ironically, Pearl Harbor was bombed that morning with mortar shells exploding all around, creating fires everywhere. Bob's new home was spared from the flames.

During World War II, Kaya served the U.S. Government Engineering Department by build-ing government structures and bomb shelters for residents.

Through the 1950s, Robert M. Kaya Builders enjoyed impressive growth in home improvement work and new home construction; the firm also constructed school buildings and performed major repair projects for the military. In 1956, Robert M. Kaya organized the Home Builders Association of Hawaii—known today as the Building Industry Association of Hawaii—to serve the needs of the industry and public. Kaya served as its first president and is credited as the "founder" by all in the industry.

With statehood for Hawaii, the decade of the 1960s saw Robert M. Kaya Builders diversify its building construction services. Expansion into the commercial, government and institutional sectors and subdivision housing took place. Incorporation took place in March 1965, paving the way for more growth in the '70s.

Because of the emphasis on quality construction at reasonable and competitive prices, the firm maintained its growth in the 1970s and garnered many awards of excellence for quality construction. Presently, Robert M. Kaya Builders is one of the major "quality" builders for residential, commercial and institutional new construction or renovation projects. The firm contracts work from small repairs and renovations to multimillion dollar projects and provides equal services and attention on all. The smaller jobs, in fact, were the stimuli to Kaya's growth. For that reason, the firm feels the importance of the small jobs to its continued growth.

As a monument to the company's skills as a builder stand the restored Iolani Palace, Tensho Kotai Temple building, Ward Centre and Manoa Marketplace shopping centers and numerous custom residences at Diamond Head, Waialae, Makiki and Manoa and subdivision homes at Hawaii Kai, Windward and Leeward Oahu.

Robert M. Kaya Builders, Inc. is headquartered at 1087 Dillingham Boulevard with 36 employees. It is a closely held corporation. Chairman of the board is Robert M. Kaya and president is James M. Higa.

Gross sales for 1983 are projected at $12 million, which will sustain or create employment for approximately 200 tradesmen among suppliers, subcontractors and equipment dealers.

Iolani Palace interior and exterior repairs and alterations were done by Robert M. Kaya Builders, Inc.

Reflections on the childhood of a new industry

On December 1, 1952, KGMB television made history in Hawaii with the first telecast in the islands. On that first evening, viewers saw interviews with many of those who had worked to make the new medium a reality in Hawaii, followed by a mix of shows that featured Gene Autry, Lilli Palmer and Hopalong Cassidy.

The days that followed included a range of programming—from test patterns in the afternoons, which aided retailers in lining up and adjusting sets, to a rich variety of mainland shows from the three major networks in the evenings.

Originally owned by the Hawaiian Broadcasting System, with J. Howard Worrall as president, KGMB television and its sister radio station became properties of the Honolulu *Star-Bulletin* in 1960. In 1965, Cec Heftel bought the properties, which became known as Pacific Broadcasting Company. The company name was later changed to Heftel Broadcasting Corporation.

With the purchase of superior color equipment and the addition of such top personalities as Bob Sevey, KGMB television moved quickly into the dominant position in the marketplace. The news department was expanded and local programming increased. Checkers and Pogo and Super Spy McPig became household names. And Hawaii Production Center was formed.

In November 1966, Hawaii entered the satellite age. For the first time, viewers were able to see live, mainland programming beamed to the islands by a primitive satellite called "Lani Bird." Even the satellite tests prompted banner headlines in the local newspapers. The test signals consisted of promotional material for the program "Flipper." The next morning, Hawaiians watched the Notre Dame-Michigan State football game, and on Sunday they saw their first live NFL game on KGMB television.

In 1976, KGMB began broadcasting the CBS Evening News with Walter Cronkite, becoming the first television station in Hawaii to bring satellite news to the viewing public on a regularly scheduled, daily basis.

In 1977, Lee Enterprises of Davenport, Iowa, purchased KGMB television. Under the auspices of Lee Enterprises, KGMB has grown and diversified. Hawaii Production Center, widely recognized for award-winning commercial work, attracts clientele from the national and international markets as well as locally.

Lee Productions, a division of KGMB formed in 1981, is responsible for numerous special programs, one of which, "Beyond the Great Wall: Journey to the End of China," won the first George Foster Peabody Award ever presented to a commercial television station in Hawaii.

KGMB also boasts the first San Francisco regional Emmy Award presented to a television station in Hawaii, given for the entertainment special, "RAP's Hawaii."

Late in 1982, another division of KGMB was opened—Lee Color, a full service color print laboratory, offering processing service to professionals and amateurs, agencies and their clients.

KGMB has lived, and been a part of, the history of the television business. It continues to be part of that history as it keeps pace with the miracles of modern technology and continues to write new chapters of its own. From the flickering, faint black and white images of the '50s to color and satellite service in the '60s to daily satellite programming service in the '70s, KGMB now looks forward to the '80s and beyond. Plans are now under way to bring Hawaii its first same-day, all-satellite, commercial network programming.

The films and kinescopes have been replaced by the most modern videotape equipment. The news-film processor is gone, replaced by modern Electronic News Gathering equipment. The film splicers gather dust in a closet while technicians ply their magic with the latest in computerized video editors. Now, letters and numbers flash on the screen in a brilliant array of colors, and pictures spin, twist and whirl at the touch of a button on the digital effects bank. The first faltering steps have become long, confident strides.

Though the business of television has changed, one thing has remained constant at KGMB. The thread that has tied it all together, and will carry it into the future, is the people of KGMB—people who have always felt that they do it best . . . but still long to do it better.

KGMB has kept pace with technology. Today's equipment provides not only the highest standard of quality, but versatility and flexibility as well.

KGMB has grown some in 30 years, and Honolulu along with it.

The first in the Pacific is the first into the future of radio in Hawaii

It was May 11, 1922, at 10:57 a.m. on the third floor of the Advertiser Building when Marion Mulrony, manager of KGU, spoke a few "hello's" into a hastily assembled transmitter and KGU became the first official station to broadcast in the territory of Hawaii. KGU's officialness had already been substantiated when it was awarded the 32nd broadcast license in the United States. Signing the license was Secretary of Commerce Herbert Hoover.

Being first is something of a tradition at KGU, a tradition that has continued for over six decades without interruption. KGU's list of "firsts" reads like a page out of world and national history.

On March 4, 1929, Hawaii listeners heard the inauguration of President Herbert Hoover. This was the first important transoceanic shortwave broadcast in Hawaii.

In 1931, the year KGU joined NBC (a relationship that lasted more than 40 years— Talk Radio KGU AM 76 is now part of CBS), a crew from KGU journeyed to the Big Island and laid three miles of lines by hand (the longest distance in the history of broadcasting at that time) to record the eruption of Mauna Loa. They even dropped a microphone down into the fire pit for a dramatic record of one of nature's most destructive events. The broadcast was fed to NBC, and the results brought praise and wonder from every state in the union and Canada.

On July 28, 1934, President Roosevelt addressed the nation via KGU, marking the first time in history that a U.S. president

Home of KGU studios for 61 uninterrupted years.

addressed the citizens of the United States from outside the continental United States.

Other events deserving special broadcasts on KGU were Amelia Earhart's historic flight, the inauguration of inter-island airmail and the arrival of the Hawaiian Clipper. KGU provided the first and only direct transpacific report on the attack on Pearl Harbor—starting when Mr. Mulrony (the same Mulrony who said the "hello's" into the transmitter nineteen years before) climbed one of the radio towers on top of the Advertiser Building and verified that Hawaii was indeeed under enemy attack. He then went on to rally staff personnel and got

President Franklin D. Roosevelt addressed the nation via KGU on July 28, 1934, the first time in history a president did so from outside the continental United States.

off to NBC a detailed report of "The Day of Infamy."

But not all was war and news in KGU's history. Entertainment has always made KGU synonymous with radio in Hawaii. Dramas, the Lucky Strike program, the big band sound and celebrities like James Stewart, Shirley Temple and countless others have all been heard from 605 Kapiolani Boulevard.

Sports have played a big part in KGU's popularity. Baseball, football, basketball, boxing, wrestling, golf and more—locally, nationally, internationally, high school, collegiate and professional—KGU's sports broadcasting has always been one of its many strong points and one that island residents have come to depend on.

Another of KGU's "firsts" happened in the 1950s when KGU became the first station in Hawaii to bring in major-league baseball on a daily basis when it broadcast the complete schedule of the San Francisco Giants.

Entertainment, news, sports, a strong sense of commitment to the community and state-of-the-art equipment and technological advances in radio have enabled KGU to continue its long string of "firsts" that Hawaii has come to expect from its first radio station.

Always watchful for quality broadcasting that reaches the widest audience, on May 3, 1982, KGU left the fickle world of music behind to become Talk Radio KGU AM 76, thereby becoming the first station in Hawaii to broadcast satellite live programming on an almost continual basis.

Talk Radio KGU AM 76, besides providing people the opportunity to listen to the most famous people in the world as they're interviewed by the most popular talk show hosts in the nation, also gives island residents the opportunity to *talk* to these same people—*free*. Island residents need only dial 949-TALK to speak satellite live to the mainland.

In addition to the exceptional talent from the mainland, Talk Radio KGU AM 76 rounds out its programming with entertaining and informative local shows.

In 61 years, Talk Radio KGU AM 76 has gone from a primitive transmitter three floors above the ground to satellite live broadcasting miles above the earth.

The list of KGU's "firsts" shows a commitment to Hawaii—a commitment that has lasted 61 continuous years and that General Manager Brian Loughran and the rest of the staff and management of Talk Radio KGU AM 76 is dedicated to continue, uninterrupted, for many more years to come.

Service and progress for more than 30 years

In December 1952, the Territory of Hawaii viewed the initial broadcast of its second television station. The owners of the approximately 10,000 television sets in Honolulu at the time eagerly sat before their sets to watch the sign-on telecast of Channel 2, then known as KONA-TV, now KHON-TV. As an affiliate of the National Broadcasting Company, Channel 2 provided further evidence that Honolulu was indeed firmly entrenched in the electronic age.

Channel 2's grand opening from its studio on Koula Street near the city and county incinerator was attended by Governor Samuel Wilder King and Honolulu Mayor John H. Wilson, who led a contingent of lesser officials. But the main attraction of the evening was one of NBC's brightest stars, Eddie Cantor. Presiding over the event were the principal stockholders of the new broadcasting venture, Jack Keating, Lorrin Thurston and Elroy McCaw.

During those early days KONA-TV's facilities were scattered throughout the city. The studio was located on Koula Street in Kakaako; the transmitter and slide and film chains were housed at a site in the middle of what is now the Ala Moana Center. The executive offices were maintained in the Alexander Young Hotel in downtown Honolulu. By the mid-1950s, the station's facilities were incorporated at a new location which still exists at 1170 Auahi Street in Kakaako.

When Channel 2 inaugurated broadcast service to Honolulu viewers, some of the most talented performers in the islands were regularly seen on the station. The "Six O'Clock News" was hosted by the late Webley Edwards, creator of the famed "Hawaii Calls" nationwide show; news and sportscaster was Carlos Rivas; a cooking show was hosted by Lucky Luck; and commercials were performed live by Hank Sims. One of the station's most popular features was a live wedding ceremony performed each week during prime time.

By the mid-1960s, the ownership of KONA-TV had changed, as had the station's call letters—to KHON-TV. As the technology of broadcast engineering advanced, KHON-TV kept pace with the latest developments of the day and provided Hawaii viewers with color video and live satellite broadcasts from all parts of the world. Today such feats are commonplace and taken for granted, but in the '60s they were remarkable accomplishments. KHON-TV is especially proud to have been in the forefront during those pioneering days of technological advancement.

Throughout the 1970s, KHON-TV continued

KHON anchorman, Joe Moore.

to play a dominant role in providing the people of Hawaii with the best in entertainment, news and information. With satellite stations on Maui and the Big Island and a translator on Kauai, KHON-TV programs serve the entire state from its transmitter and tower atop Century Center on the edge of Waikiki.

By 1980, KHON-TV began a new era of progress when the station was purchased by the Des Moines Register and Tribune Company of Des Moines, Iowa. The Des Moines *Register* and *Tribune* were founded in 1903 and

KHON president and general manager, William L. Snyder.

have operated throughout the state of Iowa—newspapers that have been distinguished for journalistic excellence and integrity. That same commitment to quality was brought to Hawaii when the company expanded its broadcast holdings with the acquisition of KHON-TV. In addition to the Iowa newspaper and KHON-TV, corporate acquisitions included WQAD-TV in Moline, Illinois; KYXI (AM) and KGON (FM), Portland, Oregon; and WIBA (AM and FM), Madison, Wisconsin.

Under the leadership and guidance of William L. Snyder, KHON-TV's president and general manager, the station has grown to a position of dominance in news and entertainment. Snyder, a broadcast veteran, came to KHON-TV after serving many years at WQAD-TV, Moline, Illinois. Since assuming his position at KHON-TV, the station has made tremendous gains in professionalism, as well as audience acceptance.

Another key factor in the success of KHON-TV and its pacesetting contributions in the field of television news is its anchorman, Joe Moore, a product of Aiea High School and the University of Maryland. A former sportscaster, Moore has gained widespread acceptance by Hawaii's news viewers and the respect of his colleagues in broadcast journalism.

KHON-TV is proud to be part of a growing, dynamic community and looks to the future with continued hope and vigor.

A colorful entrepreneur shaped an island institution

Since its incorporation, the Kilgo Company has quite naturally been closely associated with its founder, Aubra L. Kilgo, and so expressive of his ebullient personality that in the public perception there is no distinction between the man and the business.

The business, now a giant hardware, building and marine supply house on Sand Island Road, was started in 1946 to deal in surplus building materials. The man who started it is a transplanted Alabaman whom the war had brought to Hawaii in 1942. Kilgo came from a managerial job for Woolworth in St. Louis to be general manager of the messing halls and clubs for the Civilian Housing Authority at Pearl Harbor Naval Yard.

The housing authority built and operated entire temporary cities to house the many thousands of civilian workers. These essential workers (whose motto was, "We keep them fit to fight") worked round-the-clock shifts, and they had to be fed, clothed and entertained. In performing his duties, Kilgo earned the personal attention of Admiral Chester W. Nimitz. He also met his future wife—the lovely Trinidad Sanchez—as she sang in a talent show in one of his mess halls.

At the end of the war, Kilgo had to choose between returning to Alabama and staying in Hawaii. And of course, the Islands won out. Although he now had no job and only $354 in

The original store in 1946.

his pocket, the idea of leaving the beautiful islands and their languid beauties was not appealing. Besides, he saw an opportunity, and he took it.

By war's end Hawaii had become the repository of vast amounts of surplus military material. And the temporary cities now had to be demolished. As a contractor in the early postwar years, Kilgo reduced to lumber many of the same buildings he had helped create. He won the contract to raze the original Royal Hawaiian Hotel in Alakea Street, and he took down the mast on the sunken U.S.S. *West Virginia*. Not all was demolition work, though. In the early 1950s Kilgo gained recognition for

a series of custom homes he built, including his own weekend house dramatically situated at Waimea Bay.

As a dealer in building supplies, his lumber yard soon became legendary. It offered outstanding value and such unique merchandise that people would stop by to browse whether or not they actually needed anything. There was a lot more than lumber. If one needed an industrial-size generator, scores of slightly used parachutes or a 20-foot anchor, Kilgo's was the obvious and only possible place to look.

By the time of statehood in 1959, the original one-room shed and adjacent Quonset had been replaced by the first of several modern structures, and the emphasis of the business was shifting. The availability of surplus material was much reduced, while catering to the building trades had naturally led to wider, related interests—retail sales to the general public, and importing and exporting industrial materials.

As an international industrial trader Kilgo deals directly with manufacturers around the world, traveling often to consult with business and government officials.

As a retail supply house—the most visible aspect of the operation—the expanded Kilgo company was an immediate success. The building trades professionals who had long been devoted to Kilgo were now joined by throngs of new customers—mostly homeowners and do-it-yourselfers drawn by the almost encyclopedic variety of merchandise. The aim was, and still is, to provide every substance and tool necessary for the construction or maintenance of the home.

Kilgo's now has specialized departments for lumber and fencing, hardware, plumbing, rope, chain and tackle, professional power tools and garden supplies. The company's location near Honolulu and Keehi harbors as well as Kilgo's particular interest have encouraged the growth of one of the most complete marine supply departments in the state.

Though Kilgo credits the success of the company to his "team of co-workers and an understanding board of directors" others suggest it's because he stays closely in touch with employees and customers by working in the store every single day. Indeed, to visit Kilgo's and not see the boss in the thick of the action is almost unimaginable!

Kilgo's today.

Hawaiian sweet bread . . . with the taste of success

Robert Rokuro Taira was born in a sugar plantation worker's camp on the Big Island of Hawaii, one of eleven children and the youngest of his five brothers. Robert's parents, Zensho and Kame Taira, sailed from Japan in 1906 to work the Hawaiian sugar cane fields, but they encouraged their children to pursue their individual freedom through higher education.

Robert was left at home to take on the daily work responsibilities at age 13. He was recognized as hard working, reliable and dependable, though not scholarly. However, he was not afraid to speak his mind, and he was a real go-getter.

It seemed only right that Robert Taira build his career in vegetables instead of bread because he was a top-notch gardener who out-hustled everyone else. Even when Robert had to ride the bus to school, he bypassed the $6 monthly charge by filling in as a part-time school bus driver. By the time he was 18, he had his own bus route and, within a year, his own transportation company. He hauled merchandise between Hilo and the country stores until he entered the Army in 1943, when he turned over his trucking company to his older brother.

Robert's exposure to Army life opened his eyes to the regular provision of food to thousands of men. He recognized it as a business with a future. At war's end, Robert was sent to Japan. He noticed that among the

Robert R. Taira, president of Taira Management and Consultant Services.

food staples, Western-style baked goods were absent. Robert Taira set his goal to return to his parents' homeland after the war and open an American-style bakery.

After his four-year Army career, Robert attended Honolulu's first vocational baking school while also acquiring his high school diploma. With his goal still firmly set, and the Korean War making it difficult for him to return to Japan, he decided to pursue his baking career in Hawaii.

Lacking investment capital, Robert had almost come to a dead end when his father, Zensho, took all the cash reserves from his life insurance policy—some $3,000—and financed his 27-year-old son's bakery business,

King's Bakery and Coffee Shop, Honolulu.

knowing that "Bob" was someone he could count on.

In 1950 Bob opened Robert's Bakery in one of Hilo's small, older downtown buildings. The taste of success came with the first opening of the doors. Friends, neighbors and some strangers, who all shared a fondness for freshly baked sweet goods, bought everything. It was difficult to keep up with the demand. Bob Taira worked so hard that two months after opening, he was hospitalized suffering from exhaustion.

Within five years, the little Hilo bakery was selling $90,000 in sweet goods annually. This prompted Bob to purchase a half-acre of land in Hilo on which he designed and had built the first commercial building to operate solely as a bakery. He opened the doors to his new building in 1956 and rang up $120,000 in sales that first year.

Ironically, one thing missing from Robert's bakery was bread. After persistent pleas from customers, Bob decided to bake a Portuguese sweet bread for charitable fund-raising sales. Bob spent weeks making samples to produce commercial quantities without losing the unique home-made taste. Without adding preservatives, Bob found the proper solution to baking this much sought-after sweet bread while still maintaining richness and taste, even after one month without refrigeration.

In 1961, Robert's Bakery in Hilo was sold for $250,000. Bob moved his entire family to Honolulu, and after waiting a year for the right location, he opened King's Bakery on South King Street.

By 1977, King's Bakery was a $4-million-a-year business. The flood of mainland orders and his strong determination prompted Bob to open King's Hawaiian Bakery West, Inc., on the West Coast. King's Hawaiian sweet bread had now become nationally famous. There were many problems, but one by one, Bob Taira conquered them. One problem was adapting the mixing machines to the bread to maintain the original taste, which it had lost during automation.

By 1979, the mainland-made sweet bread bakery finally turned a small profit producing an estimated five million loaves.

Today, King's Hawaiian sweet bread has gained such acceptance that another bakery is being constructed in Grenville, South Carolina, to fill Eastern orders. With the development of new techniques in marketing and distribution, U.S. expansion will be complete through a network of over 86 major U.S. food brokers.

Robert Taira now acts as a consultant to all King's Bakery operation under Taira Management & Consultant Services, Inc.

Radio trendsetters of today exploded with postwar Hawaii

Kkua (AM) and KQMQ (FM), the radio stations of the Aloha Broadcasting Company, perhaps most closely typify the lifestyle of Hawaii in the 1980s. The Territory of Hawaii was just beginning its second major transformation of the century in the late 1940s. Prior to World War II it was a sleepy tropical backwater, its economy just getting along on sugar cane and pineapple and a moderate but stable level of tourism and military presence. The war in the Pacific that began with the attack on Pearl Harbor in 1941 would change all that. When the conflict was over, unprecedented numbers of servicemen and civilians had heard the siren call of "paradise" and they would soon be returning, as tourists or residents. The postwar boom was on!

In 1945 there were only two radio stations in Honolulu, but there was an immediate flurry of applications from interested groups for new facilities. One of those was the Pacific Frontier Broadcasting Company, a group of investors headed by Harold T. Kay, a military aide to the territorial governor. Their station, KULA, went on the air at 7:00 p.m. on May 14, 1947. The opening ceremonies were attended by many local celebrities, including Governor Stainback. Don McDiarmid wrote a special hula for the occasion, and a hula contest was held at the new Kapiolani Boulevard studios. The station was the most powerful in Hawaii at the time, and was the first to affiliate with the fledgling ABC Radio Network.

The station changed hands several times in later years, and for a time was co-owned with KULA-TV. One constant was Jack Burnett, who guided the station from its debut in the '40s until the '60s. However, by the mid-60s, success in radio was no longer determined

Station originates the "Jack McElroy Show" nationwide on the ABC network during Aloha Week, 1948. From left to right, Jack Burnett, Jay Stewart, Candy Vroman and Jack McElroy.

solely by which network's programs were aired, but by what kind of music was played. So in 1967, after a brief unsuccessful flirtation with country music, the newly renamed KKUA was launched into the area of contemporary music (known back then as "Rock and Roll"). That format has matured into today's mix of music, personality, sports and information that holds great appeal for young adults.

In 1968, the owners of KGMB-TV and another local AM station expanded their holdings by constructing an FM station, Hawaii's fourth. KGMB-FM went on the air on April 1, 1968; although it was quite successful, Honolulu was still very much an "AM" market well into the 1980s. KGMB-FM was subsequently named KGMQ, and in 1976 it was sold to the Aloha Broadcasting Company, which was in turn purchased by the owners of KKUA. Both stations were taken over by present management when they were bought by the Coca-Cola Bottling Company of Los Angeles.

Management attention was first directed toward the revitalization of KKUA. The equipment had been neglected for years, and KKUA was lucky to make it through each day without a serious breakdown. By 1983, nearly a quarter-million dollars would be spent modernizing both KKUA's and KQMQ's transmitting facilities. More significant was the redirection of the programming towards public

service and community involvement. A need was perceived on the part of the state's enormous running community for serious coverage of their activities, and in 1979, KKUA did its first live coverage of the Honolulu Marathon. By the end of 1982, that event had become one of the largest in the world, and KKUA was recognized as one of the country's leading stations in the area of running event coverage and support. Other new activities included the transformation of the Waimanalo Canoe Regatta into a day-long festival of entertainment and canoe racing, and bringing the World Belly-Flop and Cannonball Diving Championships to Sea Life Park at Makapuu Point.

Meanwhile, a not-so-quiet revolution was happening on the FM band. Although still outnumbered by their AM brothers by more than two-to-one, the overwhelming success of FM on the mainland was not to be denied in Hawaii. With a finely tuned combination of music and events appealing to Hawaii's young adults, 93 FM-Q, as it was known by now, became the number-one rated FM station in spring of 1982. Since fall of that year, KQMQ has been the number-one radio station in the 50th state, the first FM station to reach and maintain that position.

The stations of the Aloha Broadcasting Company were babies of the postwar boom, and have matured along with Hawaii into the communications leaders of the "Crossroads of the Pacific."

Over 10,000 runners entered the 1982 Honolulu Marathon as KKUA provided step-by-step coverage from its broadcast tower high above the finish line.

A history of caring—a future of progressive quality care

Kuakini Medical Center, 1982.

In the late 1800s, the sugar plantations in Hawaii were booming, and contract laborers were the backbone of the industry. Between 1885 and 1900, over 70,000 Japanese immigrants crossed the Pacific Ocean to Honolulu to work in the flourishing cane fields. Low wages and unexpected expenses soon placed the newcomers in destitute circumstances. During this period, relief to the needy was provided by charities such as the Hawaiian Relief Society and the British Benevolent Society, according to ethnicity. The few Japanese groups available gave limited relief and existed for only a short time. However, one group—the Japanese Benevolent Society—survived over the years to become the forerunner of Kuakini Medical Center.

The Society, incorporated in 1899, decided to build a charity hospital after thousands of Japanese immigrants were left without homes following the outbreak of bubonic plague and an out-of-control fire. The two-story wooden structure, completed in 1900 in the Kapalama district of Honolulu, contained 38 beds and was called the Japanese Charity Hospital. After two years, the structure became inadequate for patient needs and another hospital was built a few miles away. For fifteen years, the Society maintained this hospital until it, too, became rundown.

By 1917, a modern facility was built at a third location, the hospital's present site on Kuakini Street, funded by the Society and public contributions. The 70-bed hospital, called the Japanese Hospital, was equipped with up-to-date facilities on a site with abundant space for present and future needs.

By 1931, many of the Japanese immigrant men remained unmarried, were of retirement age and had no families to care for them. To fulfill this need, the Japanese Home of Hawaii was built on the hospital grounds through community donations. The 50-man facility, the forerunner of the present Kuakini Home, provided care, food and shelter for these elderly men.

A major expansion program in 1939 increased the hospital's size to 100 beds and added X-ray, surgical, pediatric and maternity facilities. As a tribute to the Japanese government, which donated 10,000 yen to the expansion, a distinctive dome was placed atop the new building. As the war began in 1941, a portion of the hospital was placed under the Army's control. Soon after, the hospital gained a new name—Kuakini Hospital and Home—

after Chief Kuakini, who was the acting governor of Oahu and brother-in-law of King Kamehameha I. The hospital was returned to civilian control in 1945. From that year on, Kuakini began planning and implementing a series of building programs that added new facilities, deleted unsuitable services (obstetrics/pediatrics) and renovated outdated areas in order to maintain adequate quality care to the community.

In 1975, the hospital was renamed Kuakini Medical Center to reflect its expanded services to the community. The most recent and significant building program was developed in the '70s and completed in increments

from 1977 to 1980. This included remodeling of the ancillary facilities, such as the pharmacy and laboratory; a 750-car parking structure; an eight-story physicians' office building and a ten-story, 250-bed geriatric care facility called Hale Pulama Mau (House of Cherishing Care), an outcome of Kuakini's long-standing commitment and concern for providing services for the elderly.

Today, Kuakini Medical Center is a 500-bed private, nonprofit eleemosynary health care institution with services for acute care, ambulatory/emergency care, skilled nursing and intermediate care facilities, residential care home, adult day care and adult day health care programs. Kuakini is accredited by the Joint Commission on Accreditation of Hospitals and affiliated with the University of Hawaii as a teaching hospital.

For 83 years the Kuakini Medical Center has diligently provided high-quality health care and has grown with the development of the city and county of Honolulu and the state of Hawaii. With the positive support of its community members, Kuakini will continue to provide health care needs through comprehensive patient care, education and research.

Japanese Charity Hospital, forerunner of Kuakini Medical Center, in 1902.

Going your way since 1922

In the early 1900s when Waikiki was a picturesque duck pond and some horse-drawn carriages still appeared on Honolulu streets, a group of Chinese immigrant merchants felt the need for a bank to serve their own credit needs as well as that of the Chinese community. Hawaii was still a territory, tourism was not yet a common household word and many Chinese residents were having difficulty arranging for banking service because of language and cultural barriers. It was in this period that Liberty Bank, the third oldest bank in Hawaii, had its beginning.

On January 31, 1922, an organizational meeting took place at a then-popular Smith Street dining establishment in Honolulu called Sun Yun Wo Restaurant. There, fifteen Chinese businessmen molded a plan to form a bank. Because America, the land of freedom and opportunity, had given these individuals so much by its free enterprise system, they dreamed of a new financial institution that would be named "The Liberty Bank of Honolulu" with the Statue of Liberty as its logo. Application for a banking charter was signed and filed the same day and approved on February 11, 1922. The newly formed bank, with Lum Yip Kee as its first president, was temporarily located at 75 North King Street, then moved permanently to 99 North King Street.

With the sounds of tens of thousands of exploding firecrackers, The Liberty Bank of Honolulu formally opened its doors on February 18, 1922. Within the first three hours

An historic moment—10:40 a.m. on July 21, 1922—at the corner of King and Maunakea streets. Note the flags of China and the United States prominently displayed side by side—and the absence of women.

On December 7, 1951, senior officers and directors, together with contractor, architect and his assistant, pose proudly at groundbreaking for a new and modern bank building at the same site of the 1922 grand opening.

200 accounts were opened by a staff of nine individuals. The first depositors were primarily the merchants themselves, their relatives and other members of the Chinese community. Few banks in the country have had such an auspicious beginning.

The Chinese community was elated and proud of its new banking facility and business flourished. Although the original depositors were predominantly of Chinese ancestry, over the years customers as well as employees began coming from a cross-section of the Honolulu community; soon The Liberty Bank of Honolulu was serving the financial needs of Hawaii's society at large.

Through the Depression years of the 1930s and the World War II era of the 1940s the bank continued its progress and development. Expansion began in the 1950s with the completion of a new bank building constructed in November 1952 at the site of the original grand opening in 1922.

During the presidencies of prominent

community leaders Wong Buck Hung and C.T. Wong—which spanned the twenty years between 1953 and 1973—the first branch was opened at 1491 South King Street near Kalakaua Avenue. Seven more branch offices followed over that period. By the time Hawaii became the 50th state of the Union, the bank had become an integral part of Hawaii's growth.

In June 1970, the bank's name was shortened to Liberty Bank and a new logo adopted. Known for a friendly and warm touch with people, this financial institution made available to its customers over 60 different services. The bank was instrumental in establishing and developing many Honolulu businesses as well as residential communities. Its interest in community affairs, demonstrated by its involvement in many civic, cultural and ethnic events, continues today.

The bank entered the world of electronic banking under the guiding hand of Lawrence S.L. Ching, who took office in 1974—the youngest president in the bank's history. With increased services to its depositors and the establishment of two additional branches, the branch system was broadened to include eleven offices. Liberty Bank maintains a tradition of a branch office in every major shopping center on the island of Oahu.

In the age of computers and high technology, Liberty Bank continues to contribute to the growth of Hawaii and looks to the future as a time of challenge, progress and opportunity. The dream of its founders realized, Liberty Bank dedicates itself to tradition, trust and dependability—but most of all, to a sincere concern for the people of Hawaii.

A century of service to Hawaii

Matson Navigation Company, Inc., has served Hawaii continuously since 1882 and is the only American steamship company to serve the same unsubsidized trade for more than a century. Matson began when Captain William Matson left San Francisco on April 10, 1882 bound for Hilo aboard the 113-foot schooner *Emma Claudina.* It was a small beginning— just one ship with 300 tons of food, plantation supplies and general merchandise—but Hilo was a port without regular service from any other carrier. Over the next two decades, Matson returned again and again, and Hilo became his principal port.

By 1900, Matson had a fleet of four ships calling on Hilo, and occasionally at other Hawaii ports. The principal cargoes were general merchandise westbound and raw sugar eastbound. There was space each way for a few hardy passengers. Only ten years later, in 1910, Matson's 146-passenger liner *S.S.Wilhelmina* entered service with accommodations to rival the finest in the Atlantic, giving birth to modern tourism in the islands.

The new liner was quickly followed by three more as Matson teamed with Castle & Cooke Agencies to serve Honolulu as well. When Captain Matson died in 1917, his company's fleet numbered fourteen of the largest, fastest and most modern ships in the Pacific passenger-freighter service.

To provide facilities for the growing number of passengers, Matson purchased and refurbished the Moana Hotel in 1926, and a year later completed construction of the Royal Hawaiian Hotel. For two decades these were the dominant hotels in Waikiki, as Waikiki, Hawaii and Matson became synonymous to the tourist.

All Matson vessels were taken over by the government for military service during the two world wars. However, as a major steamship and terminals operator, Matson was also assigned to operate a large number of conscripted vessels, and several of the older and smaller ones provided minimal service to Hawaii. After both wars, Matson spent millions to restore its ships to operating condition. The Royal Hawaiian Hotel, too, needed $2 million worth of repainting and repair after the Navy departed at the end of World War II.

In 1956, Matson revolutionized cargo handling in the Pacific by introducing freight containerization. At the same time, the company divested itself of the remaining non-shipping assets, including its hotels.

Matson's famous passenger liner *Lurline* continued to serve Hawaii until 1970 when jet air service and rising operating costs ended it.

The three-masted schooner Emma Claudina, *Captain William Matson's first vessel, left San Francisco for Hilo on April 10, 1882.*

The Kauai *departs Honolulu for Los Angeles on its biweekly run in the Hawaii-West Coast service. The* Kauai *is Matson's newest vessel, entering service in 1980 with a capacity of more than 1,200 containers.*

At the same time, the company began a $330 million shipbuilding and terminals improvement program which by 1982 had completely transformed the Matson fleet. Under this program, all World War II vintage ships were replaced by modern container or container-trailer vessels specifically designed for the Hawaii trade. Matson today has the most modern and efficient cargo carrying fleet in its history, including five vessels capable of transporting more than 1,000 containers per voyage.

It has container terminal capacity and capability to match, following construction of a new terminal in Honolulu and installation at Los Angeles of a new overhead container handling system (MATSYSTEM), another Matson innovation.

Matson also improved facilities at its other West Coast ports—Oakland, Seattle and Portland. While Honolulu has become the largest port in the Matson network of Hawaii service with more than 5,000 container moves per week, the company also serves the ports of Nawiliwili, Kauai, Kahului, Maui, and Hilo, Hawaii, with interisland vessels.

Matson was incorporated in 1901, and shares were purchased by Hawaii's major corporations in order to assure regular cargo service between Hawaii and the mainland. Alexander & Baldwin, Inc., one of Hawaii's sugar companies, became a part owner of Matson in 1909 and controlling owner in 1964. In 1969, Matson became a wholly owned subsidiary of A&B.

Matson headquarters remain in San Francisco, as they have been since 1882.

Hawaii's first nursing facility

Beautifully located at the top of Wilhelmina Rise with a panoramic view of the crater of Diamond Head and the city of Honolulu, Maunalani Hospital was located in this locale for patients to feast on this indescribable natural beauty.

During 1942, the bed capacities of the Honolulu hospitals were not sufficient to care for the civilian load thrust upon them by the tremendous influx of civilian war workers and others in the war effort. In April 1942, the first step to alleviate the condition took place, and the Office of the Civilian Defense War Casualty Hospital was opened in the Sacred Hearts Convent at Nuuanu and Bates Street to take care of the overflow of acute medical and surgical patients from the local general hospitals. In 1943, as a second step an emergency polio hospital was opened. Yet it was still clear that there were not sufficient beds in the local hospitals to care for the population at that time.

Many patients who might better have remained in the general hospital for a normal convalescence had to be discharged. Chronically ill and infirm individuals occupying hospital beds also had to vacate to make room for the more acutely ill.

In December 1943, a meeting took place at the Pacific Club to deal with the problem. Chairman of the Public Health Committee was the late Dr. F.J. Pinkerton, who was asked to take over the project and get it organized. Dr. Pinkerton presided at a meeting on April 10,

1944. C.T. Oliphant reported that he had asked the opinion of numerous men and no person opposed the plan of a new nursing home. It would bear the title of the Convalescent Nursing Home.

On September 28, 1945, through the action of Alan S. Davis, the petition for the incorporators were: Messrs. Allen, Austin, Coll, Damon, Davis, McLean, Moody, Pratt, Steadman, and Ms. Margaret Catton. The petition was accepted and was signed by W.D. Ackerman Jr., treasurer of the Territory of Hawaii. Mrs. Elaine Johnson was appointed executive secretary at a meeting held on October 3, 1945.

On February 27, 1953, the name Convalescent Nursing Home was changed to Maunalani Hospital and Convalescent Home. On February 26, 1964, the name was again changed to Maunalani Hospital.

The following is an exerpt from the 1953 Annual meeting minutes:

"The President, Lowell S. Dillingham reported that we have developed an institution which, by its accomplishments is a credit to the territory . . . . it is efficiently operated, provides excellent care at nominal rates."

At the beginning there were 42 beds available. Only eight patients were referred from a neighboring island. In 1955, 53 beds were available and all the islands were represented. Maunalani Hospital was now

indeed an integral and very important part of the health program of the islands.

In 1956 the directors decided that an expansion to 100 beds was most desirable and economically feasible. Construction was to begin by May 1, 1958.

At a meeting on April 19, 1961, the board of directors expressed their appreciation to A.A. Carswell, chairman of the building committee, in finishing one of the finest building projects in the State of Hawaii. The dedication and open house was held June 7, 1961.

In 1962, Dr. George Mills was appointed medical director of the hospital. With the retirement of Executive Director Elaine Johnson in 1979, Kenneth Halpenny was appointed successor in April 1980. James Iwatani, a very dedicated employee since 1962, was appointed associate executive director.

Extensive renovations to the building complex in 1982-83 have made Maunalani Hospital one of the finest long-term care facilities in the nation.

Current members of the board are H.C Eichelberger, president, elected in 1961 and president since 1977; David Pietsch Sr., elected in 1967, and R.E. Hager, elected in 1971, are vice presidents. Board members are A.A. Carswell, who served as secretary from 1955-67 and president from 1967-77; S.E. Woolley, H.H. Hamamoto, J.H. Goldcamp, M.A. Pietschman, E.R. Champion, H.H. Stephenson, A.J. Wriston and P.E.B. Wainwright.

Aerial view of Maunalani Hospital, 1983.

Thirty-seven years of change kept this ad agency New! and Improved!

He came from Brooklyn to serve with the Marine Corps during World War II—in an exotic world known as Hawaii. When the war ended he went back to New York, but soon he was back in Hawaii. Ray Milici has called Hawaii home ever since.

Milici/Valenti is the advertising agency he started 37 years ago in a small Waikiki office. His partner was Paul Beam, former war correspondent and a speech writer for Hawaii's Republican party. The agency opened in 1946 as the Beam & Milici Advertising Agency. It had no clients.

One of Hawaii's first live radio shows was produced by Beam & Milici as an advertising vehicle for its first client, a surplus store. Later, Beam & Milici introduced the famous Hilo Hattie Talent Hunt show. And then came radio re-creations of Madison Square Garden boxing matches. The advertiser was Alberto-Culver. The radio announcer was a young man by the name of Frank Valenti.

In 1957, Milici reorganized the agency in anticipation of Hawaiian statehood. What followed was Milici Advertising, the direct forerunner of Milici/Valenti. Frank Valenti would join Milici full time in 1968 after twenty years of sports announcing for Hawaii radio and television stations.

In 1972, another milestone was reached. Doyle Dane Bernbach, the Madison Avenue ad agency that started the advertising industry's creative revolution, offered to buy Milici Advertising. At the time, Milici was Hawaii's largest ad agency, with billings topping $7 million. Doyle Dane Bernbach was then the nation's twelfth largest ad agency. A Doyle Dane connection would bring many benefits. Milici would be able to operate on his own as before, but he would have the financial backing and support of a worldwide advertising organization. Milici agreed to Doyle Dane's offer.

Two years later, Frank Valenti was named president, and the agency was given its current name. Today, Milici/Valenti billings have reached $18 million. The staff has grown to 55 people. The agency achieved strong and steady growth by winning new accounts and benefiting from the growth of existing clients.

Milici/Valenti's account list is a roster of blue-chip Hawaii companies:

Alexander & Baldwin, Inc.; Aloha Airlines, Inc.; Amfac, Inc.; Brewer Chemical Corporation; C. Brewer & Company, Ltd.; Dillingham Corporation; Eastman Kodak Company; First Hawaiian Bank; First Hawaiian Leasing, Inc.; First Insurance Co. of Hawaii, Ltd.; Foremost Dairies-Hawaii, Ltd.; Frito-Lay of Hawaii, Inc.; Hawaii Medical Service Assn.;

A nationally recognized public service ad prepared by Milici/Valenti in 1971 to recruit new members for the Honolulu Police Department

Hawaii Pizza Hut, Inc.; Hawaii Thrift & Loan; Hawaii Visitors Bureau; Hawaiian Electric Co., Ltd.; Hawaiian Telephone Company; The Hertz Corporation; Island Holidays, Ltd.; Kenault, Inc.; Matson Navigation Co.; Mauna Kea Beach; Mauna Kea Properties; Mauna Loa Macadamia Nut Corp.; Paradise Beverages; Polynesian Cultural Center; State Savings & Loan Assn.; Webco Hawaii, Inc.; The Westin Wailea Beach.

In serving these clients, Milici/Valenti has followed in a Doyle Dane Bernbach tradition of consistently outperforming other agencies in awards competitions. Indeed, creativity is the agency's hallmark. Many people in the

creative department were imported from prestigious mainland agencies.

In a business whose inventory goes down the elevator every night, it's important to have a talented and experienced staff in every department. For 37 years, this has been one of Ray Milici's guiding principles. It is one of the reasons for his long-standing success in Hawaii's ad business.

Public service is another agency hallmark. The agency creates public service advertising on a regular basis for a variety of community organizations. Ray Milici himself spends about 30 percent of his time devoted to various civic projects. He is a past chairman of Hawaii's Chamber of Commerce; a past president of the Rotary Club of Honolulu; and he frequently travels with the governor on trips promoting Hawaii as a great place for business and tourists alike.

His primary commitment, of course, will never change. This explains why, in a business known for its instability, Milici/Valenti has been remarkably stable. Accounts have stayed, and people have stayed, as well. Many of today's employees were with the agency five, ten, even twenty years ago.

Certain changes, however, have given Milici/Valenti its unique character. Milici left Brooklyn to set up shop in Hawaii. Valenti left sportscasting to join Milici. Many agency employees left cities all over the mainland— lured by Milici/Valenti and the prospect of a new Hawaiian lifestyle. Other staffers were born and raised in Hawaii. The result is much the same as Hawaii itself—a rich blend of people working together in an environment most would find difficult to leave.

Ray Milici and Frank Valenti at the entrance to Milici/Valenti in downtown's Amfac Building.

Significant contributions to the economy of Hawaii

Among the largest insurance agencies in Hawaii today, National Mortgage & Finance Company, Ltd. received its corporate charter more than half a century ago on July 30, 1929 from the Territory of Hawaii.

The company was organized by a group of young Hawaii businessmen who felt the need for a locally oriented finance company. The organizers wanted a company which could meet the needs of islanders who were becoming increasingly active in the Hawaii business community and whose needs were not being met adequately.

National Mortgage formally opened for business in September 1929 with President Toworu Kunikiyo; Vice Presidents Woodrow T. Saito, Masayuki Tokioka (present board chairman), Wilfred C. Tsukiyama and William Kwai Fong Yap; Secretary S. Morris Morishita and Treasurer Charles S. Ching. The board of directors also included Harry Akiyama, E.B. Clarke, James K. Hoe, Dr. Charles S. Murakami, John F. Stone, Wade Warren Thayer, Tasuke Yamagata, Clifton H. Yamamoto, Takao Yamauchi and Charles T.T. Yap.

In September 1930 the International Trust Company, Ltd. became an agent for National Mortgage. Five years later, however, International Trust was dissolved during the Great Depression, and National Mortgage then acquired its insurance agency operations.

National Mortgage's principal business was mortgage financing, real estate sales and property management, and insurance. Its first location was on Merchant Street, subsequently at 1030 Smith Street and now in its own building at 1022 Bethel at the corner of King Street. It operates from that location as well as its other building at 1165 Bethel Street and a Big Island office in Hilo.

Today the company's principal activity is the property and casualty insurance general agency operations; it is among the largest independent property and casualty insurance agencies in Hawaii. The company is additionally engaged in property management, real estate sales and investment development, plus a managing insurance general agency. The insurance companies it represents include internationally known and respected industry giants as well as local insurance companies. The senior management team is composed of President William T. Hiraoka, CPCU, Executive Vice President-Secretary Franklin M. Tokioka and Vice President-Treasurer Steven T. Kodani.

International Trust Company offices in 1930, subagents for National Mortgage & Finance Co., Ltd.

Island Insurance Companies, the only active property and casualty insurance companies fully owned in Hawaii today, rank among the top ten largest premium writers in the state.

The present Island Insurance Company, Ltd. was chartered on December 27, 1939 under the laws of the Territory of Hawaii by three key men—Wade Warren Thayer, president; Masayuki Tokioka, vice president; and Clifton H. Yamamoto. The company was organized to meet a need to insure risks which were not generally accepted by mainland-based property and casualty insurance companies, using inapplicable national standards in Hawaii. These risks were actually desirable insurance risks because of differing local conditions.

Initially capitalized at $100,000, Island Insurance kept increasing its capital to $1,050,000 with paid-in surplus of $262,500. On December 31, 1982 its unassigned surplus exceeded $11.6 million, making the total capital and surplus $12.9 million.

Its subsidiary, Tradewind Insurance Company, Ltd., was incorporated on December 15, 1955. Together with Island Insurance, it is now part of the Island Insurance Companies. The group is licensed for all lines of insurance except title insurance in the state of Hawaii.

Island's financial strength, progress and professional approach to the handling of insurance has earned it the highest possible policyholders' rating of A+ from the respected A.M. Best Company, which also assigned it the financial size category Class XI.

The growth of Island Insurance Companies started after arrangements for a reinsurance program were made. The principal reinsurer is INA Reinsurance, with additional reinsurance both in the United States and through the London market.

Island Insurance Companies use the independent insurance agency system in marketing, ranking well within the top ten insurers in premiums written in Hawaii. The senior management team includes President William T. Hiraoka, CPCU; Senior Vice President-Secretary Franklin M. Tokioka; and Senior Vice President Steven T. Kodani. Chairman of the board is Masayuki Tokioka.

The management and operation of Island Insurance Companies is contracted to National Mortgage & Finance Company.

A company of growth and innovation

Oceanic Cablevision, founded in 1969, was a relative late-comer to the cable television business on Oahu. Five other companies had already established themselves in neighborhoods where off-air television reception was poor and demand for cable service high. Oceanic initially served Nuuanu, Manoa and Mililani areas.

In 1973 the state of Hawaii assigned franchise areas to the various existing companies, awarding Oceanic the metropolitan Honolulu, Central Oahu and the North Shore areas. At that time, cablevision was considered a means of bringing television to geographically isolated locations. Metropolitan areas where off-air television reception is good were considered a tough place to sell cable service. The North Shore was indeed isolated from television reception, but low population density and a location over 30 miles from Honolulu made profitability questionable.

As is sometimes the case with businesses determined to survive under adverse conditions, handicaps were transformed into motivational assets. Out of necessity, aggressive marketing, innovative programming, efficient customer service, state-of-the-art technology and solid financial planning would spell the difference between success and failure.

By 1975 Oceanic had grown—15,000 homes were receiving service. To celebrate this landmark figure, Oceanic launched its first optional pay movie channel, "Theater 26."

Oceanic's construction crews worked non-stop to increase the number of homes able to be served by cable. The marketing department followed closely with innovative sales campaigns. By 1977 subscriber count had doubled to 30,000 and the Home Box Office service replaced the old "Theater 26."

Sheer volume and the ever-increasing complexity of operations necessitated the installation of an on-line, in-house data processing system in 1977, the same year Oceanic introduced its first monthly cable magazine and had constructed Hawaii's first satellite earth station for cable television. By the beginning of 1978 live programming from San Francisco, Atlanta and New York were part of the 24-hour service.

Program expansion continued into 1979, as did geographic expansion of the system. The company had dedicated itself to growth and innovation. In June of that year, cable history was made as Oceanic was first to introduce addressable converters on a large scale. By way of a computer located at Oceanic's central office, cable converter boxes in individual homes could be selectively activated to provide services ordered. Subscribers from Kahala through Central Oahu to the North Shore could choose from four optional pay movie channels: HBO, Action Theater, Critics Choice or Family Fair.

In April 1981, Oceanic was acquired by ATC (American Television and Communications Corp.), a wholly owned subsidiary of Time Inc. ATC provided capital to allow rapid completion of the construction of the Oceanic system. The ATC/Time Inc. alliance postured Oceanic for not only economic growth in the '80s and '90s, but also strengthened its competitive stance. In March 1983, ATC acquired a neighboring cable system, adding 10,000 subscribers to Oceanic's 80,000.

By the third quarter of 1983, Oceanic was operating one of the most sophisticated cable television systems in the United States, with a total subscriber count of over 90,000. Growth and service to subscribers continue. Oceanic is presently expanding its community programming activities, making its facilities available to worthy nonprofit organizations and ethnic culture groups. Optional pay services now total seven.

Oceanic Cablevision, in a period of less than fifteen years, has developed its system of a few thousand subscribers in an initially adverse franchise area into one of the nation's fifteen largest cable television companies.

Hawaii's first satellite earth station for cable TV transmissions, built by Oceanic in 1977.

Innovation and quality—the cornerstone of a company's success

"Articles of incorporation of Pacific Construction Company, Ltd., a new construction firm, have been filed in the office of the territorial treasurer." So began an item in the January 3, 1939 edition of the Honolulu *Star-Bulletin,* heralding the birth of what has become one of the leading construction companies in the Pacific Basin.

On December 31, with capital of $100,000 and a handful of contracts totaling $276,000, Pacific's founder, George E. Freitas, filed papers of incorporation. A local boy and son of prominent Honolulu contractor, Henry Freitas, it was natural that George would follow his father into the construction business.

In June 1929, after graduating from the University of Dayton, George returned to Hawaii. The day after his arrival in Honolulu, he remembers being taken to see one of his father's latest projects, the Advertiser News Building. "My father was short of laborers so I started work immediately at 35 cents an hour."

George mastered all aspects of the construction business and in 1935, ventured out on his own. Early projects included the Mabel Smyth Auditorium, the Baldwin High School on Maui and various bridges on the Hamakua Coast of the Big Island.

The early days weren't easy, with Pacific having to bid against large construction firms to survive. But George's courage and innovative approach gave Pacific an edge over its competitors. He traveled the world extensively

George Freitas (L) and father Henry (R) are pictured with building supplier Louis Underwood at Wheeler Field—one of George's early projects. Year 1930.

to learn new methods, "not for curiosity's sake," points out George, "but to do it better!" With a reputation for bringing the job in on time, within budget and with workmanship of the highest caliber, Pacific Construction began to grow.

As the company grew, so did the people. George recognized that a company's strength lies in its employees. Like George, each man started at the bottom of the ladder and was given more responsibility until he reached his full potential. "We built the company from within, using incentive—something for the future. That's why our people stayed with Pacific. Many were with me for 20 or 30 years."

Pacific Construction Company employees in front of Baldwin High School on the island of Maui. Circa 1939.

Based on a foundation of solid business principles, Pacific prospered and its reputation for innovation and excellence strengthened.

The company made headlines for such feats as completing a 600-unit housing project 101 days ahead of schedule, despite the turbulent effect of labor disputes; and for being the first in the state of Hawaii to use the now familiar Linden Climbing Crane from Denmark. Pacific's contract load reached such proportions that an additional company, Pacific Utility Contractors, was created to handle roads, bridges, watermains and subdivisions.

In 1962, the Vonn Hamm-Young Company, Inc. invited Freitas to be its president. George accepted with the understanding that his new employers would buy his companies—Pacific was sold for $2 million.

In July 1964, Vonn Hamm-Young changed its name to The Hawaii Corporation (THC), and five years later George retired as president and chief executive officer. In 1976, THC filed for reorganization under federal Chapter XI bankruptcy statutes. As a condition of the filing, THC sold Pacific to its major creditor, the Bank of Hawaii, but only after a long court battle with the THC trustees who vehemently opposed the sale of the most profitable subsidiary.

In August 1977, the bank re-sold Pacific to Artec Corporation, a wholly owned subsidiary of Tecon Corporation. Tecon is a member of a Dallas-based group of companies owned by the Murchisons, a prominent Texan family with investments in the islands dating back to the early '60s.

The prime mover in bringing the Murchisons and Pacific together was Richard C. Baker, an Australian who had worked in the construction business in Honolulu for many years. In 1978 Baker, who today is chairman of the board of Pacific Construction, negotiated the merger of Pacific and DMA/Hawaii, a Honolulu contracting firm headed by Frederick M. Kresser.

Under Kresser's direction, Pacific reached new heights of prosperity and prominence. By 1983, the company had built over twenty percent of the state's hotel room inventory and 60 percent of downtown Honolulu's office space.

In an industry that is constantly changing, the survivors are those who dare to move with, and sometimes ahead of, the times. Pacific is that kind of company. What hasn't changed over the years is the pioneering spirit of founder George E. Freitas and the belief that a job well done brings its own rewards.

Modest beginnings, decades of growth and a man named Coney

In October 1928 a handful of prominent Honolulu citizens organized a small company to provide sickness and accident insurance for plantation workers; little could they have imagined that the seed they planted that long-ago autumn would survive the Depression of the '30s, World War in the '40s, the '50s and '60s boom years, the advent of statehood and the explosion of the island economy through the '70s and '80s. Nor in the mid-1920s could they have imagined that their company's most vigorous period of growth would really begin some twenty years later under the guidance of a Californian named Coney who in 1922 was just beginning his insurance career.

Pacific Insurance Company, Ltd. was formed October 25, 1928 by H.A. Truslow, M.R. Monsarrat, J.D. Flint, David Kalauokalani, Dr. Fred Lam, Fred Patterson, G.W. Schuman and H.A. Hahn—names still familiar to islanders nearly 60 years later. From small offices in downtown Honolulu's historic waterfront Stangenwald Building, Pacific wrote accident and sickness insurance for plantation employees—a coverage being discontinued by mainland insurers. It limited itself to this type of service for ten years and ended its first decade with assets of $85,385. Spurred on by an ever-tightening mainland market for workers' compensation insurance, Pacific began its next decade by expanding and becoming an "all lines" casualty and fire insurance company. Profits made were kept in surplus, nearly half a million dollars in new capital was invested in the company and a 1944 U.S. Supreme Court decision allowed Pacific and other companies to increase the number of general agents beyond the previous limit of two.

When Alexander J. Coney took the reins as executive vice president in January 1948, Pacific was a mature company, fully licensed, well staffed and boasting assets of $1.08 million.

Coney was a California attorney who moved to Hawaii in 1947 to organize the Hawaii Casualty and Surety Rating Bureau. Having begun his insurance career with AEtna Casualty and Surety of San Francisco, Coney would prove to be both a leader in the Hawaii community and a competitive innovator in business. In the first five years of Coney's

leadership, Pacific increased the value of its written premiums from $762,000 to more than $2 million. The company grew into larger quarters in the Kapiolani Bowl Building and then into its own building at 1677 Ala Moana. By 1953 Coney was elected president.

His leadership and innovation would fuel even further growth for Pacific.

Part of Pacific's increased prominence came from Coney's involvement in industry affairs. He served as national convention chairman for the National Association of Insurance Commissioners, the governing committee of the Hawaii Casualty and Surety Rating Bureau and the Hawaii Fire Rating Bureau. Recognition also came from Coney's public service involvement with Junior Achievement of Hawaii and St. Francis Hospital, and from leadership roles with Outrigger Canoe Club, Pacific Club and the Waialae and Oahu country clubs. But his internal leadership was perhaps most important. Under Coney, Pacific became known as an innovator; it formed Sentinel Insurance Co., a wholly owned subsidiary, in 1955. It initiated monthly financing of premiums, it

became the first Hawaii insurance company to become computerized and it introduced numerous creative marketing plans and products.

Elected chairman and chief executive officer in 1963 (the same year that Pacific joined with the Hartford Insurance Group), A.J. Coney retired in 1971. He was succeeded by Ernest H. McCaughan, 1971-77, and H.E. McCord, 1977-80.

Today Pacific Insurance Co., Ltd. occupies several floors of the Davies Pacific Center Building on the corner of Merchant and Bishop streets—the very core of Honolulu's financial and industrial district. Premiums, raised to more than $21 million before Coney's retirement, *now stand at more than $40 million.* The firm employs over 250 people. DeRoy C. Thomas of the Hartford is chairman of the board, and Paul Ables is president. The little office in the Stangenwald building where it all began in 1928 is less than a block away—fully renovated.

And A.J. Coney, still active in the Waialae Country Club, plays a bit more golf these days.

A.J. Coney

Forty years of innovative technology in service to Hawaii

Hours after the Japanese attack on Pearl Harbor, Fred Loui worked his way through the chaotic streets of Honolulu to his job at the Naval Shipyard. Loui knew that the destruction would be immense, and his dedicated nature led him to serve his country as best he could by contributing immediately to the rebuilding of the Pacific Fleet as a shipyard worker.

That attitude of service was to become an essential part of Loui's business philosophy in the years ahead.

As World War II neared its end, Loui left Pearl Harbor in 1944 to start his own business. Pacific Refrigeration Service initially serviced private and military ships from a small workyard in the Ala Moana section of Honolulu. It was from that modest beginning that Pacific Marine & Supply Co. Ltd. and the Unitek Group of Companies were founded.

Long hours, dedication and ingenuity brought quick success to the ship refrigeration firm. After six years in business, the company changed its name to Pacific Marine & Supply Co., Ltd. to reflect its full range of ship repair services to the growing market.

Navy, Coast Guard, research and commercial ships, including tankers, cruise lines, fishing and oceanographic vessels, were among those repaired by Pacific Marine. Its customers flew the flags of all nations, and included the companies of such legends in the shipping industry as the U.S.A.'s Daniel Ludwig, Greece's G.P. Livanos, and Hong Kong's Y.K. Pao.

Because Pacific Marine had benefitted from Hawaii's booming postwar economy, it was conscientious in giving back to the community.

Well aware of the significance of the ocean to both the state and the company, Pacific Marine played a major role in Bishop Museum's restoration of the nineteenth-century whaling ship, *The Falls of Clyde.*

In 1969, after the sudden death of Fred Loui, his son, Steven, took the helm of the company. The younger Loui foresaw the changes in the maritime industry and reasoned that it was time to take the company's established reputation for service and technological expertise into new industrial areas. Thus began a decade of planned diversification that has enabled Pacific Marine to become the family of engineering service companies it is today.

Steven Loui, president of the now-diversified group of technologically oriented service companies, says, "My father, Fred Loui, established a philosophy of superior service, entrepreneurial innovation and technical excellence. We have built upon that founding commitment by diversifying into non-marine areas."

A corporate name change in 1980 has unified the expanding, family-owned company and its subsidiaries under the name of Unitek. Seeing the importance of new and rapidly changing technology to business in the coming years, the company has established itself in data communications; environmental and energy services; and product distribution and representation, while maintaining its principal business in marine and specialty contracting.

Unitek Computer Services specializes in

Fred Loui, far right, and his Pacific Marine staff in the early 1950s.

custom programming as well as sales of software and hardware for DEC, Wang and Data General. A sister company, Unitek Electronics, maintains a satellite receiver station for communications and transportation clients.

Another example of the company's successful diversification into growth industries for the '80s is in the environmental and energy service area. In 1976, Unitek Environmental Services built the only waste oil recycling facility in Hawaii. Today it offers three key services which help preserve the high quality of the state's environment—waste oil and solvent reclamation, hazardous waste management and emergency chemical-spill response. To complement this business, Unitek Energy Systems has developed a market to distribute and construct alternate energy systems.

The Unitek Supply company serves as a wholesale distributor of industrial products and construction materials, with product lines including Mobil Oil lubricants and 3M.

While expansion into other fields has enabled the company to increase in size almost tenfold in ten years, ship repairing remains the largest single operation of Unitek. It, too, has modernized with the times.

In August 1983, Pacific Marine received its recently constructed $2-million floating dry dock, the first wide enough to handle modern barges. This dry dock, the only privately owned one in the state, demonstrates the continuing commitment the company has to its founding business.

As the Unitek family of companies enters its 40th year of service to Hawaii, it is well positioned for the next four decades.

Small gas flame propels energy company into world marketplace

At the turn of the century, as Hawaii was reveling in its newly acquired status as a territory of the United States, a trio of businessmen set out to establish a gas business in Honolulu.

Gas was the new, modern fuel in America. The three (a teacher, a crockery merchant and an attorney) believed that gas—that instant, clean fuel—would be irresistible competition to the hot, sooty fuels of the day. Their dream was to build a plant and make gas out of oil for cooking and water heating.

The franchise for a gas utility was granted to them by the U.S. Congress in 1904. By May of next year, their dream was realized when the Honolulu Gas Co., Ltd. began sending out gas to Honolulu homes through twelve miles of newly laid underground pipe.

As the population of Honolulu grew, the network of gas mains threaded its way into these new communities. To meet demand, the gas plant was rebuilt, expanded and improved. But when World War II was over, the plant and its people were so exhausted by the war effort that many thought it would be wiser to abandon gas service than to rebuild.

Instead, a group of businessmen led by E.E. Black took over the company and renovated the plant. The booming postwar economy, the evolvement of Waikiki as a tourist center and the impetus of statehood sparked another surge of dynamic growth. The company began supplying bottled gas to customers away from utility lines.

By 1967, the company was supplying gas to all of the major islands in the Hawaii chain. A young Seattle executive, James F. Gary, arrived to take over as president and brought a bold vision and spirit which in ten years would transform the small gas business into a major energy provider in the Pacific Basin.

At the time, Hawaii was almost completely dependent upon a single source of petroleum. To increase energy self-sufficiency, and with

The finest of gas appliances—heaters, ranges and ceiling lights—on display in modern Honolulu Gas Co., Ltd. showroom at Beretania and Alakea, circa 1915.

the blessing of public officials and the business community, Gary's management team built Hawaii's largest oil refinery. In the process, the company took a new name, Pacific Resources, Inc. (PRI), and The Gas Company became a major operating subsidiary.

PRI's new refinery subsidiary, Hawaiian Independent Refinery, Inc., began making products out of imported crude oil in 1972, just as the curtain rose on the most difficult period in the history of the energy industry. OPEC's rise to power, subsequent high crude

Honolulu Gas Co., Ltd.'s modern fleet of motor vehicles— the handcranked variety—proudly pose in 1932 before the new Kamakee Street distribution center.

oil costs and the world demand for petroleum put the young company to the test. PRI soon moved into position as one of Hawaii's top four companies and on to *Fortune* Magazine's list of the nation's top 500 companies.

PRI's petroleum operations adapted, expanded and changed to meet the needs of its growing customer base. By 1980, PRI had become a billion dollar corporation. Today, the refinery's rated capacity is 67,900 barrels per day. PRI markets energy products and services including jet fuel, gasoline and residual fuel oils in Hawaii, the U.S. West Coast, Southeast Asia and throughout the Pacific Basin.

The Gas Company built a synthetic natural gas plant adjacent to the refinery and put its old plant on cold standby in 1974. To stem the loss of gas sales stimulated by rising energy prices and conservation, the company sought new business opportunities in the field of alternative energies. By 1980, PRI was the state's leading solar sales firm. In 1983, it began marketing heat pumps, built a cogeneration plant and participated in a federal fuel cell installation test.

Now in its eighth decade, PRI has earned an international reputation as a company that treasures its Hawaiian roots while keeping pace with the technological demands of the energy industry. PRI's employees remain mindful of the company's modest beginnings and the gas flame that propelled its dynamic growth.

Keeping pace with the islands since the early 1900s

The firm that is Peat Marwick today has grown apace with the islands it serves. In 1917, a partnership was formed between Ernest R. Cameron, an Internal Revenue agent, and Ralph Johnstone, a tax representative of the Territory of Hawaii. Neither of the partners of Cameron & Johnstone was a CPA, although Cameron was issued a certificate when the CPA legislation was passed years later.

In those early days, Cameron & Johnstone's practice was confined to income tax work, primarily because few business people in Honolulu were familiar with the new federal income tax law. Cameron was widely held to be one of the most competent tax professionals available, a reputation enhanced, no doubt, by his previous affiliation with the IRS. Johnstone was not a technical tax man, but he was widely known, was well-liked, and so brought in clients for the firm. The practice grew rapidly, with a client list that included many of the larger companies engaged in business in the islands at the time.

Meanwhile, in 1923 a New Zealand-chartered accountant named Hugh C. Tennent arrived in Honolulu with his family. He had spent six years in what is now Western Samoa as treasurer of that group of islands. Within a short time, Tennent had formed a partnership with Edward J. Greaney, a former agent of the Internal Revenue Service and executive with Oahu Railway & Land.

Tennent supervised the audit practice, while Greaney directed the tax practice. They, too, developed an excellent client roster, including Walter F. Dillingham's new firm, Hawaiian Dredging & Construction Co.

The two former IRS agents, Greaney and Cameron, built fine reputations as tax professionals in those decades. Both partnerships were located in downtown Honolulu— C&J in the original Bishop National Bank Building and T&G in the Dillingham Transportation Building. Shortly after the death of Greaney in 1950, the two firms merged to form Cameron, Tennent & Greaney. The period was one of dramatic growth—for the islands and for the new firm. In a short time, Herbert C. Dunn's name was added to the masthead.

In 1956, Cameron, Tennent & Dunn became a part of Peat Marwick Mitchell & Co.,

Front, left to right, F. David Fowler, managing partner; Curt A. Boland, partner in charge, Audit. Rear, left to right, John R. Marks, partner in charge, Tax; Malcolm J. Tom, partner in charge, Management Consulting; Merle D. Crow, partner in charge, Private Business Advisory Group.

together with the Henry Davis Audit Company. Leadership of the new firm included Doris Bennett, Frank DePonte, Herbert Dunn, Fred Green, William L. Higdon, Charles Moses and Val Tennent.

The resulting firm has grown to be the largest public accounting practice in the islands. Over 100 professionals are engaged in accounting, audit, tax, management consulting and private business advisory services.

The practice now has two operating offices—the original one in Honolulu plus a location on Guamm, and is one of the major practices in the international network of the firm. The client list includes businesses and organizations located throughout the Pacific Basin. The diversity of this clientele and the growth of the practice requires that the staff be composed of professionals with an extensive and varied array of skills and experience. The client listing is a cross section of island business, public sector, institutional and professional activity.

Today, twelve partners direct activities for the firm. The services provided go far beyond the basic financial reporting and income tax

services provided by the founders. While Audit continues to be the largest department, the Tax practice has expanded dramatically in recent years. The Management Consulting department is also growing rapidly, reflecting the firm's reputation as business advisors. The Private Business Advisory Group, established in response to the needs of smaller, owner-operated companies in the islands, continues to be called upon with increasing frequency.

The Peat Marwick professional must be able to deal with a wide range of problems— from foreign tax credits to software packages. Reflecting the cosmopolitan mix of the modern island community, Peat Marwick's staff can boast fluency in over a dozen languages—from Chinese to Chamorro.

Though the firm is larger and more sophisticated in the '80s, Peat Marwick has maintained the founders' dedication to the island community. The offices may take up two floors of a new skyscraper, but Peat Marwick is still on the same corner on Bishop Street in downtown Honolulu.

A story of experience

Original oil portraits of King David Kalakaua are on permanent display in each of Pioneer's branch offices. Kalakaua, the "Merry Monarch," granted Pioneer's charter in 1890.

Pioneer Federal enjoys the distinction of being the only savings and loan association in the United States to have been chartered by a king. In 1890, the islands of Hawaii were experiencing a tremendous business expansion as businessmen, fortune hunters and laborers migrated to Hawaii. Industrious newcomers swelled the need for additional homes.

It was in this climate that Hawaii's first savings and loan association, the Pioneer Building and Loan Association, was incorporated. On June 12, 1890, Pioneer was granted its charter by King David Kalakaua, known to his people as the "Merry Monarch." The royal seal of approval gave new dimensions to the financial and economic structure of Honolulu. Founded on the concept that shelter is one of man's basic needs, Pioneer's aim was to help fill that need by giving financial help to people seeking home ownership.

During its first 50 years, growth was slow, but Pioneer remained healthy and stable. In 1941, the firm became a member of the Federal Home Loan Bank System and the Federal Savings and Loan Insurance Corporation. In the 1950s and 1960s, Pioneer was the fastest growing savings and loan in Hawaii. By 1962, the savings and loan business had become the cornerstone of home financing for the community. Savings and loan associations were making more than 55 percent of all home mortgage loans recorded. The time had come for expansion of Pioneer's facilities.

Instrumental in Pioneer's growth was Charles K. Fletcher, director of Pioneer in 1962 and president and manager in 1964. Mr. Fletcher had founded one of the largest savings and loan institutions in the nation, Home Federal Savings and Loan Association of San Diego, California.

Pioneer began a major expansion program in 1963. New office buildings, patterned after the style of the traditional Hawaiian long house, set the design theme for all of Pioneer's offices built during the next decade. At this time, Pioneer was the only financial institution in Hawaii to offer a 4.8 percent per annum dividend rate paid on insured savings.

In 1965, on Pioneer's 75th anniversary, Senate Resolution No. 142, of the Third Legislature, 1965, state of Hawaii, saluted Pioneer as "the first and oldest of all of the savings and loan associations in these islands." This anniversary also featured the unveiling of a full-length oil portrait of King Kalakaua in honor of his 129th birthday. Mrs. Adele Sommerfeld, noted Honolulu artist, devoted months of research into the monarch's life and photographs to achieve authenticity.

Pioneer initiated the practice of Saturday openings in 1968, and was the only savings and loan offering this customer service at that time. On June 25, 1970, the Federal Home Loan Bank approved Pioneer's application for conversion from a state-chartered to a federally chartered association. The official name of the firm became Pioneer Federal

Pioneer's main office in downtown Honolulu, 1967. Today, within steps of this site, stands the 22-story Pioneer Plaza.

Savings and Loan Association of Hawaii.

Another Pioneer Federal first came with the introduction of The Investor Club. The Club offered many free services, including private lounge facilities, latest financial periodicals and free safe deposit boxes. In 1972, Pioneer pioneered mobile branch offices in four communities on the Big Island of Hawaii. The mobile vans served well to bring savings services to smaller towns and would be converted to full service branches in time.

In 1976, ground was broken in downtown Honolulu for the Pioneer Plaza, a 22-story commercial and office complex. The site also includes Pioneer's location at the time of its charter in 1890.

By 1979, Pioneer was the only savings and loan with branch offices on all four major islands. In March 1983, Pioneer changed its name to Pioneer Federal Savings Bank— Hawaii's first savings bank. The change reflects, once again, Pioneer's commitment to the financial needs of Hawaii's people and a commitment to growth to fill those needs.

Since its royal beginning in 1890, Pioneer has grown, through the spirit of understanding, innnovation and the concept of people helping people. Persistence and determination . . . the Pioneer spirit.

A legacy of love

In 1854, when Alexander Liholiho ascended to the throne as King Kamehameha IV, the Hawaiian population had dwindled from about 250,000 to a little more than 60,000. This was the result of epidemics and diseases and the lack of proper health facilities and skills to care for the stricken.

King Kamehameha IV, appalled and grieved by the tragedy that had befallen the people, recognized the pressing need for a hospital.

In 1856, the King married the Ali'i Emma Rooke Nae'a, the adopted daughter of Dr. T.C.B. Rooke. While growing up in that household, Emma was witness to the suffering of the people who sought the care of her foster father. The Queen supported her husband, both in spirit and action, in his efforts to establish a hospital.

In 1859, the royal couple took it upon themselves to raise the funds to build a hospital. They were able to personally raise more than $13,500, to which the Legislature added another $6,000.

In May 1859, with King Kamehameha IV as President and 20 trustees, The Queen's Hospital (named after Queen Emma) was established.

The Queen's Hospital opened its doors to the public in December 1860 with 124 beds and two physicians on the nine-acre site where it stands today. The two-story coral building cost $14,000.

The first years of the hospital were not easy ones. Its continued existence during those years was due largely to the generosity

The Queen's Hospital, 1907. "New" Pauahi Wing at left, Main Building at right.

of Charles Reed Bishop. Mr. Bishop not only served as trustee but donated large sums of money and equipment, including a two-story brick building in 1893 and the original Pauahi Wing in 1905 in the memory of his wife, Bernice Pauahi Bishop.

The Liholiho Wing, which contained large wards and some private rooms, was dedicated in 1922, at which time the original coral structure was demolished to make way for the Queen Emma Building in 1924; today this wing is called Nalani, a nickname for Queen Emma.

Subsequent years witnessed the construction of additional wings to house the increasing number of new programs and services offered.

In 1967, the Board of Directors changed the name of the hospital to The Queen's Medical Center, reflecting the broader scope of health care services.

The Medical Center has been a leader in the State in introducing new technology and implementing progressive surgical and therapeutic procedures, developing innnovative training programs and offering insightful human services. Among the programs and procedures which Queen's has initiated in Hawaii are the following: 1955—brain surgery using the techniques of hypothermia; 1959—open heart surgery; 1960—use of a two million-volt radiation therapy machine; 1964—establishment of a medical intensive care unit;

1968—establishment of a coronary care unit; 1972—acquisition of a Computerized Tomography Head Scanner; 1979—opening of a primary care unit; and 1980—establishment of a microsurgery training program.

Today, The Queen's Medical Center, a private, nonprofit institution, is a major acute care teaching facility for the University of Hawaii John A. Burns School of Medicine. The Center has a licensed capacity of 506 beds, and has approximately 2,400 employees and 1,200 members on the medical-dental staff. Located at the "Crossroads of the Pacific," Queen's has hosted visiting professors, physicians and students from all over the world, particularly the People's Republic of China and Japan.

Queen's has had a tradition of dedication and service from its Board of Directors and administrators, beginning with King Kamehameha IV and Dr. William Hillebrand. In recent years, E.E. Black Sr. (immediate past Chairman of the Board), Malcolm MacNaughton (Chairman of the Board) and Will J. Henderson (immediate past President) have provided strong leadership in today's complex health care environment.

The Queen's Medical Center represents the fulfillment of a "legacy of love" dedicated to the people by its founders Queen Emma and King Kamehameha IV, who, in their wisdom and benevolence, envisioned a health center which would serve the people of Hawaii with concern and compassion.

A legacy of caring

St. Francis Hospital opened as a 50-bed hospital in 1927.

On November 8, 1883, at 1 o'clock in the afternoon, the *Mariposa* docked in Honolulu Harbor. Among her disembarking passengers were Mother Marianne Cope, Mother Superior of the Sisters of the Third Order of St. Francis of Syracuse, New York, and six Franciscan Sisters. All had willingly accepted the challenge of a new mission, without regard for their personal welfare.

They had come in response to a plea from Hawaii officials for nursing Sisters to provide comfort and care for people afflicted with that most dreaded of diseases, leprosy.

Upon their arrival in Honolulu that November day in 1883, the Sisters were welcomed royally. Five carriages of state were dispatched by King David Kalakaua to meet and transport them to the Cathedral of Our Lady of Peace, where Bishop Hermann Koeckemann offered benediction.

Mother Marianne accompanied the Sisters on their journey intending only to help them get settled in their assignments, but she never returned to Syracuse. She died on August 9, 1918 at the leper settlement at Kalaupapa, Molokai, where she spent the last 30 years of her life.

For many years the Sisters also served at the government hospitals in Wailuku, Maui, and Hilo, Hawaii.

The selflessness and caring of these first Franciscans in Hawaii is the legacy on which St. Francis Hospital is founded.

The hospital itself began as a dream in the hearts of a few Sisters of St. Francis in the early years of this century. While deeply involved in their schools and in their work with lepers, the Sisters saw the need for a community hospital, one that would serve the medical needs of the people.

Prominent among the hospital's early supporters was the beloved Hawaiian Princess Abigail Campbell Kawananakoa, who organized the St. Francis Hospital Guild and, as its first president, planned fund-raising activities and enlisted the support of friends. One of the Guild's successful activities was a bridge party, held at the newly opened Royal Hawaiian Hotel.

The 50-bed hospital opened on May 9, 1927 and admitted its first patient, an 8-year-old girl, whose total bill for a tonsillectomy came to $15.

In 1929 the hospital opened its School of Nursing; hundreds of Hawaii's nurses graduated from this program before the school closed in 1966.

It soon became apparent that a larger hospital was needed, and expansion of hospital facilities and services became a way of life at St. Francis. Wings were added to increase the hospital's bed capacity and provide space for needed services. Two major additions were the five-story Mother Marianne Wing in 1959 and the five-story Sullivan Wing in 1975.

Today, St. Francis has 256 acute care beds and 52 skilled nursing facility beds. Beds, however, tell but a part of the story, for under the leadership of its chief executive officer, Sister Maureen, St. Francis has introduced several programs that serve many thousands of people outside its walls. The hospital pioneered home care on Oahu and Kauai and hospice care for the terminally ill and their

Nurses Sister Pancretia and Judy Akina in the hospital's first surgery.

families. It provides health screening for senior citizens at fourteen sites on Oahu, health education programs for patients and the community, and medical and dental services at a health center in the low-income Chinatown and Iwilei areas. St. Francis Hospital's Women's Alcohol Treatment Center offers a residential treatment program for women who have problems with alcohol. The hospital staff performed Hawaii's first bone marrow and kidney transplants and operates kidney dialysis units on Oahu, Maui, Kauai, Hawaii and Molokai.

CT body scanners, radiotherapy, laser treatments, total hip replacements, rehabilitation services for cancer patients, pastoral care services, counseling and therapy . . . these are but a small part of the hospital's commitment to meeting the medical, physical, spiritual and psychological needs of its patients.

St. Francis Hospital is affiliated with the University of Hawaii and other institutions dedicated to educating the care-givers of the future. The hospital is also accredited by the Joint Commission on Accreditation of Hospitals and by other state and national bodies.

Commitment, service and quality care. These are the legacy of the pioneering Franciscan Sisters who first set foot on these shores in 1883.

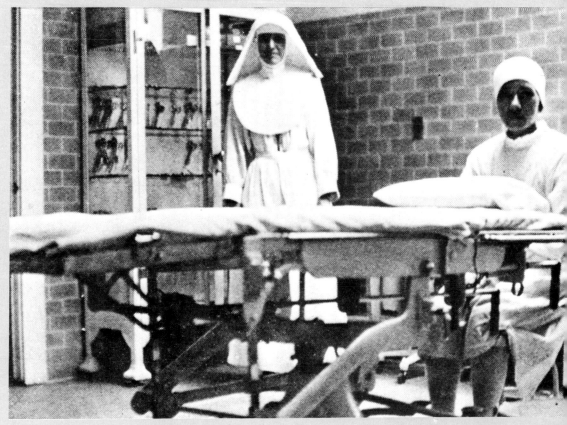

A local miniconglomerate

Servco Pacific had its humble beginnings in a small sugar plantation service community called Haleiwa on Oahu's north shore in 1919. An ambitious immigrant, Peter Fukunaga, purchased a small two-car garage for $1,500 (with a down payment of $25). Convinced that the automobile industry was the key to his destiny, Peter Fukunaga worked very diligently to build his business. Two years later, he incorporated his garage with two others as Waialua Garage Company; and then, in 1926 obtained General Motor's Chevrolet distribution franchise, now the oldest such franchise in the state of Hawaii. Back then he sold only a few new cars a month.

As the '30s approached, Peter Fukunaga branched out and moved his headquarters to Wahiawa in central Oahu. With this expansion, he purchased an acre of strawberry farmland and expanded his dealership facilities. Peter Fukunaga wanted a new name to go along with his new move. Rather than make up a new name, he had a contest offering a $25 prize. As a result, the name Service Motor Company emerged—because "service was the heart of the company's policy."

As his automobile dealership grew, Peter Fukunaga began to diversify his business. He got involved in the wholesaling and retailing of home appliances and musical instruments, giving birth to a new business venture—Easy

Appliance Company and Easy Piano and Organ Company.

Peter Fukunaga's success continued spiraling, extending into the financial arena. Knowing that many of his customers would need financing for their purchases of goods, in 1931 he started Service Finance, Ltd. Known today as Servco Financial Corp., it is very active in the industrial loan business.

But the automotive industry remained the cornerstone of Fukunaga's activity. He opened a second GM-Chevrolet dealership—Waipahu Auto Company—in 1951. That same year he incorporated Hawaii's first profit-sharing plan, patterned after Sears, Roebuck's, and created the Fukunaga Scholarship Foundation which currently is assisting 26 students at various universities and colleges.

Peter Fukunaga's last major business accomplishment was the negotiation of exclusive import distribution franchise for Toyota vehicles (cars, trucks and forklifts) for the state of Hawaii. This business franchise acquisition made in 1958, two years before his death, resulted in significant growth for Servco Pacific.

Under the continued guidance of the Fukunaga family (Peter's two sons, George

and Tom, are chairman and president), the company—now called Servco Pacific Inc.—has diversified even more. The insurance, leasing, advertising, real estate, electronics, audio-visual, office automation, tire, department-store, leisure marine, shopping center, plant nursery and fast-food industries now all include Servco in their numbers. The Servco automotive interests have swelled to include Lincoln-Mercury, Ford and Mazda in Guam, and Suzuki, Alfa Romeo and Maserati franchises for Hawaii; and Servco's other operations have extended to Guam, Saipan and, in the near future, the Marshall Islands.

Servco's founding father, Peter Fukunaga, had mastered the intricacies of business management and business success—a personal commitment to hard work, dedicated employees and the ability to satisfy customers.

Today, Servco Pacific boasts over 1,300 employees in Hawaii, Guam and Saipan, working in no less than 50 disparate locations, in numerous fields of endeavor, and enjoys annual consolidated revenues well in excess of $100 million.

Surely, Peter Fukunaga would be proud.

Waialua Garage Co., Ltd. in 1925, forerunner of Servco Pacific.

May 1925

Quality fresh produce since 1908

Tai Hing Co. with partners, staff and customers in 1918. Wong Buck Hung, 24, is second from the right.

Tai Hing Co., Inc. is the oldest and one of the largest fresh fruit, vegetable and grocery enterprises in Hawaii. It was established by three immigrants from China on January 3, 1908.

The company began as one stall in King Market, an open-air market in Chinatown at 733 Kekaulike Street—Honolulu's main marketplace—before the advent of supermarkets. Customers came from miles around, crowding the market where the fresh roasting aroma of Tai Hing's "Red Heart" pure Kona coffee wafted in the air. Turkeys were sold live, papaya sold for 3 cents a pound and 100 pounds of pineapple could be purchased for 75 cents!

The two individuals responsible for the development and expansion of Tai Hing are the late Wong Buck Hung and Leonard Dai Ying Wong—father and son.

Wong Buck Hung arrived in Honolulu from Canton, China, in 1911 at 16 years of age. He did not speak a word of English, but was destined to play an important role in the future of Tai Hing and Hawaii. He made deliveries for the company on foot with a pushcart from 4 a.m. to 6 p.m., seven days a week. His destinations were Kamehameha School, the old Alexander Young Hotel and stately homes of missionary families such as the Dillinghams, the Castles and the Athertons.

By working hard and living frugally Wong soon saved enough money to purchase shares in the company. When the original partners began retiring to China in 1919, he became manager and eventually senior partner. By the time he became president of Liberty Bank in 1953, he was a well-known community leader. The story of his achievements have been recognized in the *U.S. Congressional Record.*

Wong's life story—as told by George Chaplin, editor of the *Honolulu Advertiser,* at Wong's 71st birthday party in 1965—was entered into the *Congressional Record* by U.S. senator from Hawaii, Hiram L. Fong. Another story was entered by U.S. representative from Hawaii, Spark M. Matsunaga, on the occasion of the Wongs' golden wedding anniversary in 1967.

The future success of Tai Hing was assured when Leonard, the older son of Wong's eight children, took the helm. He had gained a working knowledge of the business from working there since he was a youngster. With acumen and foresight, he developed and directed the business along wholesale lines. Under Leonard's dynamic leadership, the firm expanded from primarily a retail store to a modern wholesale produce house, presently located at 1023 Kawaiahao Street.

Today Leonard runs his business with canny expertise gleaned from a lifetime of dealing with highly perishable items. He takes frequent trips to West Coast farms and markets to seek the finest products for his customers. Long years of experience is the key to his ability to locate specialty items for a demanding clientele. The first to have fresh strawberries and the popular "honey" tan-

Wong Buck Hung, 35, proudly rests a hand on the shoulder of his 10-year-old son Leonard, in 1930. They fulfilled an American dream.

gerines flown to Hawaii, he is regarded in management circles as the "prime produce procurer"—the pioneer in air-freighting new products for the Hawaiian market.

Community-minded like his father, he has been president of all the major Chinese organizations. He is president of the Wholesale Produce Dealers Association and secretary and director of Liberty Bank.

Tai Hing, incorporated in 1963, has built up a prestigious list of institutional customers over the years, including many of the better hotels, restaurants and military clubs. It is also a ship chandler and a supplier of fresh produce to the airlines. Its staff prides itself in offering fine personalized service and quality products as exemplified by the corporate logo—the "Red Heart" of quality.

Transporting of goods has changed greatly from the early 1900s when Chinese truck farmers made deliveries of fresh produce to Tai Hing by horse-drawn wagons traveling on dirt roads in the wee hours of the morning—with kerosene lanterns lighting the way. Three-quarters of a century later, fresh produce is made available to appreciative patrons not only through island growers but from mainland farms, arriving by surface bulk shipments in refrigerated vans and daily by air container service.

Tai Hing Co., Inc. is a family business that has progressed and grown with Hawaii and the nation. It is a story of a Chinese immigrant who pursued an American dream and of a son who helped to make that dream come true.

Theo. H. Davies — his Hawaii

Late in the morning on November 14, 1856, the Dutch vessel *Quatre Bras* was several hours out of Liverpool harbor. Aboard was a youth of 22, lonely, homesick and seasick. Theophilus Harris Davies, the eldest of five children of a poor Congregational minister, was on his way to seek his fortune in the unknown Sandwich Islands.

Davies arrived in Hawaii to fulfill a five-year employment contract with the island trading firm of Starkey, Janion & Co. In 1862, upon the completion of his term, Davies returned to England as he promised his father he would. He had discovered the island *aloha,* however, and the following passage from his journal indicates the depth of his feelings and the difficulty of parting:

My five years in the Pacific are gone — gone to the eternal past and now, within two days' sail of New York, I write their epitaph. I cannot look back on this bright chapter of my life without a glistening eye and a throbbing pulse, for I love Hawaii Nei. No years of my history have been happier, no friends more lavish of their kindness and no signs of the loving kindness of my Heavenly Father more marked than those I have known in the Sandwich Islands.

Within a year, Theo. H. Davies returned to Hawaii, where he would establish one of the "Big Five" companies and play a key role in the islands' economic, social and political history.

A friend of the Hawaiian royalty and supporter of the monarchy, Davies and his wife were appointed legal guardians of the Princess Kaiulani when she was 13 years old. In 1893, the monarchy fell, and Davies, as Kaiulani's guardian, felt it his duty to take the princess to Washington, D.C., to make a personal appeal. When they arrived, the city was celebrating the inauguration of a new president, Grover Cleveland. Davies and Princess Kaiulani visited the President and First Lady in the great white-columned house on

Pennsylvania Avenue. The extent of the effect that call had on President Cleveland has never been determined — but for the rest of his life Cleveland favored the restoration of the monarchy in Hawaii.

Though his attempts to aid the restoration of the monarchy were never successful and the Princess Kaiulani would never rule as queen, Davies saw her become a beloved symbol of the heritage of the Hawaiian people.

In business, Theo. H. Davies prospered. Guided by keen business insight, he acquired 100 percent ownership of Starkey, Janion & Co. within eleven years from the time he started as a clerk. In 1894 the company was incorporated as Theo. H. Davies & Co., Ltd.

The original site of Davies' business, leased from Kamehameha III for 299 years, was at the foot of Kaahumanu Street near the waterfront in downtown Honolulu. Davies himself steadily expanded the company's interests to include transportation, insurance and sugar, as well as trading. He became a pioneer of the Hawaiian sugar industry, taking a leading part in the creation of several plantations, including Hamakua and Laupahoehoe on the Big Island. Davies' sugar business would continue to grow to eventually include the Philippines. Through much of

The Davies Pacific Center.

the first half of this century, his company also remained one of the foremost merchandisers in Hawaii.

The 1970s were to bring dramatic change to the company. The decade opened with a bang as the ornate four-story "Hawaiian Renaissance" warehouse/office building which had stood as the company's corporate headquarters for a half-century came crashing down to make way for the new 23-story Davies Pacific Center in the heart of downtown Honolulu. Three years later, in late 1973, negotiations between the Davies family and Jardine, Matheson & Co., Ltd., a large British trading company headquartered in Hong Kong, culminated in the sale of the company to Jardine, Matheson.

Today, Theo. H. Davies & Co., Ltd. ("TheoDavies") is still known as one of the Big Five — the largest established businesses in Hawaii with major landholdings and roots in the Hawaii sugar industry. The company employs more than 1,600 people engaged in a wide range of activities, including agriculture, engineering, distribution, agency, property and energy businesses.

Through such operations as TheoDavies Hamakua Sugar Co., Pacific Machinery and TheoDavies Euromotors, the company represents some of the most respected names in business, including C and H Sugar, Mercedes-Benz, Caterpillar, Toro, Michelin, Lykes Lines, Del Monte and Lloyd's of London.

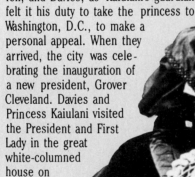

Princess Kaiulani and her guardian, Theo. H. Davies, on their trip to Washington, D.C., to ask for restoration of the Hawaiian monarchy.

A family business grows with the Islands

In 1911, 21-year-old Ching Sing Wo opened a small general store on King Street in downtown Honolulu. The store carried all kinds of merchandise, including furniture, hardware and even toys. Back then, Hawaii was a young and prosperous territory of the United States. Along with Hawaii, C.S. Wo's business grew.

Ching married and raised a family of three sons and two daughters. The eldest son, Robert, left the islands in 1941 to attend college at Stanford. When World War II broke out shortly thereafter, Ching decided to close up the store and move to San Francisco, where the whole family could be together.

With the war over, the Wo family happily returned home and reopened its business. In 1946, Robert graduated and joined his father in running the company, which then became known as C.S. Wo & Sons, Ltd. When the other sons, James and William, graduated several years later, Ching was able to retire, leaving the store in the capable hands of his enthusiastic sons.

Almost immediately, the young Wo brothers showed great business instinct. They reasoned that certain industries were ideally suited for Hawaii's rapidly growing population. One of these industries was furniture. The Wos therefore focused the company's expertise in one direction—home furnishings. This move marked the start of C.S. Wo's determined effort to gain the reputation as "Hawaii's #1 furniture store." Obtaining that reputation was not easy.

The Wo brothers faced their first major crisis in 1949 when Hawaii suffered its worst dock strike ever. After two long months without any mainland shipments of furniture, the brothers were desperate for a solution. Instinct prevailed; together, they gathered all the local lumber they could find, hired some local craftsmen and carpenters and started a small furniture manufacturing shop on Ward Avenue. Robert Wo recalls, "Just as a temporary measure to keep our store going, we decided to try our hand at manufacturing. And it worked."

"The dock strike was actually a blessing in disguise," adds James Wo, "because it changed the direction of our company. With the experience that we gained from setting up the Ward Avenue shop, we then became extremely confident of our ability to succeed in furniture manufacturing."

This confidence of the Wo brothers revealed itself in 1953 with the purchase of Van's Furniture. On this piece of property, the Wos set up both a manufacturing facility and a retail showroom. Destroyed by fire in

Ching Sing Wo in his store, circa 1920s.

1958, the site was rebuilt and renamed BJ Furniture, the first of C.S. Wo's six BJ outlets.

The establishment of the BJ Store was perfectly timed. Along came the Waikiki hotel boom and booming furniture sales. For C.S. Wo & Sons, it was time for further expansion.

The Wos had a plan. They realized that the Far East, with inexpensive, skilled labor and modern production, offered the perfect opportunity to manufacture furniture. And they were right. In Japan and later in Taiwan, Singapore and Hong Kong, the Wos produced furniture components which were then sent to Honolulu for distribution. In 1971, C.S. Wo entered a partnership with Hong Kong

Downtown Honolulu in the 1920s.

Teakwood, an established furniture manufacturer specializing in dining sets. Under the guidance of Chairman Robert Wo, Hong Kong Teakwood improved its production tremendously. Within just ten years, it has grown from a one-factory operation to the number one dining room furniture maker in the world.

Things have changed since 1911. What once was a small general store in Honolulu is now a multinational corporation. The future looks bright for this island company, whose third generation of management leads the way. Executive Vice-president Robert Bub Wo Jr. remarks, "Over the years, we have changed a great deal . . . but we're still just a family-owned company with Hawaii roots, offering the very same quality, value and service that has made C.S. Wo & Sons the place 'where beautiful homes begin.'"

A past woven into Hawaii's future

Arthur Young & Company, one of the "Big Eight" international accounting firms, entered the Honolulu market on October 1, 1971 when it merged with two established Honolulu accounting practices, Kadowaki & Leong and Hough & Miyaki.

A full-service organization, Arthur Young provides its clients with accounting, audit, tax and management consulting services and is one of the largest professional service firms in the world. Arthur Young's U.S. practice comprises more than 7,000 people in over 85 cities. In addition, Arthur Young International, the firm's overseas arm, serves clients with 252 offices in 67 countries across the globe, including several important to Hawaii's business community such as Australia, Hong Kong, Japan and Singapore.

Prior to merging with Arthur Young, the firm of Kadowaki & Leong had served the accounting needs of Hawaii businesses for a quarter of a century. Founded by Theodore Char in 1946, the firm was originally named Char & Fromm.

Char, a second-generation Chinese-American, had the distinction of being the first person of oriental descent to become a certified public accountant in Hawaii. He was a graduate of the University of Illinois.

Over the years, Char's business interests broadened and he was increasingly involved in real estate development. Accordingly, he reduced his participation in the firm, handing over responsibilities to other partners. The practice continued to prosper, evolving through several partnership changes prior to merging with Arthur Young.

The other accounting practice involved in

Theodore Char.

the merger, Hough & Miyaki, was originally formed in 1963 when CPAs Frank Hough and Michael Miyaki teamed up together. Both men had long and distinguished business careers in Hawaii, Hough having been president of the Hawaii Society of Certified Public Accountants in 1959, the year of statehood, and Miyaki being a former state controller.

Following the merger of the two local firms with Arthur Young, Gordon Kadowaki became office managing partner, a post he retained until 1974 when Walter Lohman, a long-time Arthur Young executive formerly based in Los

Arthur Young & Company Honolulu office partners—Karl A. Haushalter (left) and Gordon Kadowaki.

Angeles, joined the Honolulu office as managing partner. In 1975, Lohman returned to the mainland and Karl A. Haushalter, audit principal of the Honolulu office, became the office managing partner. Kadowaki semi-retired from the firm in 1980, although he continues to retain an office at Arthur Young's Honolulu headquarters on the eighth floor of the Amfac Building at 700 Bishop Street. At 32, Haushalter was the youngest office managing partner in the Arthur Young system. Under his leadership, the firm grew and prospered, presently serving over 200 private companies and several government agencies in Hawaii. On October 1, 1983, Haushalter became the senior partner of the Honolulu office.

Lawrence D. Rodriguez, the Honolulu office's fourth managing partner, also heads up an informal and conscientious team of accounting and audit specialists. The group has earned a reputation for working with clients, rather than for them, developing an insider's understanding of the client's business that enables Arthur Young to provide sound, practical recommendations and advice.

The management consulting division, under the direction of Edward F. Andrew, consists of highly qualified specialists who advise businesses on a variety of topics ranging from electronic data processing systems development and review to organizational development, executive compensation and profit planning.

In 1979, the firm was also among the first to institute a small business division, a move aimed at providing consultation and services for fledgling businesses at an affordable price.

The firm's tax practice, under the leadership of Richard J. Saas, partner, quickly established a reputation as a leading tax practice in Honolulu. In addition to a substantial personal tax planning practice, the tax group's areas of specialization include real estate development, retailing, foreign investors and financial institutions.

As the firm approaches the mid-80s, it has garnered its share of major accounts in Honolulu, including Pacific Guardian Life Insurance Company, Aloha Airlines, Liberty Bank, Territorial Savings & Loan, Shirokiya and the Halekulani Corporation. Arthur Young Honolulu continues to expand, winning new clients and adding fresh talent to its ranks. In a survey by *Fortune* Magazine, peers singled out Arthur Young among all other "Big Eight" accounting firms as the firm that is "widely respected and super professional." It's a reputation that Arthur Young is proud of and that it will continue to earn in Honolulu for many years to come.

J.I. Silva Homestead Store was important to the daily lives of villagers in Eleele, Kauai, at the turn of this century.

AUTHOR'S ACKNOWLEDGMENTS

In writing a history there is a kind of osmosis effect that must be recognized if you have lived a long time in the place you are writing about. The locale's sights and smells and tastes are absorbed through the senses, of course, but also through the heart. Since I have lived a long time in the islands, my historical viewpoint is shaped by deep feelings for a place which has given so much to me, and thus my history of Hawaii is, inevitably, subjective to a certain degree. Objectivity, once the goal of every reporter, suffers somewhat in this book but not, I hope, to the extent that the reader also suffers.

The history of Honolulu and the history of Hawaii are inseparable, which is the reason for their intertwining here. A history of Honolulu could be written that would nail down the time and place of every new building's dedication, and how many cubic yards of concrete were poured into the basement of the new capitol, and perhaps be interesting—but it would miss the pulsing heart of a city that has grown like no other, whose history has been vibrant and vital, and whose characteristic has been that of change. Honolulu has been and probably will be a city in transit, for in spite of the wonderful Polynesian laissez-faire, there is a sense of movement and motion that is a part of Honolulu's charisma.

So all history is selective. What I have chosen to include here are illustrative moments connected by a general narrative, designed to give the reader a feel for the sweep of Hawaiian history and its high drama. To include all of the events and personalities that shaped the islands would be to write volumes, not a single work.

But to draw the islands as cleanly as possible within time and space limitations—that is both a challenge and a labor of love.

I wish to acknowledge some valuable help: Walelu Stone, advisor, critic, typist; Doug Carlson, for his critique of the manuscript; Laura Figueira, for her advice and suggestions; John McGowan for his support and his fine editor's eye; Mary Ann Akao for her fine historian's eye for detail and accuracy; Mazeppa Costa, for advice and for her artist's vision; and others too numerous to mention whom I interrupted from time to time with questions about aspects of this history. Naturally, I assume responsibilities for any errors.

Listing sources for this work presented a problem. My primary source is more or less continuous residence in Hawaii for more than a quarter-century. Important sources have been interviews with newsmakers and long talks with friends of all races over many years; the newspaper on which I worked for nearly ten years; the closeness with politicians, newsmen, artists, sailors, crooks, laborers, farmers and scores of others; and pleasurable moments spent sailing, diving, hiking, camping or riding in the midst of spectacular scenery. There were also many pleasurable moments spent on beaches lit by brilliant sunsets, staring over the sea toward the origins of the Hawaiian people, lost in the misty genesis of a proud and intelligent race.

In a quarter-century of reading about Hawaii some works stand out as especially valuable. They are listed here, along with a few others that a reader might find helpful or interesting.

BIBLIOGRAPHY

Anthony J. Garner. *Hawaii Under Army Rule.* Honolulu: University of Hawaii Press, 1975.

Armstrong, R. Warwick, et al. *Atlas of Hawaii.* Honolulu: University of Hawaii Press, 1973.

Aspects of Hawaiian Life and Environment, commentaries on significant Hawaiian topics by fifteen recognized authorities. Honolulu: The Kamehameha Schools Press, 1965.

Barker, A.J. *Pearl Harbor.* New York: Ballantine Books, Inc., 1969.

Barrot, Theodore Adolphe. *Unless Haste is Made.* Oahu, Hawaii: Kailua Press Pacifica, 1978.

Buck, Sir Peter (Te Rangi Hiroa). *Vikings of the Sunrise.* New York, 1933.

Bushnell, O.A. *A Walk Through Old Honolulu.* Kapa Associates, Honolulu.

Carlson, Doug. *Hill of Sacrifice, The National Memorial Cemetery of the Pacific at Punchbowl.* Honolulu: Island Heritage, 1982.

Christensen, John. "A History of Firsts." *The Sunday Star-Bulletin and Advertiser,* Honolulu, April 4, 1982.

Coffman, Tom. *Catch a Wave: A Case Study of Hawaii's New Politics.* Honolulu: The University of Hawaii Press, 1973.

Daws, Gavan. *Shoal of Time, A History of the Hawaiian Islands.* Honolulu: The University of Hawaii Press, 1968.

Day, A. Grove, and Stroven, Carl, editors. *A Hawaiian Reader.* New York: Popular Library, 1961
The Spell of Hawaii. New York: Meredith Press, 1968.

PICTURE EDITOR'S ACKNOWLEDGMENTS

Researching and collecting photography for *Honolulu: Heart of Hawaii* has been a challenging and satisfying undertaking. None of it would have been possible without the support and assistance of the Hawaii community whose commitment to preserving the history and enchantment of the Islands shines forth in the pages of this book.

My special thanks to the **Bishop Museum**, specifically Director Dr. Edward C. Creutz, Manager of Operations David R. Huffman and, most especially, Photo Librarian Betty Lou Kam and members of her staff.

Mary Ann Akao and other staff members of the **Hawaii State Archives** unhesitatingly gave of their time and knowledge. **The Kamehameha Schools** opened their files and gave generously of their assistance, particularly in the efforts of Luryier Diamond and Bruce G.S. Lum.

Many organizations generously provided photographs and assistance—Boys Club of Honolulu; Hawaii School for Girls at La Pietra; Hawaii Visitors Bureau; Hawaiian Historical Society; Hawaiian Mission Children's Society Library; Honolulu Academy of Arts; Honolulu Community Theatre; Honolulu Symphony Society; Honolulu Theatre for Youth; Office of the Mayor, City & County of Honolulu; Pan American World Airways; Photoplant, Inc.; R.M. Towill Corporation; Wimberly Whisenand Allison Tong & Goo Architects, Ltd.; and the U.S. Navy.

The contributions of these individuals made the project rewarding...and a great joy—Bob Awana, George Bacon, James Campbell, Joe Carini, Roger Coryell, Monte Costa, Page Costa, Robert Costa, Tony Costa, Jeff DePonte, Arlene Duncan, Bob Ebert, Charlotte King Ebert, David Franzen, Betty Hirozawa, Ron Jett, Nadine Kahanamoku, Mark Lofstrom, Terry Luke, Ah Quon McElrath, Douglas K. Mukai, Pepi Neiva, Gretchen Reyes, Richard Rothrock, Gordon Sakamoto, Allan Seiden, A.A. Smyser, Scott C.S. Stone, Brett Uprichard, David Yamada and Greg Vaughn.

To all of you, many thanks.

PHOTO CREDITS

Sources of photographs, maps and art appearing in this book are noted here in alphabetical order and by page number (position on the page is noted). Those photographs appearing in the chapter "Partners in Progress" were provided by the represented firms.

Apio, Alani: 154/55.

Bishop Museum: 17; 18 top; 24; 46 full page; 50; 57; 58/59; 66; 68 top; 69; 70 left; 72 top; 78 top right; 80 bottom, right center; 86 top left; 86/87; 92; 94 right; 128 bottom left; 130; 134/35; 135 top; 136.

    A.T. Agate engraving: 26 bottom.
    Jacque Arago lithograph: 18 bottom.
    G.H. Burgess, original lithograph: 64/65.
    Crepin engraving after Arago: 30 top.
    Robert Dampier: engraving, 43 bottom; engraving after painting by, 46 top.
    Menzies Dickson: 80 top left.
    Robert Elwes original watercolor: 10/11.
    John Williams Gear: 43 top.
    Laurence Hata: 140 top.
    John Hayter: 31.
    Thomas Heddington: 29 top.
    C.J. Hedemann: 88, 112 top.
    Henry W. Henshaw: 19 top.
    Seth Joel: 16 top.
    Joseph W. King: 67 top.
    Barthéleme, Lauverge: 47.
    L. Massard: 42 top.
    Louis-Jules Masselot: 44/45, 48/49.
    Pellion, engraving after: 28, 30 bottom.
    August Plum: 52 bottom.
    John Webber: Original pencil, pen and wash, 20 top left; drawing, 20 top right; engraving, 16 full page, 23 bottom; original pen and wash, 23 top right, top left, 26 top; original sketches, 19 bottom, 178/79.
    Charles L. Weed: 68 bottom.
    Wood: 25 bottom.

Bishop Museum, Carl Andrews Collection: 103.
    Donald Angus Collection: 20 bottom (William Bligh map), 25 top.
    Ray Jerome Baker Collection: 1 bottom, 29 bottom, 32, 34, 56, 87 top, 104/05, 108 top, 118 top, 124 bottom, 127 top.
    Leningrad Museum of the Academy of Arts (N. Tikanov portrait): 27.
    Tai Sing Loo Collection: 131, 132.
    United Japanese Society: 133.

Carini, Joe: 158, 161 bottom, 165 bottom left, 167 top right, 168 all, 176, 178/79 inset.

Costa Family Collection: 113, 137, 142 top left, 177.

Costa, Mazeppa: 169 inset, 171 center inset, 172 top left, 174 left.

Costa, Monte: 4/5, 166/67, 171 bottom inset, top inset, 174 right.

Costa, Page: 8/7.

Ebert, Bob: 13, 140 bottom, 142 bottom, 144.

Hawaii State Archives: 6/7, 14, 38 top, 43, 54, 55 all, 60/61, 62, 67 bottom, 70 top, 72/73, 75 all, 76/77, 78, 79 all, 81 bottom, 82/83, 83 top, 85 top left, top right, 89 top right, 90 top left, 94 left, 95, 97, 98, 99 top, 100, 101 top, 105 top, 106 all, 110/11, 111 top, 118 bottom, 120 top, 146, 147, 148, 149 all, 160 top, 161 top, 180/81, 269, 271, 272.
    Bingham sketch, woodcut after: 42 bottom.
    Auguste Borget: 53 bottom.
    Louis Choris: 37; lithograph after, 36 all; lithograph 38/39.
    James Dwight Dana: 52 top left, 52/53 top, 53 top right.
    Fisquet: 41 full page.
    John Hayter, from painting by: 45 top.
    F. Howard: 41 top.
    Hulsart, after drawing by: 39 top.
    August Plum: 53 center inset.

Hawaii State Archives, Mary Ann Akao Collection: 143.
    George Bacon Collection: 150/51, 152 top left, 152/53.
    Ray Jerome Baker Collection: 73 top; 74 top (Rulofson); 77 top right; 89 bottom left, bottom right, center right.

Fuchs, Lawrence H. *Hawaii Pono, A Social History.* New York: Harcourt, Brace & World, Inc., 1961.

Goodman, Robert B., et al. *The Hawaiians.* Honolulu: Island Heritage, 1970.

Gorshkov, Sergei G. "Navies in War and Peace." U.S. Naval Institute Proceedings, March, 1974; and Berg, L.S. *Ocherki Po Istorii Russkikh Geograficheskikh Otkyrytiyi* [Sketches on the History of Russian Geographic Discoveries] revised and supplemented. Publishing House of the Academy of Sciences, USSR.

Grant, William. "How Downtown Evolved Into Its Present Form." *The Sunday Star-Bulletin and Advertiser,* Honolulu, April 11, 1982.

Graves, William. *Hawaii.* Washington, D.C.: The National Geographic Society, 1970.

Hodge, Clarence L., and Ferris, Peggy. "Building Honolulu." Chamber of Commerce of Honolulu, Hawaii, 1950.

Hoefer, Hans, et al. *Insight Guides—Hawaii.* Hong Kong: APA Productions, 1980.

Li, John Papa. *Fragments of Hawaiian History.* Honolulu: Bishop Museum Press, 1963.

Joesting, Edward. *Hawaii, An Uncommon History.* New York: W.W. Norton & Co., Inc., 1972.

Judd, Gerritt P. *Hawaii, A Student's Guide to Localized History.* New York: Teachers College Press, Teachers College, Columbia University, 1966.

Krout, Mary H. *Hawaii and a Revolution.* London: John Murray, Albemarle Street, 1898.

Kuykendall, Ralph. "Hawaiian Kingdom." Honolulu, 1938-1967.

Lewis, David. *We, The Navigators.* Honolulu: The University of Hawaii Press, 1972.

Macdonald, Gordon A., and Abbott, Agatin T. *Volcanoes in the Sea.* Honolulu: The University of Hawaii Press, 1970.

Macdonald, Gordon A., and Kyselka, Will. *Anatomy of an Island.* Honolulu: Bishop Museum Press, 1967.

MacLean, Alistair. *Captain Cook.* New York: Doubleday & Co., 1972.

Mellen, Kathleen. *Hawaiian Heritage.* New York: Hastings House, 1963.

Murphy, Tom. "Ambassadors in Arms." Honolulu, 1954.

Sheehan, Ed. *One Sunday Morning.* Honolulu: Island Heritage, 1971.

Stone, Scott C.S. *Pearl Harbor, The Way It Was.* Honolulu: Island Heritage, 1976.

Twain, Mark (Samuel Clemens). *Letters From the Sandwich Islands.* San Francisco, 1937.

Wriston, R.C. *Hawaii Today.* New York: Doubleday, Page & Company, 1926.

Yardley, Maile. *Hawaii Times and Tides.* Lawai, Kauai, Hawaii: The Woolsey Press, 1975.

Zalburg, Sanford. *A Spark Is Struck!* Honolulu: The University of Hawaii Press, 1979.

Pearl Harbor.

Henry L. Chase Collection: 84/85.
C.B. Cooper Collection: 71 left.
Davey Collection: 110 top left, top right.
J.W. Egeser Collection: 90 top right.
Milton Esberg Collection: 76 top.
J.A. Gonsalves Collection: 99 bottom.
Hadley Collection: 77 top left.
Kalanianaole Collection: 108 bottom, 124 top.
R.S. Kuykendall Collection: 2/3, 108 bottom, 115 all, 116/17 all, 119 all, 124 top.
Eaton Magoon Collection: 120/21.
Monsarrat Collection: 74 bottom.
J.T. Phillips Collection: 90/91.
Mabel Phillips Collection: 112 bottom.
Taylor Collection: 96, 102.
Ed Towse Collection: 71 right.
J.J. Williams Collection: 81 top, 101 bottom.
Hawaiian Historical Society, D.R. Malden sketch: 35.
Honolulu Star-Bulletin: 126 (Warren Roll), 141.
Honolulu Symphony Society: 165 bottom right.
Honolulu Theatre for Youth: Pepi Neiva: 165 top.
Jett, Ron: 12/13.
Kahanamoku, Nadine, Collection: 114.
The Kamehameha Schools/Bernice Pauahi Bishop Estate: De Ponte 155 inset, 175 bottom.
Lum, Bruce: 11 top, 182.
Pan American World Airways: 122/23 all.
Seiden, Allan, Creative Focus: Cover, 1 top, 164 bottom, 170/71.
Sutton, Ty: 156.
U.S. Navy: 128 top, 128/29, 127 bottom.
Uprichard, Brett: 163 top.
Vaughn, Greg: 162 left, 162/63, 169 full page, 172 center left.
Wimberly Whisenand Allison Tong & Goo Architects: 160 bottom.
Yamada, David: 159, 175 top.
Young, James Y.: 164 top.

Groups assemble before a Mormon church at Laie in the early 1880s.

Concept and design by
Continental Heritage Press, Inc., Tulsa.
Typeface is Cheltenham.
Text sheets are Warrenflo.
Endleaves are Multicolor Antique.
Cover is Kingston Linen.